WHEN
MIRACLES
HAPPEN

EDITORS OF GUIDEPOSTS

WHEN MIRACLES HAPPEN

TRUE STORIES
of God's Divine Touch

Guideposts
New York, New York

When Miracles Happen

Published by Guideposts
16 East 34th Street
New York, New York 10016
Guideposts.org

Acknowledgments

Every attempt has been made to credit the sources of copyrighted material used in this book. If any such acknowledgment has been inadvertently omitted or miscredited, receipt of such information would be appreciated.

Scripture quotations marked (NIV) are taken from *The Holy Bible, New International Version*. Copyright © 1973, 1978, 1984, 2011 by Biblica, Inc. Used by permission of Zondervan. All rights reserved worldwide. www.zondervan.com

Scripture quotations marked (NKJV) are taken from *The Holy Bible, New King James Version*. Copyright © 1982 by Thomas Nelson, Inc.

Scripture quotations marked (RSV) are taken from the *Revised Standard Version of the Bible*. Copyright © 1946, 1952, 1971 by Division of Christian Education of the National Council of Churches of Christ in the United States of America. Used by permission.

Scripture quotations marked (TLB) are taken from *The Living Bible*. Copyright © 1971 by Tyndale House Publishers, Wheaton, Illinois 60187. All rights reserved.

Cover and interior design by Müllerhaus
Cover photo by Shutterstock
Typeset by Aptara, Inc.

Printed and bound in the United States of America
10 9 8 7 6 5 4 3 2 1

CONTENTS

CHAPTER THREE | *Miracles of Faith*

CHAPTER FOUR | *Miracles of Christmas*

CHAPTER FIVE | *Miracles & Animals*

CHAPTER EIGHT | *Miracles of Prayer*

CHAPTER NINE | *Miracles of Joy*

INTRODUCTION

*"Remember the wonders he has done, his miracles,
and the judgments he pronounced."*
—*1 Chronicles 16:12* (NIV)

L IFE OFTEN SEEMS TENUOUS AND UNCERTAIN, A PERCEPTION that causes us to worry and fear. Yet God promises we are not beyond His reach. Our needs will be met. We will be cared for.

When Miracles Happen is an inspiring collection of true accounts of the extraordinary ways God helps meet our needs. Whether we require a material necessity, emotional and spiritual support or protection from danger, our prayers never go unanswered. Indeed, God provides just what we need, though often unexpectedly and only in His time.

A curious son helps his mother understand the miracle of charity . . . a mother, newly and painfully single, experiences the miracle of church and community . . . a judge, hardened by life on the bench, witnesses the miracle of forgiveness.

We hope these stories will bring the unqualified assurance that God is with you, ready to help you shine even in the darkest night, triumph against the toughest adversity and rejoice in those around you, as He instructs us to do.

*M*IRACLES OF KINDNESS

*Therefore, as God's chosen people, holy and dearly loved,
clothe yourselves with compassion, kindness,
humility, gentleness and patience.*
—Colossians 3:12 (NIV)

Midnight Magician

Fulton Oursler

———

UNABLE TO SLEEP ONE DECEMBER NIGHT, I GOT OUT of bed and roamed the house. Somehow my cares and concerns always seemed to loom larger in the gloom. Then, as I stared out the window, I remembered someone else who had insomnia long ago: my father.

My father had many careers during his lifetime. He had been a magician, a ventriloquist, a reporter, an editor and a news broadcaster. But most of all—and throughout all of these endeavors—he was a writer. He wrote plays, movie scripts, newspaper columns, magazine articles, mystery stories and many books. In 1949 his most popular book was published, *The Greatest Story Ever Told*, a telling of the life of Jesus. It was around that time, when I was sixteen years old, that I began to help him in his office at our New York City apartment.

Every morning before I left for school, it was my task to make sure his desk was in order. Were the pens filled with ink? Did he have enough paper clips? Mountains of paper passed across that desk—correspondence, drafts of articles, lectures, chapters of new books. But it was never untidy, and my father kept the surface immaculate. So I was stunned one morning to find a glass ashtray overflowing with a huge pile of ashes. As I tried to imagine what had happened, I heard my father's footsteps behind me. I turned. There he stood, in bathrobe and slippers, with a curious smile.

"What happened?" I asked. "Was there a fire?"

"Only a little act of arson," he said, mischief in his eyes. "In the early hours of the morning, I put on a magic show!"

As he prepared to shave in a small bathroom beside the study, he told me the story. He had awakened from a bad dream and found he could not get back to sleep. He then went to the study to read. But just as he was about to turn on the light, something caught his eye. With the shaving brush, he pointed across the room. "Out that window," he said, "I beheld a vision."

Behind his desk was a large window that faced an air shaft, a column of space that soared between buildings like an invisible skyscraper. We lived on the eighth floor, and directly across from us was the window of another apartment some fifty feet away. "As I stood in my darkened study," my father said, the razor moving across his chin, "I saw a little girl gazing out that window. She was about eight years old, and she was a picture of sorrow!"

His words made the scene come alive. In my mind I could see the little girl, elbows on the sill, her face cupped in her hands and dimly lit by a small lamp. "She had long hair," he said, "and eyes that hardly blinked. I have never seen such a sad face."

He told me he watched her for a moment, wondering what stories lay behind the sadness. Or had she too awakened from a bad dream? "One thing was clear," he said. "That little girl needed something to make her smile."

When he first started to write about Jesus, my father was an atheist. At one point, as a magician himself, he had thought he could explain away Christ's miracles as artful magic tricks. But after years of study and trips to the Holy Land, he had become a Christian. He often said he had written his way into faith. Nestled among the books in his study was a shelf filled with his paraphernalia of tricks. In the darkness, he hurriedly assembled some items on his desk and put on his magician's robe and a tasseled hat. "I said a prayer that I could do something to make that child feel happy," he said. Then he turned the shade of the light on his desk so it would serve as a spotlight.

"Oh, you should have been there!" he said. His shaving done, he continued the story as he dressed. "The instant I switched on the light, her eyes became wide as saucers! I bowed to her and began the show." All my life I had watched my father perform magic, and I could almost see the tricks as he described them. First he took three hoops of steel and juggled them in the air until one linked effortlessly with another and the third disappeared. Suddenly all three were back in his hands, linked in a chain that he dropped to the desk. Then he picked up each hoop, separate once again. Next came a red ball. It moved through his fingers until there were two balls and then three and four. In the next instant the four became two balls, rolling through his fingers with a life of their own until he gave a clap of his hands and the balls vanished.

"I don't think I have ever had such an audience," he said. "The little girl's eyes were so wide, I could see the whites. Still, her expression did not change. At first I thought she was frightened, but then, at the end of a trick, she actually jumped up and down! That little girl had given me the magician's dream: pure, simple delight at my performance."

My father described the rest of the show while he put on his shirt and tie. "I pulled coins from my ears. I did card tricks, shuffling entire decks up and down my arms. I poured water out of a pitcher into my hat and then put the hat on my head to show that the water had vanished. I whipped off the hat and lifted out the missing red balls. And then—I sneezed!"

Now I was smiling, because I knew what came next. He sneezed a shower of silver coins into the hat. "I had a sneezing fit," he said, "and kept on until the hat was full of coins. By now she was not only smiling—she was laughing and clapping!" "But what about the ashes?" I asked.

"That was the grand finale." In the ashtray, my father had arranged a pyramid of flash paper—specially treated tissues that blaze up brightly and then go out in a second. He made a slow, dramatic bow of farewell. "I blew her a kiss," he said, "lit a match and touched it to the paper as I switched off the light—and disappeared in a great flash!"

Ready for work, my father swept the ashes into the wastebasket. "She was still smiling when she turned out her own light," he said. "I went back to bed, thanking God for a successful show."

Somehow my own troubles seemed to disappear in a flash as I remembered that story. My father had forgotten his insomnia the moment he'd seen that sad child's face. He had put all this thought and skill into making her happy. Wasn't that kind act the sure way to inner peace—losing one's self in caring for others? I went back to bed and thought what I might do the next day. I would call a friend whose son was sick, to see if he was any better. Then we were going to visit my daughter—and I thought of Sophie, her eight-year-old, who always wanted a new story. I would tell Sophie about the middle-of-the-night magic show. And as I fell asleep, I knew that my father's kindness, once again, would make a little girl smile.

The Good Samaritan

Christy Lowman

IT WAS EXTREMELY WARM FOR A FALL FRIDAY. MY MOM picked me up from school early so I could help with a craft show. Mom, an oil painter and antiques restorer, had just started venturing out from the local area to try craft shows a little farther from home.

Mom had just bought a beige van from my uncle. It had already been in the shop several times for repairs. New spark plugs and a tune-up were just some of the minor things it needed. We got it back Thursday and packed it full that night with Mom's hand-painted antiques for the show. The craft show was in the mountains, about an hour and half from home. Mom and I rode in silence, listening to the old AM radio.

I admired the scenery on the way. The trees were beautiful in all their variety of shapes and colors. The leaves danced on their way down and were all over the interstate. Then, all at once, Mom slammed on the brakes. Up ahead in the distance, a transfer truck had jackknifed, and both lanes of traffic were backed up as far as we could see. We could not see the wreck but heard the traffic report on the radio. I was worried for the driver, so we said a prayer for his safety. It was starting to get really hot in the still of the traffic. The van didn't have air conditioning, just the windows and the vents at our feet, which were really nice when we were moving. We sat there twenty minutes at least before we moved a car width, and maybe went five miles in an hour. Mom looked down at the dash gauges and panicked. "Oh my, the van is overheating!" she said, pulling off to the side of the road. "I'll turn the van off and let it cool down; then we'll try it again."

"Okay," I said with an uneasy look on my face. We sat there in silence as the minutes seemed like hours. The people in the vehicles that passed barely glanced at us and kept moving. We were forty minutes away from home; the next exit was several miles away. This was before cell phones, so we had no way to call for help.

"Mom, how are we going to get back on the road?" I asked. "The line goes back for miles."

"I'm sure someone will let us back on," she assured me. After about thirty minutes Mom tried to crank the van, but nothing happened—just a click. "Come on, Betsy," Mom said to the van and tried it again. She tried several more times and still nothing happened. At this point I was getting nervous. We decided to stand outside the van in hopes someone would stop or at least roll down their window and ask if they could help us. The interstate was packed for several more hours, but no one offered to help. A police officer came to a halt beside us in the line of traffic. We waved to get his attention but were ignored.

"I cannot believe this," I said. Not long after the police officer went by, a transfer truck slowly crept up. There was a big gap between him and the car in front of him. He was talking on his CB. "I'm going to try to get him to stop and see if he will call someone to help us on his CB," Mom said. "You stay put."

Mom came back with a scared look on her face. Later she told me he jumped out of the transfer with his pants undone. "Madam, what seems to be the problem?" he asked Mom.

"I'm not really sure; the van overheated and now it won't crank," Mom said.

The man went back to his transfer to get his tools, but he returned empty-handed. "Got any tools, like a wrench?" he asked Mom.

"No," she said.

"Me neither, but I'll call the police out for you on my CB," the man said.

"Okay, thanks."

We decided we would wait the remainder of the time in the van because that guy scared both of us. After the wreck was cleared, traffic started going at regular speed again. Each time someone passed us, the entire van shook and rattled.

There wasn't much room between the interstate and the small piece of pavement where we were parked. I was afraid we were either going to be hit by a vehicle or the van was going to flip over on its side. None of the drivers bothered to slow down when passing or stop and offer to help us. The police officer the man called never showed up, and it was getting dark and cold outside. Mom hung a white plastic bag out the window, and we sat there and prayed for someone to come and help us.

I was hoping that after Dad didn't hear from us, he would come looking; that seemed to be our only hope at that point. But then, to our surprise, a young man pulled off on the side of the road and walked to Mom's window. Mom rolled down the window but kept the door locked.

"Can I do something to help?" the man asked.

"My van overheated and after it cooled down it won't crank."

"Okay, I'll turn my truck around and hook my jumper cables to it and see if I can jump it off," he said. The young man looked behind his seat and then came back to the van.

"Someone must have taken my jumper cables because they're not in my truck. I'll go grab a friend's cables and be back," the man said. We watched him get back on the interstate with hopes of his return.

"Mom, I don't think he's coming back, do you?" I said.

"I don't know, but I hope so," Mom said. I was too nervous and worried to have an appetite, and my thin jacket wasn't enough to keep me warm. We hunched up in our seats to get warmer and waited as the sky turn black before our eyes. Soon all we saw were bright headlights and felt the shaking of the van when cars sped by. I had become quite used to the shake and wasn't bothered by it anymore.

To our surprise, the man came back. He turned his truck around carefully so he could hook up the jumper cables.

"Sorry it took so long; I couldn't find anybody with cables," the man said smiling. "You and your daughter can climb into my truck and get warm."

"Christy, go ahead and get in while I open the hood and help him hook them up," Mom said. "It will be okay; he's a nice guy, so you'll be fine."

I didn't say anything, but my fear must have shown on my face. I scooted over in the middle of the bench seat and appreciated the warmth that was pouring out of the vents and stinging my cold cheeks. My mind raced. *What if he hurts Mom, or what if he jumps back in the truck and speeds off with me in it. I'll just open the door and roll out on the interstate if he does that.*

Mom and the young man got in the warm truck and waited for the battery to charge. They talked for a while, and I just listened. Mom seemed comfortable with him, but I was still leery. I think Mom just knew from the start that he was a good guy, had that feeling about him, but it hadn't passed over to me yet. His name was Roy, and he was on his way home from work. He was a hairstylist and lived in the next town.

"We have been sitting here almost all day, and no one would help us," Mom said.

"That's probably because this is a very bad place to pull off. In the past, some women had been pulling off and pretending to have car trouble; then guys that were hiding in the woods would come out and rob whoever stopped to help them," said Roy.

"Oh my, so that's why the police kept going," Mom said. That was hard to believe. It sounded like something you would see on TV or read in a book.

Once the battery had fully charged, the car started and Roy followed us to the first gas station. The mechanic told us to stay at the motel for the night and wanted to charge us a ridiculous price to replace a belt and the alternator.

"That is way too much. I think I can fix it good enough for you to make it home," said Roy.

"I agree, and we can't stay the night," said Mom. Mom happened to have a belt under her seat that was too small, but Roy made it work.

"You should make it home all right now, but I'm going to follow you to make sure," Roy said.

"Oh, are you sure? It's a pretty long way," Mom said.

"Yes, I'm not leaving you guys till I make sure you get home okay," said Roy.

"Okay, thank you very much," Mom said.

I looked from time to time in the side-view mirror to see if he was still behind us on the drive home, and sure enough he was. That's when I decided he was a good guy. We turned off on our exit and pulled over to tell him we would be fine the rest of the way.

"How can I ever repay your kindness?" Mom asked. "Let me pay you something."

"No, you don't owe me anything," Roy said. "If you're sure you will be okay the rest of the way, I'll go on home."

"Yes, I'm sure we'll be fine. If you won't let me pay you, at least let me make an appointment to get my hair fixed at your place," said Mom.

Mom made an appointment but later on had to cancel it. It was the last time we saw or heard from Roy, the "good Samaritan" who stopped and helped us when no one else would.

Do Unto Others

Betty R. Graham

WHEN I WOKE UP LAST WEEK, I LOOKED OUT THE WINDOW and saw nothing but white—the entire yard was blanketed with snow and ice. It wasn't a surprise; the newscasters had been forecasting the winter storm for days.

I groaned, anticipating the struggle of clearing my long walkways to the street, both front and back. The weather had been very mild until that day, but now winter was here in all its glory. In years past I had jumped into the task at hand, shoveling myself out without too much effort, but this year the task seemed enormous. The older I get, the harder the job becomes. It had been getting harder and harder every year since I'd had back surgery a few years ago. I was dreading the task before me.

I fixed myself some breakfast and lingered over the second cup of coffee, postponing the dreaded exercise as long as possible. I knew I'd have to get to work soon or the mail carrier would have trouble getting to my front porch where my mailbox is. Then I heard a noise in the backyard. When I looked out the window again, I was surprised to see my young neighbor shoveling my walkway. I couldn't believe my eyes. Although I knew those neighbors well, we didn't spend much time together. I waved at them when I saw them walking their dogs several times each day, and I chatted with the wife at times when we saw each other in the yard, but other than that, we didn't socialize. They are much younger than I.

Quickly, I fixed a cup of hot chocolate and took it downstairs to the back door.

When I opened the door, Gary stopped his work and gratefully accepted the hot cup I extended to him. I tried to thank him, but he said it was nothing. *Nothing!* It was a miracle for me.

When he finished his hot chocolate, he went right back to work, finishing a wide path to the street. Now I'd be able to get the garbage can out for the trash truck to pick up the next day. Then he went around to the front and repeated his labors, making a path for my mail delivery. Shoveling wasn't an easy job because on top of the snow was a solid sheet of ice, making the walkways and streets treacherous. But that didn't stop Gary; he worked hard until the job was finished. Then I saw him go to the house on the other side of his own, where another elderly widow lived, and repeat his efforts. And when it was all finished, he got in his car and drove to work. His wife Cathy also left for her job.

What could I do to repay their kindness? I decided to make a big pot of soup for their supper. All day I peeled and chopped vegetables and browned beef to stew. When it was finished in the afternoon, I felt good. Cathy would not have to fix a meal when she came home from work, and hot soup would hit the spot on such a cold day. But the street between our houses was still very icy, and I am not too steady on my feet. I was afraid I would not be able to deliver my offering to them safely. So when I saw Cathy come home, I called and told her I had some soup for them. When she came over to pick up the soup, she seemed as grateful as I felt when I saw her husband shoveling my walkways. It was a small thing I had done—much smaller in my mind than the gigantic blessing they had given me.

After Cathy left, I started thinking of what else I could do to help others in difficult times. I saw the mail truck come slipping and sliding down the street. The temperature had plummeted to the teens and immediately I felt sorry for the mail carrier, having to deliver mail and walking on icy sidewalks in the freezing cold. Again I fixed a cup of hot chocolate and presented it to him as he handed me my mail. He was surprised, but very grateful. For the rest of the week, I met him with a cup of hot chocolate when he delivered my mail, and he said to me, "You are a blessing." His words warmed my whole spirit.

It wasn't much to do, but it seemed like a lot to that young mail carrier.

Now I am constantly looking for ways to make others happy, especially those people we take for granted every day. Gary had started a chain reaction in my soul. By helping me out without being asked, he sparked a similar feeling within me. Who knows who the mail carrier will help along his way? It's really a kind of miracle, don't you think?

I don't know who else will come along who might appreciate a helping hand, but at least now I am consciously aware of those I meet. In fact, it gives me joy to watch for opportunities to help someone else, especially someone I might not have even noticed in the past. Because of my age and health, there are always some things I'm not able to do, but often enough I can do something to lift another's spirit.

The Red Shoes

Susan Farr Fahncke

～──────◈◉◈──────～

S HE WAS IN THE LAST STAGES OF HER YOUNG LIFE. TWENTY-
eight and losing her battle with a brain tumor, my sister
seemed to be a people-magnet wherever she went. Although
she would become much weaker and soon lose her ability to talk, walk and do anything on her own, Angel had not
yet reached that stage. As our dad walked with her into the
University of Utah Medical Center, my sister beamed and
struck up a conversation with anyone who made eye contact
with her. Signing in for her daily radiation treatment, she
spotted a woman nearby who was wearing something Angel
had coveted and had searched for for months: red shoes. They
were sneakers in my sister's favorite color, and she grinned at
the woman and complimented her on her shoes.

"I love your shoes," she told her. "I've always wanted red sneakers."

I don't know what it was in her voice, or maybe it was her obviously scarred, bruised and bald head—the tell-tale signs of cancer combat and not a winning fight. Or maybe it was her frail, vulnerable body; her right side was paralyzed from the brain tumor, her arm hung limp at her side and her leg dragged as she struggled every moment just to keep upright and keep walking. Dad stood with his arm around her, helping her keep her balance and letting her know he was right there with her. It also might have been her beautiful sparkling eyes. She always looked you right in the eye and made you feel you were an incredible gift to her. Her friends were every person she ever met: every shape, size, type and age— she loved all people. She was completely loving and genuine with everyone, so maybe that made the woman do what she did.

Reaching down, without a word, the woman unlaced those red laces on her sporty red sneakers and handed the shoes to my sister.

Embarrassed, my father stepped in and refused the woman's gift.

"No, that's okay. Really!" My father said, pushing the red shoes back to the woman. I think he was mortified at a woman in public taking off her shoes.

"I want you to have them." The woman insisted, gently placing them in my fragile sister's only good hand. She reached around and gave Angel a gentle squeeze and looked into her eyes with what must have been a very understanding heart.

Somehow she just knew, and although it left her in her stocking feet, she gladly gave this gift that was so wonderful to my sister.

Shocked, Angel stood gaping at the stranger who had, without a thought, given her the very shoes off her feet. She stammered her thanks and in amazement watched the woman walk away, her shoes now clutched in my sister's arm. The woman seemed totally unself-conscious at her shoeless state, and I can only imagine the glow she must have felt at seeing my sister light up. As she disappeared, my father wondered what she had been waiting for, as she left as soon as she had offered her gift. It was almost as if she were a red-shoe angel, magically waiting to give Angel this odd gift.

My father, still terribly embarrassed, nevertheless was deeply moved at this selfless gift from a complete stranger. Angel stood, clutching her new red shoes and wearing a big grin that reached all the way to her deep blue eyes.

"You don't even know if they'll fit." Dad attempted one last weak argument against the gift.

"They will." Angel assured him with a confident smile. "Help me put 'em on."

Dad got her seated and then loosened the laces and tried them on her size five-and-one-half feet. Like Cinderella, it was a perfect fit.

"I told you," she grinned up at him. "They were meant for me." My sister had an almost magical belief in everything.

After her treatment, Dad brought her home and they told me the story of the mysterious woman and her generosity.

I listened in amazement and wondered if the woman had any idea of the impact her gift had on our family. That a total stranger would take the shoes off her feet and, without hesitation, give them to my sister was incredible—I think maybe even the gift of an angel.

It's been almost two years since my sister passed away. I often reflect on her great impact on the world and of the impact of the world on her. She looked for the good in people and found it more than most of us ever do.

I sometimes think of those red shoes too. Angel never got to wear them much, as her feet swelled from her medication and the red shoes didn't make it onto her feet again. But they stayed prominently displayed in her bedroom, right up until the day she left for bluer skies. Always a reminder of the good in people and the earthly angels who walk in and out of our lives all the time. Angels bearing gifts of red shoes are probably a rarity these days, but I know of at least one.

Michael and
the Window Washers

Pam Proctor

———————— ❊◦❁❈❁◦❊ ————————

Nine-year-old Michael and I were on our way home from our thrice-weekly trip to the Bronx for his tennis lessons. As we stopped for a red light near the entrance to the Third Avenue Bridge going to Manhattan, the usual thing happened: The car windshield was sprayed by an aggressive vagrant, who cleaned it off whether I liked it or not.

"No!" I shouted through the closed window. The idea of a scruffy man with a dirty bottle of soap or Windex or who-knows-what crawling all over my windshield didn't appeal to me.

As the light changed, Michael asked, "Mommy, why do you yell 'no' at those window washers? Why don't you let them wash the car window and give them some money?"

"These men are trying to force us to give them money," I explained. "They will end up spending it on liquor or drugs. We'd just be feeding their habits."

But Michael wouldn't let me off the hook. "You don't know that, Mom," he said. "I feel bad for them. How would you like it if someone yelled at you? How would you feel if you were hungry and didn't have any money?"

His relentless questions prompted a family discussion at home. "Michael thinks we should give money to the window washers," I said to my husband.

Bill, who usually shouts the loudest at the window washers, listened intently to Michael's importuning. Immediately he remembered an interview he'd had with Mother Teresa of Calcutta for a book he wrote nearly a decade earlier. Retrieving the volume from the bookshelf, he turned to her answer to a question he had asked her about how to deal with panhandlers—especially those who may be using the donations for unsavory purposes. "Whenever we give, we give to Jesus," said Mother Teresa simply. "I'd rather we made mistakes in kindness than work miracles in unkindness."

I looked at Michael. Instinctively he had known what to do. Right then and there we made a decision to welcome the window washers joyfully.

The next time we stopped at the red light, it was pouring rain. Nevertheless, I rolled down the window and said to the nearest window washer, "Could you please clean my rear window?"

His mouth broke into a gap-toothed grin. He wiped the window spotless, and just as the light turned green, I gave him some change and said, "Thanks."

That night in bed Michael prayed for the window washers. Then he had another inspiration: "Why don't we give them Bibles?"

So now we come prepared with a pocket Bible, a home-made muffin and fifty cents. Who knows what effect our son's instincts may have?

Gifts of Kindness

Darlene Crowford

I WAS TERRIFIED I WAS GOING TO HAVE A NERVOUS BREAK-
down. Nothing was going right that morning. Fighting back
tears, I couldn't even get the twisty off the end of the bread bag
where I had saved heels from loaves gone by in case of emergency. *This is surely an emergency,* I thought as I angrily tore
the plastic from the tangled twisty and retrieved the heels. The
last bread in my house was going for my three children's school
lunches made from scrapings from the peanut butter jar and
the final drops of grape jelly.

I didn't know what I would do for their lunches the next
day—a day I had never thought would come. Not even the
most inspired homemaker could put together a meal from the
odds and ends in my almost-empty cabinets. I held back my

tears for the sake of the children, slapped together the heels with their meager smears of peanut butter and jelly, wrapped them in used plastic wrap and put them in the lunch boxes. Thank God for Kool-Aid, I thought as I checked the lids of the thermoses.

When the kids were finally out the door, I fell on the sofa and let out the tears I'd held back all morning. I cried over my failed marriage. I bawled out loud over the lovely house I'd given up to get rid of my unfaithful husband. And I found myself screaming as I remembered the stuffed pantry and overloaded cabinets I'd always taken for granted in my former home.

Totally spent from my outburst, I fell to my knees and begged God to show me what to do. I felt He was with me when I finally couldn't take my former husband's infidelity any-more and sued him for divorce. What I'd failed to consider was the power my husband held in the small town where we lived, his childhood home where he and his father and grandfather had practiced law for generations. I was never totally accepted by his family or the townspeople because I was an "outsider." Even our children were shunned, probably because they were the fruit of my loins instead of the woman my ex was expected to marry.

The final blow was when I caught him with that woman at a local motel. No, the final blow was really when the hometown judge ruled for my husband in the divorce suit and gave him everything but custody of the children. I thanked God for that blessing and knew, with His help, I could make it. We moved to another state, where I found a great teaching job that would begin at the next term, a mere three months away. Meanwhile, I worked at a dry cleaner's to get us through the summer.

Although we'd lived in this fairly small town almost two months, I still hadn't made any real friends. We were lucky enough to find a nice house with a decent rent in a seemingly safe neighborhood. But I'd been busy getting the house ready, settling the kids in a school they appeared to like, and looking for a job, so I hadn't gotten acquainted with anyone. A priority was to find a church, and the one we joined seemed wonderful, but again I hadn't made any friends in spite of the many ladies who urged me to join their morning prayer group. I couldn't wait till my teaching job started so I could have a decent schedule and have time to take part in church activities.

Meanwhile, I struggled like crazy to stretch the meager settlement the judge had allowed me to "take care of the children." That cash was now gone—totally gone.

"God, what do You want me to do?" I cried out loud. If I could just make it for two weeks until my first paycheck came from the dry cleaner, we'd be all right. In fact, if I just had enough food, we'd be okay, because the children walked to school, I walked the few blocks to my work and church was just around the corner.

I told God how I'd humbled myself to the point of looking for a food bank and even asked about one at the church, but the town was too small. Growing up in a family that always had tons of food and extras, and coming from an attorney's income, I'd never known what it was to go without life's necessities. I was rather proud of having humbled my pride enough to look for help—but that was an oxymoron, wasn't it? However, making the settlement stretch so far was a good feeling, and I mentally patted myself on the back. *But what am I supposed to be learning now?* I asked God.

As I burst into helpless tears again, I was amazed to hear God's words, clear as a bell. I didn't believe in God actually speaking, but there was no doubting His words: "I have never let My children go hungry. Look it up in the Scriptures," He said. "Trust My Word."

Had I really heard His voice? I was beginning to doubt my sanity. Maybe I *was* having a nervous breakdown. Or maybe I should do what God said and look in the Bible. I grabbed my Bible off the coffee table, glad I'd been faithful in my daily reading. I thumbed through the concordance, looked up the first *hungry* I came to, and there it was!

"I have never seen the Lord forsake a man who loves him; nor have I seen the children of the godly go hungry" (Psalm 37:25, TLB).

"Oh, God," I whispered, "forgive me for not believing You could speak to me. I trust You to be my Father and my children's Father."

A new energy seemed to come over me as I rose to my feet. I hurried to get ready for work, determined to trust God. As I walked the two blocks to the dry cleaner, I kept remembering

God's promise that my children would not go hungry. I didn't know what I'd fix for supper that night or what the kids would eat when they came in from school clamoring for snacks. But I held up my head, told God the food problem was His and marched into work.

As I trudged back home that afternoon, I tried to push the picture of the empty larder from my mind and focus on the nice paycheck I'd get in a couple of weeks. Even so, I was near tears as I unlatched the gate and entered my yard. And I was so consumed with trying not to fret that I didn't notice the front porch until I'd mounted the steps.

Dozens of cardboard boxes and plastic bags lined the porch. In amazement, I peeked into several and saw they were packed with meats and breads and staples and even goodies, and a cooler held gallon jugs of milk and juice. One bag even held plastic wrap and baggies. *Who knew? Who did this?* I asked myself. Then I noticed the note stuck in the screen door. Scrawled in bold print was the most beautiful message I'd ever seen. Through my tears I read, "Enjoy. Love, Your Father."

The Post Office Angel

Joy Scrivener

OUR FOURTEEN-YEAR-OLD DOG ABBEY DIED LAST MONTH. The day after she died, my four-year-old daughter Meredith cried and talked about how much she missed her friend. She asked if we could write a letter to God so that when Abbey got to heaven, He would recognize her.

She dictated and I wrote:

Dear God,

Will you please take special care of our dog, Abbey? She died yesterday and is in heaven. We miss her very much. We are happy You let us have her as our dog even though she got sick. I hope You will play with her.

She liked to play with balls and swim before she got sick. I am sending some pictures of her so when You see her in heaven You will know she is our special dog.

But I really do miss her.

Love,

Meredith Claire

P.S. Mommy wrote the words after I told them to her.

We put that in an envelope with two pictures of Abbey and addressed it to God in heaven. We put our return address on it. Then Meredith stuck some stamps on the front (because, as she said, it may take lots of stamps to get a letter all the way to heaven) and that afternoon I let her drop it into the letter box at the post office.

For a few days, she would ask if God had gotten the letter yet. I told her I thought He had.

Yesterday we found a package wrapped in gold paper on our front porch. Curious, I picked it up. It had a gold star card on the front and said "To Meredith" in an unfamiliar hand. Meredith took it in and opened it. Inside was a book by Mr. Rogers, *When a Pet Dies.* Taped to the inside front cover was the letter we had written to God, in its opened envelope.

On the opposite page, one of the pictures of Abbey was taped under the words "For Meredith."

We turned to the back cover and found the other picture of Abbey, along with this handwritten note on pink paper:

Dear Meredith,

I know you will be happy to know that Abbey arrived safely and soundly in heaven! Having the pictures you sent to Me was such a big help. I recognized Abbey right away.

You know, Meredith, she isn't sick anymore. Her spirit is here with Me—just like she stays in your heart—young and running and playing. Abbey loved being your dog, you know.

Because we don't need our bodies in heaven, I don't have any pockets, so I can't keep your beautiful letter. I am sending it back to you with the pictures so you will have this book to keep and remember Abbey. One of My angels is taking care of this for Me.

I hope the little book helps. Thank you for the beautiful letter. Thank your mother for sending it. What a wonderful mother you have! I picked her especially for you.

I send my blessings every day and remember that I love you very much. By the way, I am in heaven, but wherever there is love, I am there also.

> *Love,*
> *God and the special angel*
> *who wrote this after God told her the words*

As a parent and a pet lover, this is one of the kindest things I've ever experienced. I have no way to know who sent it, but some very kind soul is working in the dead letter office.

CHAPTER TWO

MIRACLES & MYSTERIOUS VISITORS

"For I was hungry and you gave me something to eat,
I was thirsty and you gave me something to drink,
I was a stranger and you invited me in."
—*Matthew 25:35* (NIV)

The Shimmering Visitor at Lake Balaton

Renie Szilak Burghardt

I WAS A CHILD OF WORLD WAR II, BORN IN HUNGARY. MY young mother died two weeks after my birth, and my young father was away because of the war, so my maternal grandparents raised me.

When you're a child of war, you're never sure what the next minute, next hour or next day may bring. All you can do is hope and pray it will be over soon. That is what I did, day after day.

We lived in the Bacska region of Hungary near the Serbian border, and when, in the spring of 1944, the communist partisans were closing in, many Hungarians decided to leave. We were no exception. Grandfather conferred with his younger brother

Tamas, and our two families made plans to go to Kalocsa where Great-uncle Peter, my grandfather's oldest brother, lived. I was seven at the time and was happy we'd be going together because Uncle Tamas' daughter Anni was my age and the closest thing to a sister I would ever have. We had been inseparable all our lives.

The following couple of days were taken up with packing a few things we would be taking along. Most of our belongings were to be left behind. Grandmother agreed I could take two of my favorite storybooks with me; the rest of my toys and books would stay.

"We can read to each other on the train," I told Anni. Reading was my favorite pastime.

"Yes, and we can watch the scenery. The train will go right by Lake Balaton," Anni said excitedly.

Lake Balaton was Hungary's largest lake and well known for its scenic beauty. We had learned about it in school but had never seen it, so we looked forward to it. Anni and I also looked forward to seeing our cousin Agi, Uncle Peter's youngest child, although we hardly knew her. She was nine and had written in a letter that she couldn't wait to see us.

The night before we were to leave for the train station, Grandfather made a sudden abrupt change of plans because of a feeling he had. "We are not taking the train. We are going by horse and wagon instead," he announced.

"But it will take you five days by wagon. By train you'll be there in two days," Uncle Tamas said.

"I know, I know. But we can pack so much more into the wagon and take it along. We have very little money left. Things are expensive. Why leave behind the few things we have? Besides, as I already told you, I have a bad feeling about taking the train."

"Oh, Jozsef, we are taking the train just as we planned. So we will be seeing you in about five days," was the last thing Uncle Tamas said before he left for home, and Anni and I said our sad good-byes.

Of course, I was upset by Grandfather's change of plans. It meant Anni and I would not be traveling together. And it also meant that Anni would get to see Agi days before I did. But I knew that once Grandfather made up his mind about something, there would be no changing it.

All that night my grandparents worked on packing things into that horse-drawn wagon. Then early the following morning, while the guns of the partisans could be heard in the distant hills, we boarded the wagon and left the village of our birth behind.

Once the wagon was on the road and I was comfortably snuggled into my featherbed in the back of the wagon, the journey got interesting. Hundreds of people were on the road with their wagons, all of them hoping to find safety somewhere in our country. When we heard warplanes approaching, we'd all scramble out of our wagons and run to lie down in a ditch, just in case those silver cigars would decide to drop some bombs on us.

At night we camped together somewhere along the road, and the men built little fires so the women could cook their meager suppers. And again, if we heard that warplanes were heading our way, people rushed to put out the fires and run for some kind of safety, with prayers on their breaths!

On the fourth day of our journey, we reached Lake Balaton. I gazed at the shimmering waters and thought about Anni and how she and Agi must already be having fun together. There were beautiful villas along the shore, and I wondered if the people living in them felt safe in their placid lake homes.

We found a public area of the lake and took the horses for a drink while we washed our hands and faces for the first time in days. Then we settled down to spend the night there before joining the line of wagons again in the morning. We'd be finally arriving in Kalocsa later in the day. As I lay on my featherbed in the wagon, I could see the moonlight casting silver beams on the waters of the lake. It was such a beautiful, tranquil setting that I forgot all about the dangers and hardships of war. Suddenly, I heard a voice calling my name and I sat up and saw her. It was Anni, smiling and waving to me from the edge of the lake, her entire being shimmering, as if she was an angel. She looked so happy and beautiful!

"Anni, you're here! I thought you were in Kalocsa already," I called back to her happily. At that point, my grandmother, who was sleeping next to me, woke up.

"Anni is out there by the lake," I said. "I just saw her. She was waving to me."

"I don't see anything," Grandma said. "You must have been dreaming. But you will see Anni later tomorrow, sweetheart. Go back to sleep now."

I looked to where I had seen Anni standing, but she was no longer there, so I decided Grandma was right; it must have been a dream. I fell asleep remembering Anni's smiling, shimmering face, happy we'd be together soon. And the following morning we were back on the road again before the sun was up.

After what seemed an eternity to a seven-year-old, we arrived in the city of Kalocsa and pulled into Uncle Peter's property. Uncle Peter and Aunt Rozsi came running out of the house to greet us, followed by cousin Agi.

"Where are Tamas and his family?" I heard Grandfather ask as I was ready to jump to the ground.

"You mean you haven't heard?" Uncle Peter asked, his expression turning grave. "The train they were traveling on was hit by bombs. Everyone on that train was killed. Blown beyond recognition. It was on the radio. I thought you had heard by now."

I'll never forget my grandfather's reaction upon hearing the news that his baby brother was gone. He buried his face in his hands and sobbed uncontrollably. It was the first time I had ever seen him cry. "I told him I had a bad feeling about taking the train. But he wouldn't listen," Grandfather kept saying, while Grandmother held me close and tried her best to comfort me, for I was crying too.

But I could feel no comfort in anything anyone did or said. Anni was gone. "But why, why did it have to happen to Anni and her family?" I kept asking my grandmother.

"Only God knows the answer to that, sweetheart," Grandma answered solemnly. Later that evening, Grandma took me in her arms and once again tried to console me. "Remember the dream you had of Anni at the lake?" she asked gently.

"Oh yes, I remember," I sobbed.

"Well, I was wrong; I don't believe it was a dream after all. I believe God sent Anni to you. He wanted you to know she was all right and happy. He wanted her to say good-bye to you, because she loved you and you loved her. And to show you she was whole and happy and with Him now."

Grandma's words did console me; they brought me much comfort. Anni was with God now, and she was happy and whole and beautiful. And that's how I would always remember her.

I don't know why Anni and her family perished at that time while we made it safely, but I can still see her in my mind's eye, shimmering and smiling and waving at me at the edge of Lake Balaton in the spring of 1944.

A Hand in the Water Pipe

Charlie W. Shedd

THE CEDAR RIVER RUNS THROUGH MY HOMETOWN. Wide, deep, winding, this has to be one of America's most beautiful rivers. And I should know; I grew up on it. As the Cedar passes by downtown, there is a churning section of water called the millrace. Standing on the river bank you can plainly see why they labeled this a race. Fallen limbs from the upstream trees, worn-out and broken boats, old tires and trash of many kinds battle each other in the millrace.

More than sixty years ago, when I was a boy, one landmark at the millrace was a giant pipe. Purpose of the pipe? To keep the millrace from rushing its debris downstream. Manufacturing plants, factories and businesses had been built along the river's edge. Their foundations of concrete, brick and wood were important to both owners' and employees' pay-checks. For this reason, a giant screen was attached to the pipe's outlet. Here the debris could be halted to protect the downstream walls and underpinnings. Every few months the screen was removed and cleaned and the rubbish hauled harmlessly away.

Almost every boy who grew up along the Cedar River became a good swimmer. Swimming was our thing. Showing off was our thing, too, and all those signs along the millrace bank were a magnet drawing us on. Danger, Strong Current, Undertow, Swimming Strictly Forbidden. But you know how boys are. For us the taunting question was, "How close can you get to the big pipe?" This day I decided it was my turn. I would show them something, and I did.

It was full-river season, with extra danger because the water was high. What I didn't know was that water would also be high in the pipe. At the top there would be no more than a few inches of air. Six? Ten? Sometimes the line between good sense and plain foolishness is very fine, and this day I crossed the line. Into the water I went and started toward the pipe, one eye on the current and the other on my friends. But the current was powerful enough to pull even an accomplished swimmer into the tunnel. Before I knew what had happened, I was swept into the pipe, sucked under the water by the powerful rush of the millrace! Truth: I was about to drown.

If you were about to drown, you would have an amazing experience. Like a fast-forward video, everything you ever did would go racing through your mind. The good, the beautiful, the bad, your hopes and dreams—all speeding by. Awesome. Unbelievable. At thirteen, boys don't think of dying. But I did then. Boys don't pray much either, but I did that too. Then suddenly I felt a lift, as though a hand was taking me up to the air.

I filled my lungs and fought against the undertow, but I was little competition for the downward pull. Down to the bottom I went again. All this time I was struggling—struggling against the current, struggling to get back where I came in. There would be no escape at the other end; the heavy screen was much too stubborn to let a boy through.

Then back came that hand. Something, someone lifted me up for air again. Three or four times it happened. And each time, when the hand was gone, it was back to the bottom for me, no match for the pull.

Still, I kept struggling, turning around, heading back toward the entrance. Yet with each turn now I seemed to hear a voice saying, "Forget the screen! Head for the outward exit!" And once more I felt the hand, this time turning me hard, hurling me toward the screen end. With one mighty shove, up, up and out of the tunnel, up to unlimited air.

"See the wooden fence, Charlie? Go for it. Hold on. Hold on till the lifeguards come. See them coming fast to the rescue?"

I do not remember all that happened then, but this one thing I will never forget. As they pulled me into their boat, the captain said, "Were you ever lucky, kid. Yesterday we took the screen off to clean the thing. Real lucky."

Why did the lifeguards take the screen off yesterday? Pure routine? Or did it happen yesterday to save the life of a teenage show-off today?

The lifeguards asked a barrage of questions: "What's your name? Where do you live? Why were you swimming so close? What was it like in there? How do you feel?"

Then the captain asked one final question: "Weren't there two of you in there? Somehow we got the idea there were two."

How many times through the years have I asked myself, *Why didn't I answer?* "There really were two. But the other one had to leave early to answer another call."

Angel on the Slope

Tom Hendrickson

I HOPPED OFF THE SKI LIFT WITH MY SON SCOTT. IN A MINUTE I'd left him behind, zooming along the slick snow. Smooth riding . . . until I hit a rock and toppled over. Hard.

Pain shot through my lower back. I needed a hand. "Help," I yelled to someone a few feet away. As he came closer, I noticed his odd outfit. No skis and not a winter coat or gloves. The man was wearing a suit and dress shoes!

I reached up for his outstretched hand and he lifted me to my feet effortlessly. By then Scott was at my side. I showed him what I'd tripped on.

"I'm okay now," I said to the man. But he was no longer there.

"Where'd he go?" asked Scott. He'd seen him too. We scanned the slope, but the man had disappeared. I guess you don't need a ski lift when you have a set of wings.

In Momma's Room

Mary Lou Schwada

BOXES WERE STACKED EVERYWHERE. THE FIREPLACE needed a cleaning. Padding hid the piano. Yet when I looked around on this moving day, I knew we'd found the perfect home. There was a big master bedroom for Terry and me, separate bedrooms for the girls and, best of all, a guest room for my parents. Now we wouldn't always have to travel to their house for visits. My whole life I'd felt safe and loved in Momma's house. More than anything, I wanted to make her feel that way in mine.

She'd been diagnosed with Alzheimer's, and osteoporosis slowed her down. I wasn't sure how much longer she'd be able to travel, so I wanted to get right to work decorating. Singing to myself, I sliced open a box. *Just wait till I fix up the guest room,* I thought.

The bed was delivered, one with a nice firm mattress, just like Momma liked. The wallpaper and curtains suited Momma to a T. The window looked out on our front yard. Everything was ready. But when I called Daddy to arrange a visit, he didn't think it was a good idea.

"It's the five-hour drive," he said. "We just don't think we can make it right now."

Momma spent more and more time in the hospital. "The chances of her ever making the trip are slim," my sister Karen warned from back home. That didn't stop me. I added a comfortable chair to the guest room, singing as I arranged it just so.

God, let Momma see this room I've prepared for her, I asked. *Just once.*

The new chair gave me an idea. Momma was a big fan of the Marjorie Dean book series. I used to snuggle under my blankets as a child while Momma read volume after volume to me. She had been heartbroken when her set was destroyed in a flood. I'd replace them! I scoured used bookstores and garage sales for early editions. Meanwhile, Karen investigated nursing homes for our momma. Daddy could no longer give her the round-the-clock care she needed.

"You don't have many more to go," Terry said as he watched me put my newly purchased Marjorie Dean, *High School Freshman*, on the bookshelf. I nodded and ran my finger over the spines. Whenever we drove to Momma's house for a visit, I brought a volume with me. By the time we'd really settled into our new house, the Marjorie Dean set was long since complete.

Karen called one afternoon and told me she'd found a place for Momma. I drove up to help with the move. The nursing home was immaculate and the staff caring. Still, when I saw Momma's room, I couldn't help but think of the one I'd prepared for her.

A few weeks later I got a call: Momma had taken a turn for the worse. Terry and the girls helped me pack a bag. I left the next morning.

By early afternoon, Daddy, Karen and I were together at the nursing home. The doctors told us Momma probably did not have much time left.

Karen took Daddy home for a few hours' rest that evening, while I settled in the chair beside Momma's bed. The oxygen tank hissed behind me. Momma took a labored breath. "I'm right here, Momma," I said.

How different this place was from the sunny room she had at my house. I imagined her sitting on the couch in the living room while the girls played piano. Terry would make a fire. Then before bed I would read to her from her brand-new Marjorie Dean collection.

God, she'll never know the love I had waiting for her in that room, will she? I thought wearily. I had to accept it. I jerked my head up. "Is someone there?" I craned my neck to see the door. No one had come in. I squirmed in my seat. Something was definitely different. The air seemed thicker, as if a throng of people had suddenly crowded into Momma's hospital room. *My mind's playing tricks.* I pulled my chair a little closer to

Momma's bed. She was sleeping peacefully, but I wanted to do something nice for her. "I'll sing you a song," I whispered. "I am standing on holy ground . . ."

What was the next line? It was so hard to concentrate. I had the strange sensation I was singing before an audience. I scooted even closer to Momma, as if I needed to make room. *For what?* "I am standing on holy ground," I began again. I looked around. The words came. "I am standing on holy ground," I sang. "And I know there are angels all around!"

The air seemed to burst with joy, but not like any joy I had ever felt. This was joy I could almost touch. The joy of perfect love. The joy of heaven. Angels were all around me—I knew it! A host of angels had come for Momma. Was this what God had waiting for her? Momma's home on earth paled in comparison!

I leaned close to her. "I love you, Momma," I said. "And God loves you even more." Momma took two last, sharp breaths and then exhaled. The presence I had felt all around me faded.

On my way to get a nurse, I remembered my prayer. I had asked God to give Momma a glimpse of my home. He had instead given me a glimpse of hers. God had prepared a place for Momma in heaven. A truly perfect place.

A Journey of Cynics and Saints

Kristi Hemingway

I SET MY JAW IN DETERMINATION AND ROLLED BACK MY shoulders, preparing for the marathon ahead. Stacked on the curb next to me was my embarrassing mountain of luggage. I whispered my mantra, "I can do this. Lots of women do this. I *can* do this."

Although I was a well-seasoned traveler, I was still fairly new to motherhood, and I was facing a three-and-a-half-hour plane ride, just my two kiddos and me. My son Levi was a bouncy two-year-old, having celebrated his birthday just four days earlier. He had many nicknames, but the most fitting was his Viking name, Levi the Loud. My daughter Eden was approaching three months old. She was a refreshingly tranquil child normally, but she was running a fever on this day and was uncharacteristically fussy.

Five months earlier the world had witnessed the horror of 9/11, and airport security was at its panicky peak but still full of kinks and not yet well implemented. I spent a couple of sleepless nights rehearsing my strategies for getting through security, getting to my gate and onto my plane, and I was more than a little stressed about my ability to pull this trip off smoothly. My carefully constructed plans would only succeed if Levi cooperated with my every directive, if I didn't forget or drop anything and if there were no diaper bombs along the way. By the way, don't say "diaper bomb" when you are at the airport—just a little FYI.

After recently moving to Denver, Colorado, from Paris, France, my family was taking a break to spend a month with our closest friends in Florida. We had a fantastic time and it seemed like no big deal when my husband left a week early to go wrap up some business back in Europe. The kids and I would return to Denver on our own. I didn't really think about it. I had traveled a lot, including long trips to various parts of the world where people eat things that don't come anywhere close to my definition of food, where street names are ridiculously long and funny sounding and where I couldn't figure out how to flush the toilet or even how to ask where it's located. But a few days from departure, this particular trip started to seem scarier than any of those. The reality of my two unpredictable and irrational little adventurers loose in an airport and on a plane hit me. I had visions of the three of us being thrown out the emergency exit door for bad behavior.

I imagined the disapproving stares from fellow passengers when my children demonstrated the prowess of vocal chords and the irritation of the flight attendants at the mess we could generate. Especially I imagined the frustration of all involved when I would hold up the security line for a record fifty-two minutes while I unbuckled and collapsed my stroller, unstrapped my car seat, unhooked my baby carrier—rudely awakening the sleeping Eden inside, removed my backpack with my teeth while holding a now screaming child with both hands, removed the shoes and jackets that had taken all morning to get on, chased Levi—who is now free from the stroller constraints, coaxed Levi's blanket from him to put on the conveyor belt, persuaded the now screaming Levi to walk through the metal detector toward a stranger, and reached the other side of the security check with my frantic children to face a literal mountain of disassembled paraphernalia that took three days to organize in the first place. And, yes, that was all one sentence. That's the way I dreamed it.

In my pre-trip nightmares, no one was helpful or sympathetic. After living in France for nearly six years, I had reverse culture shock anytime anyone was polite or friendly to me. I guess I had become sadly cynical, because it never crossed my mind that we would be cared for. I didn't even pray for assistance; I just prayed we would survive. On the morning of departure I put on a brave face. I assembled my entourage on the curb like a puzzle: Levi strapped in his stroller; Eden strapped on my front; a backpack of diapers, wipes, extra clothing, toys, snacks and sipper cups on my back; and the car seat balanced precariously on the handles of the stroller.

"Have a good trip!" chirped my friends, barely veiling the anxious doubt on their faces. They were all touched when I burst into tears, thinking we were just having a weepy good-bye. They waved and escaped in their minivan, not daring to look back. I wobbled unsteadily toward the ticket counter, making it peacefully through that line and the next one leading to security. This is where my nightmare would begin.

I approached the belt knowing that total chaos was about to break loose in that airport. As if I wasn't already freaked out enough, the businessman behind me stepped forward suddenly and reached for my bag. *Holy smokes*, I thought. *This guy in a three-piece suit is going to try to mug me right here in front of security! A mom with two babies! What is the world coming to?* I shame-fully realized what an utter cynic I'd become when I understood that he was loading my bag onto the belt for me, followed by my car seat and my stroller. I mumbled a thank-you. The lady behind him followed up his good deed with her own by chat-ting with Levi, distracting him while his blanket and teddy bear disappeared into the X-ray machine. The security lady waved her beeper wand over me and allowed me to carry my sleeping daughter through the gate without unstrapping or disturbing her at all, and then she even set up my stroller for me.

My cynicism was melting away. I loved these people. I felt weepy and wanted to hug them all. Perhaps my children and I would make it back to Denver alive after all. I wobbled down the aisle, shoulders burning as I strained to keep everything balanced and moving. I was weaving like an inebriated pack mule as I hurried, just missing the train to the terminal. As I stood waiting for the next one, I thanked Jesus for His unexpected favor at security and rallied enough faith to ask Him to help me the rest of the way. It was then that I heard my name called out. It wasn't a loudspeaker; it was a voice, speaking my full name loud and clear.

I turned toward the voice and there was my husband's old boss from college days. Joe and his family had been wonderfully gracious to us as we worked our way through school, and they had made a point to stay in touch with us all our years overseas. I hadn't seen him for years. For a minute I had to remind myself where I was.

"Joe! What a surprise to see you. This is so weird. What are you doing in Orlando?"

"I was here all week for a convention . . ." We chatted, catching up. He was delighted to meet my children for the first time. I was delighted to discover we were on the same flight!

Without a word or a question from either of us, Joe took us on. He carried my bag and my car seat to the gate. He became instant buddies with Levi, who never even blinked when I left him with Joe to go to the bathroom. He collapsed my stroller at the gate, buckled my car seat onto the plane and switched places with the man who was seated beside us. I'm sure that guy was at least as grateful as we were!

Joe kept the flight attendant hopping, bringing us juice, captain's wings and coloring books. He walked Levi up and down the aisles and stayed with him while I maneuvered diaper changes in the two foot by two foot bathroom stall. The flight was flawless, without a single moment of stress or panic. What are the chances, of all the flights and all the people that pass through the Orlando airport every day, that I would meet Joe at the precise moment I had asked for help?

He had us off the plane as smooth as butter and never left my side until he deposited all three of us safely in the arms of my waiting brother in Denver. I hugged Joe good-bye, gushing my thanks. He smiled, brushing aside my gratitude, and disappeared toward the baggage claim. I haven't seen him since that day.

"How was your flight?" asked my brother.

"Divine."

"That good, huh? Who was that guy?"

"St. Joe, patron saint of traveling mothers and restorer of goodwill toward men."

"Okay. St. Joe, huh? Don't you have to be dead to be a saint?"

"Apparently not," I replied, surreptitiously. "You're not a cynic, are you?"

Rescued from the Jaws of Death

Laura Hatch

I SHOULD BE DEAD. PLAIN AND SIMPLE. I SHOULD NOT STILL be alive, except for a miracle I didn't deserve. For some reason, God wanted me to live.

My junior year of high school didn't begin with the sense of anticipation and excitement most seventeen-year-olds experience. In spite of being chosen homecoming princess and affirmed by my classmates as a popular student, I was battling depression and low self-esteem. Seattle's long winter days of limited daylight and seemingly nonstop parade of gray drizzly days made me feel claustrophobic. Even on those occasional days when the skies were clear and the snow-capped mountains circle Seattle, I felt no joy as I witnessed the beauty of God's creation.

In retrospect, I can see that much of my emotional malaise was due to the disconnection between my faith and my actions. I was a card-carrying Christian, but you would have never known it by my choices. Since turning fifteen I'd dabbled in drugs after school and gotten drunk on weekends. My parents had no idea I was the party girl my friends could count on for a good time. Come Sunday mornings, I knew how to turn on the compliant charm and go through the religious motions. They had no idea I'd been date-raped and was secretly drinking to cover the shame I felt. They hadn't a clue I was losing my desire to live.

The night of October 2, 2004, I was in bed by eight o'clock. Although it was a Saturday night, I didn't want to go anywhere. My twin sister and a friend from school barged into my room and flipped on the light. They told me they were headed off to a party and wanted me to go with them. I turned over and grunted out a "no thanks."

They insisted and started to pull me out of bed. Reluctantly, I pulled on a pair of faded jeans and a T-shirt. For the first time in a long time, I chose not to drink at the party. Nothing could numb the inner pain that burned like acid in my soul. I really didn't want to be there and I locked myself in a hall bathroom. With the music pulsating against the walls, I planned how I could leave the party without interrupting everybody's fun.

Feigning a smile, I emerged from the bathroom, found my twin sister and told her I was going home. Pretending I was headed for the kitchen where the food was, I sneaked out the front door and got a ride to where my sister had parked our 1992 Toyota. I turned the key in the ignition and peeled out of the driveway. Turning in an opposite direction from the short road that led for home, I decided to just drive through the countryside and try to clear my head. So many thoughts collided between my ears that I felt dizzy. As I took a corner at high speed, my car flew off the road and down a steep embankment crowded with Douglas fir trees and blackberry bushes. The flight down the ravine took place in slow motion. With eyes wide open, I was aware of everything, and for some reason, I wasn't afraid.

Whack! The car caromed against a massive tree trunk. At once, life resumed normal speed. A branch pierced the windshield and struck me in the face. Although I had buckled my seat belt, I was thrown into the backseat and sandwiched inside the crunched frame of the car. A searing pain penetrated my body as I lost consciousness.

What must have been several hours later, I came to my senses and realized I was in real trouble. My eyes were so swollen from the impact that I was looking through tiny slits. I could feel blood all around me. The pain was so intense I knew I must have broken bones throughout my bent body. I tried to push open the door, but it refused to budge. I was trapped.

Unless someone finds me, I will die. Somehow that inevitable destiny was okay. Life had not been worth living anyway.

Meanwhile, I had no idea what was happening at home. When I had not returned in twenty-four hours, my parents reported my absence to the authorities. As the police gathered information about my troubled state of mind and where I had been the night of my disappearance, they assumed I had run away. Convinced I didn't want to be found, they didn't launch a full-fledged search. My family and my friends from school and church looked for me, but they didn't have much to go on. Because I had not braked when I failed to navigate the curve, I had left no skid marks on the road, and there was no guardrail to show I had gone through. After a few days, my mom assumed I was dead.

Every few hours I awoke from the interminable sleep that masked the pain. I was only wearing a T-shirt and jeans, so I was shivering and not able to relax fully. I tried to mark the number of days that passed by noting the darkness and light outside. On what seemed like the fourth day of my ordeal, I called out to God: "Lord, I am so sorry for the mess I've made of my life. I've messed up really bad. Please rescue me or let me die here and go to be with You."

Amazingly, I heard God speak to me. The words weren't audible, but I knew exactly what He was saying. "You aren't going to die. I will rescue you because I want you to be My disciple, witnessing to My power around the world."

During this time, my friend Bethanne and her mom Shay had been on an out-of-state trip. Upon returning, both were shocked to learn of my disappearance. Fearing for my whereabouts and condition, they joined one of the informal search efforts that by that time were losing momentum. When no evidence surfaced, Shay told Bethanne that the only real hope they had to find me was to ask the Lord for help. They both prayed.

That night Shay had a recurring dream about an intersection she knew well not far from her home. In addition to a visual image of the location, a voice in the dream implored Shay to "keep going."

The following morning was the eighth day I'd been trapped in my car barely alive. Shay told Bethanne about her "word from the Lord," and the two drove to the area Shay had pictured in the dream. Parking at the side of the road, they got out of their car. While Bethanne stayed there, her mom inched her way down the steep embankment. Her hopes of finding something that would point to me were dashed. She saw nothing.

Shay called back to Bethanne that she couldn't see anything. When she indicated she was going to climb back up, Bethanne called out, "No! Keep going!" It was the very phrase from the dream, although Shay had not told her daughter about it. Taking it as validation of the dream and the location, Shay persevered down the rugged ravine. Just beyond a thick patch of wild vegetation, she saw the mangled car. Looking in, she found me, looking lifeless.

Shay used her cell phone to call 911. Within minutes, medics and rescue personnel were scaling the cliff and evacuating me to safety. My parents were notified as I was transferred to the nearest hospital, where I was placed in the critical care unit. The doctors didn't know if I would survive. Although my mom and dad were extremely grateful I had been found alive, they feared I would never recover completely. Two days later, it appeared my vital signs had stabilized and I would live. What didn't seem likely, however, was that I would ever walk again.

While hospitalized, I learned I had lost forty pounds in those eight days from not having had anything to eat or drink. And whereas people can go that length of time without food, it is unthinkable to go without water for that many days.

Ironically, it was that deprivation of water that kept me alive. The doctors discovered a blood clot that had developed on my brain as a result of the crash. The lack of fluids prevented the clot from growing. Drinking any water would have caused the clot to expand and put fatal pressure on my brain. Amazingly, the Lord spared me from certain death by preventing me from finding a bottle of water that was on the floorboard of the car.

Two months after my miraculous rescue, I went home to the bedroom in which this surrealistic adventure had begun. Within a few weeks, I was walking again. A year later, I graduated from high school and enrolled in a Christian liberal arts university in suburban Seattle.

I smiled as I recalled God's whisper in my heart while I was trapped at the bottom of that embankment: *I want you to be My disciple witnessing to My power around the world.* I'm happy to say it's already taking place.

Stranger at the Spring

Tom Douglas

MANY PEOPLE TAKE WATER FOR GRANTED. YOU TURN ON the tap and out it comes. But my wife Robbie and I remember the days when water was not so easy to come by.

During the Depression, Robbie and I and our two young daughters lived in a two-room house close to Robbie's father's farm in Daysville, Tennessee. I worked doing construction on a new road, and I was glad to have the job, even though it meant walking five miles each way.

We had a big wood stove to cook on and to keep us warm, but we didn't have electricity or running water. We washed with water from a nearby creek and carried drinking water all the way from a spring in the pasture. That meant walking some three-hundred yards up a hill and through a gate, filling a couple of two-and-a-half-gallon buckets and trudging back to the house again. It tired us all out, especially Robbie, who usually had the girls in tow. Still, we were thankful to God for what we had and somehow sensed that He knew what we were going through and was in it with us.

One warm Saturday, Robbie took the girls to visit her parents while I stayed home working in the vegetable garden. I was hoeing away, trying to get over feeling tired and discouraged, when something made me stop and look up. A man was standing in the front yard. He was tall and wore black trousers and the whitest shirt I had ever seen. Our house was isolated, and I always knew if anyone was coming, so I was surprised.

"Good morning," the man said in a deep, pleasant voice. "I'm very thirsty. Could you give me a drink of water?"

Any drinking water taken from the buckets in our house meant we would have to climb back up to the spring sooner, and even the thought seemed exhausting. But then it occurred to me that this stranger might be pretty exhausted himself.

"Sure can," I said, shoving aside my own weariness. "Want something to eat too?"

"Just water," he said.

By now our water supply had been sitting for a while, and I suddenly thought of how much a tired and thirsty man would like a drink of fresh, cool water right from the spring. "You sit down and rest," I said, taking a bucket. "I'm going to get some fresh water for you." I climbed the hill, came back and poured the stranger a tall, sparkling glass. He drank it right down.

"Wonderful water," he said. "Too bad you have to go so far to get it."

"It would be nice if the spring were closer," I said. "But we have many other blessings."

The stranger smiled, said thanks and walked off down the road into Daysville. I stood staring after him, feeling good—and a little peculiar. Where had the man come from? Where was he going? I had felt so peaceful in his presence I hadn't even asked.

But I couldn't get him out of my mind. I decided to go into town. Daysville was so small that everyone would notice a stranger, and I would be able to learn more about him. But my friends on the porch at the general store said I was the only one who had come down the road. "We couldn't have missed him," they said.

A few days later there was a downpour. About thirty feet from the house, water began seeping out of the ground. When the rain was over and the earth dried, the trickle was still there. I took my shovel and dug in. Water bubbled out, fresh and fit to drink. It was a new spring—right at the spot where I had first seen the mysterious stranger.

We never had to make that climb up to the pasture again. Our new spring didn't go dry for the two years more that we lived there. After we finally moved, there was another downpour, and the spring vanished. Years have passed since then; today water flows right into our house. And yet I'll never forget that long-ago source of refreshment and peace. The Bible says, "If you have done it to the least of these, you have done it unto me." Well, I guess we did. And got a wellspring in return.

Five Miracles in One Day

Jody Murphy

I CAN'T KEEP DOING THIS," I TOLD MY HUSBAND KEVIN. After three years of painful fertility treatments with no results, enough was enough. The strong medication and the extreme hormone surges brought physical pain and put me on an emotional roller coaster. I did not want to live like that anymore.

Even before I married, I knew conceiving a child would be difficult. When I was a teenager, I was diagnosed with polycystic ovarian disease. My health was fine, but my chances of ever getting pregnant were slim. Kevin and I shared a deep desire to raise children, but we agreed it did not matter if they were our own flesh and blood. We prayed to God for children and asked Him to lead us to the ones who needed us. Kevin and I felt drawn to foster care. Our caseworker understood that our ultimate dream was to adopt, so when she learned of twins that were free for adoption, she called us immediately.

Five-year-old twins Brittany and Brandon came to live with us on July 3, 1997. I was a little scared at the enormity of my instant responsibility, even while my heart sang, "I'm a mom, I'm a mom!" Our prayers had been answered.

But within the week, we received crushing news. The caseworker had been mistaken. The plan was eventually to reunite the twins with their birth mother. My responsibility was to make the one-and-a-half hour drive into Buffalo once a week for a two-hour visit with their mother. I wanted to be a mother to these kids, but I would do whatever was best for them. I had asked God to send me children that needed me, and whatever the outcome, Brittany and Brandon needed the love and care I had to give them.

Within three weeks of coming to our home, Brittany asked: "Is it okay if I call you Mom?" It was what I yearned for.

"Yes, I would like that," I told her. By the next week, Brandon also began calling us Mom and Dad. I loved them more and more each day, but my heart had to hold back; they were not mine to keep. The hope that I could one day be their mother for real grew deep within me. Four months after they came to live with us, we celebrated Thanksgiving.

As we went around the table explaining what we were all thankful for, my heart melted when it got to the twins. "I'm thankful for my mom and dad," Brittany announced, smiling at us.

"Me too," chimed in Brandon.

Six months after the children had been placed with us, their birth mother stopped showing up for visits. She also had never enrolled in the court-mandated treatment necessary for her to gain back custody of her children. "If this continues, she could have her rights terminated and they would be free for adoption," the caseworker told us.

When the year was up, we met with the birth mother and the caseworker. The mother decided she would relinquish her rights if she knew we would adopt them. My heart soared. I no longer had to hold back my love; I could truly be mom to the the twins—forever. All that was left was paperwork and final court proceedings; then the kids would be ours. Returning home, we excitedly told the twins their wish to become "Murphys forever" would come true. That was in July of 1998. But in September I received a phone call from the caseworker that cut through my heart.

"I have some bad news," she began. "The birth mother has an aunt who has come forward and is pursuing adopting the twins."

"No," I cried. "They barely even know her! Somehow you have to stop this!" I ran outside to be with my children. I hugged them close and cried. "I love you both so much," I told them. "Your mother's aunt wants to adopt you, but I'm not going to let her."

We held each other tight. "We don't even know her," they cried. "We don't want to go to her!"

Kevin and I retained a lawyer and were ready to fight with all we had. Because the law at that time decided heavily in favor of any biological family members, our case did not look good. The thought of losing my children was unbearable. They had made me realize how much I loved being a mom. "Please God," I prayed. "Don't let me lose my children." I could not imagine being childless again, and yet I had to face that very likely possibility.

In October I returned to my fertility specialist. Even though I knew it was a long shot, I decided to try one more time to get pregnant. But by November I was again experiencing terrible problems with the treatment to increase ovulation. One day I felt so sick, Kevin stayed home from work. When I called my doctor, he told me to come into his office. Shortly after I hung up with the doctor, our lawyer called. "I need to see you and Kevin," he said. Both offices were in Buffalo, so we arranged to see them one right after the other that morning.

Our lawyer had unbelievable news: "The aunt has stated she will withdraw her petition on the condition that you two agree to adopt the children." We were ecstatic. In spite of still feeling ill, my spirits soared. God had answered our prayers. The children would really be ours! No one would ever take them from us. I cried tears of joy.

When we went on to the doctor's office, I was so happy I did not even mind failing at achieving a pregnancy again. The doctor had me do some blood work and then went over the results with me. "I have some great news," he announced. "You're pregnant." Before the unbelievable announcement could sink in, he continued: "But there is a slight problem. It's probably twins"

"No, I'm *adopting* twins," I laughed.

"Yes, and you are *pregnant* with twins," he laughed in return. "Your hormone levels are so high, it must be twins."

Initially, medical complications threatened to end the pregnancy. I had prayed so hard to keep Brittany and Brandon, I feared that now I would lose my other babies. "Please God," I pleaded, "let me have them all."

Within the month, my situation improved and the pregnancy progressed. At six weeks, I went in for an ultrasound. "There are three heartbeats!" the doctor announced. I could not wait to call Kevin at work. "How does three sound?" I asked him.

"You mean the twins and one more baby?" he asked.

"No, I mean the twins and triplets." We were both too excited to be scared. Before I knew I was pregnant, I had prayed to conceive. I had prayed it three times in a row. The family joke now is that it is good I did not pray it seven times.

Kevin and I had the name Kiley picked out for one of the babies. We wanted to include the twins in our family situation so we asked each one to name one of the babies. Brittany picked out the name Emilee for one of her new little sisters and Brandon selected the name Matthew for his little brother. The triplets were born on April 27, 1999.

Nearly a year later the triplets were with us when the judge banged down her gavel to symbolize the adoption proceedings were complete. Brandon beamed and announced: "Now we're forever Murphys!" And now I am forever thanking God for giving me five miracles all in one day. Being a mom to my five little Murphys is a greater blessing than I ever could have imagined.

CHAPTER THREE

MIRACLES OF FAITH

Let love and faithfulness never leave you; bind them around
your neck, write them on the tablet of your heart.
—Proverbs 3:3 (NIV)

The Witness

Judge Fred M. Mester

I HAD WANTED A LAW CAREER EVER SINCE I WAS A BOY growing up in Royal Oak, Michigan. My father, a tool and die maker, came from Springfield, Illinois, Abraham Lincoln's hometown, and from Dad I drew a love of our sixteenth president, this nation's most celebrated lawyer. I admired Lincoln's ideals, his moral tenacity, his respect for the truth and his underlying compassion for people trying to live together peaceably under a complex system of laws. Fourteen years ago, when I became a judge on the Sixth Circuit Court in Oakland County, Michigan, I made sure to bring my portrait of Lincoln from my law offices. Not too long ago, though, my faith in the judicial system wavered. It took a young man named Kenneth, who witnessed an abominable crime, to bring my beliefs back.

Seeing the misery and inequity that pass through a court-room is not easy. The Sixth Circuit covers both the affluent northern suburbs of Detroit and the blue-collar city of Pontiac. Neither area is free of the monsters of drugs and crime. A divorce case in my court is as likely to involve a successful professional couple as it is a couple on welfare. Income is no barrier to crime and tragedy, and in so many cases—both civil and criminal, rich and poor—children are the real victims. It can get to you after a while.

Late in 1989 I heard two horrendous murder cases, virtually back to back. In the first—the Tarr case—two middle-class kids, Joe and Chris, kidnapped Mrs. Tarr, a hardworking wife and mother; they stole her car and forced her to withdraw funds from a cash machine. Then they drove her to a deserted location and executed her in cold blood. The two boys went back and abducted Mr. Tarr, assuring him they would free his wife if he cooperated. He, too, was forced to withdraw funds. Ultimately, Mr. Tarr met the same fate as his wife, on the same lonely dead-end road.

But what really got to me was that these boys drove the Tarrs's automobiles to teen hangouts, attending group activities such as a roller-skating party while barely concealing their crime, and no one contacted the police. No one had wanted to get involved.

The other case was of a young woman who wanted nothing more than to get her car washed on her way to work early one morning. The twenty-one-year-old manager of the car wash

assaulted her, beat and raped her and then locked her in the
trunk of her car and parked in the driveway of his girlfriend's
house. There the car sat for five days while neighbors and
others did nothing about the muffled cries emanating from the
vehicle—pitiful cries that grew weaker and weaker till they faded
altogether.

Nothing is more serious than a murder trial, and a judge
learns to tune out everything but the law. The criminal behavior in these two cases was shocking enough, but the apathy of
people who had been in a position to do something really threw
me. I had never seen anything like it in my years on the bench.

"How could people stand by and do nothing?" I asked
Lynne, my wife, one night near the end of the second trial. "Don't
they care about their fellow human beings?" On a deeper and
more troubling level, I wondered how God could stand by and
do nothing. The woman at the car wash was a recovering alco-
holic, building a new life for herself and her children. The two
boys in the Tarr case were good students and athletes, raised in
Christian homes. How had evil so completely seeped into their
lives? Were we becoming powerless as a people to combat it?

Then I met Kenneth Briggs. I saw Kenneth for the first
time when he took the stand in my courtroom as a witness for
the prosecution in a notorious crack-house rape trial. Kenneth
was a fourteen-year-old orphan at the time, living hand to
mouth on Pontiac's tough east side. His father died when he
was two, and his mother, who worked two jobs and still managed to get Kenneth to church every Sunday, died when he

was twelve. Kenneth was shunted from relative to relative, into less and less healthy environments. That is how he came to witness the brutal assault and gang rape of a thirteen-year-old runaway. Testifying in court that day, Kenneth pointed his finger at the leader of the assault, who was sitting with his lawyer at the defense table. The defendant was a big man, six feet five and two hundred twenty pounds. Anger smoldered behind his hard eyes.

"Are you sure that is the man?" the prosecutor asked, his voice cutting through the shocked silence in the crowded courtroom.

Kenneth nodded. He had identified his nineteen-year-old brother Michael.

There was more to the story. Unlike so many witnesses I see, Kenneth had not plea-bargained his way out of a prison term in exchange for testifying. He had come only by default to live with Michael in the crack house. The first night Kenneth walked through the door, without so much as a toothbrush to his name, he witnessed something horrible: a thirteen-year-old girl being savagely abused by six young men, the youngest four years older than Kenneth. The six urged Kenneth to join in on the rape, "to become a man," they said. Kenneth refused. The assault went on for hours, and Kenneth was petrified.

"She was covered with blood," Kenneth said. Somehow the girl's eyes focused on Kenneth. "Please help me," she whispered.

Kenneth did. When Michael threatened to shoot people and ran upstairs to get a gun, the other men followed him. Kenneth freed the girl, put her in a car and sent her to the police station. He then ran as fast as he could to a friend's house, more scared than he had ever been in his life. He had violated a code of the street, and he knew he would have to pay. Eventually his friend's mother helped Kenneth go to the police. That's when they arrested Michael.

When Kenneth finished testifying and the jury was deliberating, I turned to the detective in charge of the case, Eleanor Mickens, and expressed my astonishment—formed in part by the cynicism that had crept up on me. "What made him go through with this?" I asked.

"He's just a good kid, Judge," Eleanor replied. Here was a young man who might have thought he had all the reason in the world to turn his back on society, to conform to the law of the streets. Yet something made him draw a moral line, get involved and do the right thing. I had seen so little of it recently in my courtroom. I have no doubt that in great part his religious training had guided him, had saved him.

I understood fully how much Kenneth had risked taking the stand. "They'll eat him alive out there," I told Detective Mickens.

She nodded. Already people had turned away from Kenneth, Eleanor explained. A great-aunt had ordered him not to testify. No one wanted a snitch living with them.

It's time to get involved! I thought suddenly and a bit angrily. I had been so disheartened by seeing people reject their responsibilities to society—people who were more interested in protecting family members than their fellow citizens, people who refused to trust the police or testify truthfully in court. But what about me? I had to do something for Kenneth.

Word of Kenneth's courageous testimony quietly spread through the courthouse and beyond. Secretaries, clerks, cops, even defense attorneys offered help. I talked to my church, First Presbyterian of Royal Oak, and they took up an offering. The cousin of a friend found a family in Ontario, Canada, for Kenneth to live with and a good high school for him to attend. Many people pitched in, and we were able to get him away from the streets of Pontiac.

Seven years have passed. Kenneth now attends Oakland University, not far from the courthouse, and we stay in touch. He is a psychology and biology major and wants to counsel inner-city youngsters like those in Pontiac. He has grown from a good kid to a good man. A year ago the Detroit Lions football team heard about him and passed the hat around the locker room to help with tuition. Now he has a part-time job with the team as an assistant equipment manager.

Kenneth's brother Michael is serving life in prison. After a difficult struggle, the victim is making a life for herself. I once asked Kenneth what made him come forward. He shrugged and gave me a look that said he really didn't have much choice in the matter. I know Kenneth loved his mother very much. I think he did what he knew she would have wanted, however painful the consequences.

I still see tragedy and sorrow in my courtroom. Yet I now believe the vast majority of people in this society want to be kind and do right, just as Kenneth did that day on the stand. God, I know, does not stand by idly. On the contrary, what Kenneth showed me is how God has given us all the tools we need to serve Him, for if there was ever anyone for whom doing the right thing carried a heavy cost, it was that young man. Each of us, including judges, needs to stand up and be involved—in our neighborhoods, at work and through our churches and synagogues. We must help those whose obstacles in life are greater than ours.

It has been said that the only thing needed for evil to triumph is for good people to do nothing. Kenneth saw evil and did something. My old friend Lincoln said it well: "Let us have faith that right makes might, and in that faith, let us, to the end, dare to do our duty as we understand it."

Fire and the Football Player

Charlie W. Shedd

IN OUR UNIVERSITY TOWN, A BIG AND POWERFUL ALL-American football player was jogging early one morning. It was still dark, and from the hill where he ran, he saw a fire by the side of the road. Speeding up his pace, he ran as fast as he could, and because he could run all-American fast, he saved a woman's life.

She had been in a single-car accident with no one anywhere near. She didn't know how it happened. She was on her way to work, very early, and she must have fallen asleep. But one thing she did know: When she hit the telephone pole, her car burst into flames. The crash also crushed the front end, fender and floorboard and bent the driver's door. The woman was trapped inside, one leg pinned to the floor.

You should know, before I tell you the rest of the story, that this particular football player is a devout believer. From childhood, his mother taught him many things about the Lord. She taught him that God has a plentiful supply of all the strength anyone could ever need—a strength available to him if he stayed in tune with the Divine.

Arriving at the fiery scene, he knew this woman needed his help badly. So with his mighty arms, he ripped the broken door from the woman's car, freed her leg and saved her life.

By now others had come, including the police. Seeing that everything was in good hands, the football player continued his jogging.

When the woman told the police what had happened, they asked, "Who was he?"

"I have no idea," she answered. "I wonder if he was an angel."

But the story doesn't end there. Someone at the scene knew the football player's customary morning route, and they tracked him down. "Were you at the scene?" the police and reporters asked.

"Sure," he admitted.

"Then why didn't you stay to tell us what happened? Give us your name."

"Why should I?"

"You were there."

"I needed to finish my run and hurry to class."

When they interviewed him on television, he was his usual self. Again he quoted his mother to the effect that God provides strength for life's emergencies. *Pure kindness and humility. Do what the Lord needs doing. Thank your mother and move along.*

To finish the story on a touch of whimsy, one of the coaches, the staff clown, quipped, "What our team needs is more mamma's boys."

His Mercy

Vicki Graham

———— ❦ ————

WE HEARD A SERIES OF LOUD THUMPS COMING FROM the vicinity of our front porch, and then our two dogs began to bark. When we rushed to the door we discovered a bedraggled-looking man holding on for dear life to the porch post. We approached him carefully as he moaned and slid to the floor. We dragged him into the living room and checked his vital signs. He had no apparent injury, although his pulse was racing and his bloodshot eyes were hugely dilated.

We'd never met him, but we knew immediately who he was, because our tiny town was famous for gossip, and he'd been pointed out to us many times. His long hair was pulled back in a straggly ponytail, and his moustache drooped well below his chin. The skin on his face was drawn so tightly on his skull bones that he appeared emaciated, even though he was tanned and his body seemed fit.

John David was well known around town as a former drug dealer who had already served two terms in prison in his thirty-odd years on this earth. His mother was also well known for her faithful service in the local church. Many hearts went out to her for the years she had suffered embarrassment from her son's wild lifestyle. The only good John David had done was to marry a girl who produced for him two beautiful sons, who, even at their young ages, attended church with their grandmother every time the doors were open. No one knew what had happened to the wife, who hadn't been seen around the area for several years.

As John David lay moaning on our floor and we pondered what we should do, we wondered out loud why he had ended up at our house. We soon found out as his groans turned to coherent words. "Help me," he slurred. "You know what to do. Save me."

Maybe he chose our house because I was a fairly well-known drug and alcohol counselor. Or because my husband and I shared a reputation among the locals as being fairly radical Christians who went so far as sporting front license plates on our cars that proclaim "Jesus" in bold red letters, not to mention our habit of wearing T-shirts emblazoned with Christian messages. Whatever the reason, John David was here and we needed to take action.

We were certainly in agreement as we went to the Lord in prayer for John David and for guidance in the situation. And we prayed earnestly for John David's recovery and for his salvation, because his reputed lifestyle didn't reflect any morals or beliefs.

Then we followed the legal rules mandated for my agency. We called the mental health doctor, who was also a family friend, and relayed the circumstances to him. He immediately came to our house and, after examination, declared that John David was not in critical condition but was likely suffering a drug overdose or the opposite, severe withdrawal symptoms from the lack of feeding his habit. "Watch him, feed and hydrate him and wait for his mind to clear enough to talk," he advised. Or we could call the police to take him off our hands.

We didn't want to call the law because none of us had heard of any warrants out on John David. We wondered if divine intervention had placed him on our doorstep, because we knew he had such a praying mother. Our motto had always been "When in doubt, wait." So we waited and tried to make our unexpected houseguest comfortable while he came to his senses.

Meanwhile, we discussed how crazy we were to take in a virtual stranger who could be dangerous considering the stories we'd heard about him. *What would Jesus do?* we wondered. All the examples of Jesus' kindness seemed to revolve around not judging based only on someone's looks and being aware we could be entertaining angels dressed in a poor man's clothes. Above all, we believed in "fear not." So we carefully waited for John David to revive.

When he finally was able to sit without shaking and speak without slurring, John David told us his story. In a recent drug haze, he had felt sure God was telling him to get away from the lifestyle of most of his adult life. From his childhood Sunday school experiences and the constant preaching of his mother, his conscience told him he was bound for hell if he didn't get right with God.

"But how could God ever love me or forgive me after all the bad stuff I've done?" he asked through the tears that had begun at the onset of his story. "I've done things you wouldn't believe: beat up people, stole stuff, cheated, lied, abused women. I've even cussed God. No way my mom's God would take me in."

My husband and I agreed silently that our work was cut out for us. Over the next few days we took care of John David's physical needs and tried our best to take care of his spiritual needs, explaining over and over that he didn't need to clean up his act before coming to God. The Father would clean him up after he came to Him.

Although John David hungrily took in every word we said, soaked up the scriptures we read to him and listened to our music, he wouldn't budge from his lost position. The only progress happening was his body cleansing itself of the drugs. We prayed his soul would also cleanse itself of the darkness that seemed to fill him.

We knew that when Monday arrived and we had to return to work, John David might leave before we returned. He let us pray over him that Sunday night, all the time shaking his head *No*. We went to work Monday morning with a sense of foreboding but determined to leave him at the foot of the cross.

Sure enough, Monday evening there was no John David. He had left the guest room spotless and the bed carefully made. On the kitchen counter lay a note: "Thanks for all your kindness. I'm sorry I'm such a hopeless case. J. D."

We were devastated and concerned for his life, but we once again offered our prayers and left him in God's hands. For ten days we and our little prayer group at church remembered John David and asked for God to remember him too. We had planted the seeds during his weekend with us. We just hoped the Mighty Gardener would water those seeds. We knew the Word promised that it would never return void, so we asked for fruit to come from John David.

We found out where John David lived and drove by his little house often. We saw no sign of life and no truck parked in the driveway. Even at night, no lights were on.

During a Wednesday night church service, when John David had been gone ten days, my husband and I turned to each other at the same time and decided we must be hearing from the Lord when we both said, "We need to check on John David." We hurried to our car and drove straight to his house. Sure enough, we could see the living room lamp on and his truck was parked in front of his porch. We hurried to the door, and through the screen we saw a sight we will never forget: John David was lying on the couch with a gun stuck in his mouth. If we screamed, would he pull the trigger? If we went for help, would it be too late when we got back? We did the only sure thing we knew to do. We threw open the screen door and yelled, "In the name of Jesus, stop!"

Almost in shock, John David withdrew the gun from his mouth and burst into tears. We expected him to be in a drug-induced state, but immediately we saw he was cold sober as he cried his heart out and fell into our arms.

"I couldn't take life anymore," he sobbed. "I told God I was going to kill myself."

"No, God wouldn't want that," I said as I carefully took the gun and put it away from his reach. "God loves you, John David, no matter what."

"No, no, you don't understand," he rasped. "I know God loves me."

We looked at each other, puzzled. When John David recovered enough to continue talking, he told us that as he put the gun in his mouth to end his troubled life, he told God what he thought were his last words on this earth. "If You love me, God, if there's hope for a skunk like me, You'll stop me." He wept again. "Just as I was starting to pull the trigger you two slammed in the door and something stopped me."

We wept, too, as we held this poor prodigal and thanked God for His mighty mercy. John David joined us in thanksgiving and confessed his belief in Jesus and his hope for new life.

We didn't linger long, because John David was, at last, caught up in praying his heart out to the only real Father he ever knew—someone, he said, who cared whether he lived or died. We felt confident as we left, amazed at what God had done, knowing that John David was safe in the arms of the One who would complete the work He'd started the night we found him on our front porch. Yes, God was faithful.

That Sunday we were running late for church, and the singing had already begun as we made our way to our usual front-row seats. "Someone is looking for you," the usher said. "He said you'd know him when you saw him, so I told him where you sat."

And next to our seats, there was our beloved prodigal. His hair was cut short, his moustache was neatly trimmed and he was decked out in a handsome, although ill-fitting, suit and tie! And when the altar call came, John David didn't hesitate to hurry to the front and kneel at the cross.

In the next few weeks, this born-again man exhibited his faith. He went around town apologizing to people he had wronged; he reconciled with his mother; he never missed a church service. And he arranged with the district attorney to turn state's evidence on the drug dealers he knew about in an effort to make up for all his own drug deliveries.

This true story has a bittersweet ending. Just days before John David was to appear in court, his gunshot-riddled body was found sealed in an oil drum, floating in a river. But his murderers were brought to justice and their drug rings were busted, thanks to his courage. And we are at peace, too, because we know our new brother is loved at last and safe at home with his Father.

Blue Ice, Wild Irises and a Kiwi

Susy Flory

Remember the old Sesame Street game? A bouncy little song chirped "One of these things is *not* like the other." Onscreen would flash four objects, one at a time. A boot. A sandal. A tennis shoe. A ball. Of course, the ball didn't belong. But the rest were related objects with a common purpose. The answer was usually pretty obvious. You could tell that the fork, knife and spoon went together or that the pencil, pen and crayon were a group.

Life is more confusing, however, than a Sesame Street game. You can't always see how the boots, forks and pencils of everyday life connect.

One spring day, at Bean Hollow State Beach, I couldn't see beforehand that all of these things belonged together, but they did: A sleeping bag. Blue Ice. A sailboat. Wild irises. A car in a parking lot; in it, a man with a New Zealand accent, waiting, watching the waves, patient. I get the sense now that the events of the day were planned long in advance, but all I knew early that spring day was that I wanted to get on the road. Gini and I had loaded the car in a hurry; we were friends, both fledgling writers, heading down the rugged California coast to my first writers conference.

As we carried duffle bags, pillows and sleeping bags to the car, I teased Gini. "After all our time together this weekend, we'll either become best friends or we won't be able to stand each other."

She laughed, mischief crinkling around her electric blue eyes. "You'll think I'm crazy after you see me hanging up like a bat tonight." She held up a clinking concoction of long steel bars and chains hanging from a vinyl sling. It was a device that temporarily installs in a doorway. As you hang upside down, it stretches your spine and relieves pain. I rolled my eyes as she wrestled the device into a tote bag. Suddenly one of the long steel bars detached, flipped and fell with force, the blunt end striking her toes.

"Ouch," she yelled. She whipped off her sock and shoe, and we watched her toes flush red and begin to swell. "Can you grab an ice pack?" she said. "It's just a bruise."

I poked around in the freezer until I found a big Blue Ice pack the size of a manila envelope. We grabbed the rest of her things and took off in the car, Gini's toes chilling under the ice pack.

The Pacific was blue today, the color of lapis lazuli, rich and deep. A warm breeze surfed up and over the bluffs, a rare event for the foggy coastline below San Francisco. It was the type of spring day where everything looks clean and new and more real than you remembered. As the car swung along the curves of Highway One, we passed creamy beaches peopled with surfers, picnickers, dogs and families. Finally, we couldn't stand it any longer; we had to stop.

"Here. Let's stop at Bean Hollow." Gini pointed to a metal sign on the side of the highway. "We used to come here with the boys. There are tide pools and they loved climbing on the rocks."

We pulled into the parking lot. A van full of kids passed us on its way out. The lot was now empty except for one other car. The man inside caught my attention because he sat, doing nothing. He had wavy brown hair and looked to be in his late twenties. He was relaxed, his window down, looking straight out at the waves. Probably daydreaming.

"How's your foot?" I asked Gini.

"Great," she said. "That Blue Ice did the trick. Let's go!"

We headed down to the beach, the waves purring as they nosed up the sand into the cove. Bean Hollow was a crescent-shaped beach of cappuccino-tinted sand with low rocky cliffs on each end. The far end of the beach was our destination, a little rocky trail just barely visible as it angled up the cliff.

"The tide pools are on the other side," said Gini, grinning. She favored her sore foot a bit as she walked ahead. I followed, slipping off my shoes. My feet plunged into the warm sand, hitting the cool, damp, hard-packed layer below the surface.

We reached the trail and, shoes back on, hiked up the side of the cliff, sometimes grabbing rocks alongside to steady ourselves. At the top was a field of wild irises. The blossoms looked like a thousand fluttering violet birds about to take wing.

The trail wound along the rocky bluff, loose gravelly sand under our feet. Each side dropped off to rocks and beach, the ocean sparkling ahead of us. I led the way as we walked, and I felt dreamy, distracted, lulled by the rhythm of the waves. Then I heard it—a subtle sliding sound, like coarse sandpaper rubbing across a board. Something made me turn around just in time to see her in the air, falling away.

"Gini!" I yelled, too late to grab her or do anything but watch. She hit the rocks below a split-second later, and lay in a heap, feet down, her body whiplashing against a jagged wall.

It was good I didn't see her foot. I was standing on the cliff above, looking straight down at her, but somehow I still didn't see her foot. She untangled herself, sat up slowly and then cried, "Oh, Susy . . . don't look. I think . . . I broke my foot *off*."

She told me later that when she fell, her foot had hit the rock first, taking all of her weight. Her lower leg collapsed sideways, breaking. The doctors called it a compound, complex, dislocated fracture, her foot hanging off of her leg, bone out, blood seeping through her sock. Instinctively, she grabbed her dangling foot, clamped it back on and sat awkwardly, holding it in place.

I quickly climbed down but already I knew I would have to go for help. Although Gini looked okay for the moment, she was pale and I worried about shock. After a few words and a quick prayer, I climbed back up the cliff and down the other side to the beach. I seemed to be running in slow motion, the sand sucking my foot down with each step. I breathed hard, the ocean's purr now a growl.

Back at the car, I tried my cell phone. Nothing. I ran toward the bathroom, a little concrete building at the back of the parking lot, but there was no pay phone. Suddenly I saw the guy in the car. I had to ask for help.

There was no one else. He was still looking out at the waves, motionless in the car, waiting. I ran over to his open window, panicky. He looked at me, eyes friendly, eyebrows raised. "We were hiking on the rocks," I waved at the cliffs across the beach. "My friend fell . . . broke her leg." I felt breathless. My words came out quick, choppy. "It's really bad. She's bleeding!"

"What do you want me to do?" he asked. I noticed an accent, a lyrical up-and-down quality to his voice. He was a New Zealander, a Kiwi. I had a church friend from New Zealand with that same accent. The music of his voice calmed me a bit. "My cell phone doesn't work and there's no pay phone. Can you go for help?"

Quickly agreeing, he started his car and left. He turned right on Highway One and headed south. I took a long breath and watched him go. I knew he would be back, but Gini was waiting. She could be in shock by now. I grabbed a sleeping bag to keep her warm. Then I saw a flash of blue on the floor of the passenger seat. The Blue Ice! I grabbed the big ice pack, still very cold. *Thank you,* I breathed.

Running back along the beach, awkward with the sleeping bag, I prayed that Gini would be okay, that our New Zealand Samaritan would get help, that we'd soon hear an ambulance siren.

She was there, upright, white now, still gripping her foot and holding it onto her ankle. I could see a splash of dark blood under her foot on the ground, maybe a cup.

In a thin voice, she said "Susy, it will be okay. God was here with me."

Back down in the hole, we iced Gini's ankle and arranged the sleeping bag for her to sit on. "Would you hold my hand?" she asked. I could only grip her cold wrist, both of her hands still holding her ankle together. Every few minutes I climbed up the cliff and looked for an ambulance.

Then the New Zealander returned. From across the beach, he waved his arms, cupped his hands to his mouth and shouted above the waves, "Help is coming. I'll wait here." He stationed himself at the side of the highway, waiting once again.

Again that lilting voice, the comforting voice of this friend I had met in a lonely beach parking lot. The echo of the New Zealander's voice wove a blanket of comfort around me as I turned around to climb back down into the hole.

I took Gini's hand again. As we looked out at the ocean, a sailboat came into view. The large sail in the front was bright yellow at the top, and the wind had filled it out fat. Rocking gently up and down, the boat spit bits of foamy sea as it cut through the swells. I climbed the cliff again, saw the New Zealander, climbed down. We watched the sailboat, talked quietly, prayed.

The sailboat disappeared and finally they came. Firefighters, sheriffs, park rangers, paramedics—nine vehicles in all. They stabilized Gini, gave her morphine, immobilized her ankle in an inflatable splint and carried her up the cliff on a stretcher.

On her way through the field of wild irises, she smiled huge and sang out, "Stop! Did you know that irises are my *favorite* flower? Aren't they beautiful?" I knew then that everything was going to be okay.

When Gini was on her way to the hospital, a sheriff took me back to my car. It seemed like years since I'd seen it. Amid all of the uniformed personnel still milling around their emergency vehicles, I looked for the brown wavy hair of the New Zealander. I wanted to see him up close, grab his hand, thank him, but he was not there.

Nevertheless, I know he was part of a plan. On that day, God knew what Gini would face, and He prepared a table for us in the presence of our enemies (see Psalm 23:5). On that table? A sleeping bag. Blue Ice. A sailboat. Wild irises. A car in a parking lot; in it, a man with a New Zealand accent, waiting.

The Hitchhikers

Ray Cripps

I'D LIKE IT TO BE A VACATION GOD COULD USE," SAID MY wife Jean the night before we set off to tour Scotland three summers ago. It was the first time in twenty years we had been able to plan a break for just the two of us. Dave and Pete, our two sons, were camping in France, while our thirteen-year-old daughter Mary had just gone on a hiking trip with the Girl Guides.

So it was with light and thankful hearts that we piled our luggage into our old Morris and set off in glorious sunshine, up to the M5 and M6, two of Britain's new motorways, on the first leg of the long journey to the north. The roads became more congested the farther north we went, and we began to notice numbers of youngsters standing at the roadside, waiting hopefully for lifts. Although British drivers have had fewer bad experiences with hitchhikers than Americans, my wife and I were reluctant to pick up riders. But on this trip we had asked God to use us, so we had to have an open mind about it. As we approached one young couple, Jean suddenly said, "Let's give them a lift."

The bearded young man and the girl with close-cropped hair hadn't been in the car a minute when we realized we were going to have a communication problem. They were Czech, and the girl could speak just a little English, the boy scarcely any. But as the miles sped by, we slowly and painstakingly elicited something of their story.

The girl's name was Marta Zemanovz and the boy was Alec Pokorny, though he answered to the name of Ben, a nickname given him by some English students he had met the year before in Prague. They had left home about two weeks before, with the three pounds ($7.20) allowance permitted them by their government. Ben had managed to earn a few pounds cleaning the windows of an English country house, but this and their meager allowance had gone for food and bus fares, and their only food that day had been a bottle of milk for breakfast. Despite the differences in language and customs, this young couple grew on us. We ate our evening meal together in a Chinese restaurant in Glasgow, took them outside the town so they could camp for the night, gave them a little money for bus fares and food and then drove off to find somewhere to spend the night ourselves. Next day we spent the morning with some friends in Glasgow and on their advice decided to visit the coast resort of Oban by way of Loch Lomond. As we rounded a corner about four miles out of Glasgow, who should be thumbing a lift but Marta and Ben, who had just that minute gotten off a bus.

"Well," said a surprised Jean, "this was meant to be!" We picked them up again and spent the next two days with them. We took them to Fort William, greatly enjoying the Czech folk tunes they sang on the way, and after regretful good-byes left them to make their way home to Czechoslovakia, while we spent the rest of the week on our own.

We hadn't been back home a day or two before the news of the Russian invasion of Czechoslovakia came over the radio. A few days later we received a letter, postmarked Germany.

"Dear English parents," it began. "We are in West Germany, but we cannot go to our home because there is the war! Please, help to us! We wish to go back to your free country and work and live there in the time of the war in our country. It is possible to get a room (anywhere) and live there? We are very unhappy of it. It is very terrible for us and for all our people. The foreign soldats we all hate to have in our homes. Please, can you ask a work and room for us and write the answer very soon to us? We hope it will be possible to go back to your land. What do you mind about it? With the hope and love are waiting. Marta and Ben"

"Well," said Jean, "we asked God for a meaningful vacation, and He allowed us to share the lives of Marta and Ben, perhaps just so they might have somewhere to come."

Within ten days, our Czech children had hitchhiked back across Germany and France and were in our home. They stayed with us for two weeks while friends and well-wishers provided them with clothes and supplies. With the help of some Czech people who already lived in England, we found them jobs in a London clothing factory.

To our delight, Marta and Ben decided to get married. Without too much hope that she could get a permit, we invited Marta's mother in Czechoslovakia to visit us in England and attend the wedding. She was able to get a permit to come and brought with her for the ceremony a wedding veil that had long been in the family.

At one point before the wedding, the young couple expressed amazement at the series of coincidences that had brought us together. As wisely and lovingly as we could, we told them of our belief in God and the fascinating experiences He brings us when we turn our lives over to Him. "God makes these coincidences happen," we said. I'm not sure they understood our words, but they read our hearts and knew we cared. And I'm content to leave it there, knowing what miracles God will work in the future through people who let themselves be used by and for Him.

An Angel Named Faye

Nancy B. Gibbs

⟡

W ELL, IT'S JUST ME AND YOU, GOD," I WHISPERED AS I lay in the dark hospital room.

Four days earlier I had what was considered minor gallbladder surgery, returning home only a couple of hours later. As the next few days passed, however, I felt something was severely wrong. I couldn't get a deep breath. All the aches and pains associated with surgery had subsided except for a sharp pain in my right side. Instead of getting better, the pain was becoming more and more intense.

"I'm about to call the doctor," I informed my husband Roy.

"Go ahead," he agreed. He was probably tired of hearing my complaints.

After I explained what was going on, the doctor told me to call him the next day if I wasn't any better. The next morning I woke up with chills. I called his office, but he wasn't there. Later that day he called me back. When I explained the chills, he asked me to come right to his office. That move caused a flurry of events.

Before I knew it, I was having chest X-rays and receiving frightening news. A spot showed up on the X-ray.

"I'm sorry to have to put you through this, Nancy," the doctor said, "but we have to take care of this tonight. I'm sending you to the hospital."

Words such as *blood clots* and *pneumonia* were being whispered all around me. There were release-of-responsibility forms to sign and tests to be run. Every face I saw carried a solemn expression. I have to admit, I was as afraid as I was sick.

I placed my life in God's hands and listened closely to what all the doctors and nurses were saying. A chest scan was performed. I asked questions, but nobody seemed to have definitive answers. "We just have to wait to see," I was told over and over again.

"Do you understand how sick you are?" a nurse asked. I guess I didn't, but I took her word for it and prayed even harder. After a great deal of company the next day and telephone calls from dozens of friends, I was exhausted.

Everyone returned home later that evening. Night had fallen. My husband prayed with me and went home to get a little sleep. That's when I finally let the tears go and had a heart-to-heart talk with God.

"God," I whispered out loud, "please send your hope to me through the next person who walks through that door." I looked over at the door. The words were just out of my mouth when I heard a knock.

"Come in," I said as loudly as I could speak.

A nurse, Faye, who had recently come on duty, stuck her head inside my room. "Is there anything I can do for you?" she asked.

"There surely is," I responded. I needed to get up for a few minutes and asked her to help me with my IV pole. She noticed a Christian book on my bed and commented on the title. That opened up a conversation about God between the two of us. For the next ten to fifteen minutes we talked about God's power, prayer and our relationships with Him. She left the room, and I was still afraid.

Less than five minutes passed before I heard another knock. Faye walked back into my room. "Oh yeah," she said, "can I tell you something else?"

"Sure," I answered.

"A pastor once told me that when I am going through painful times and feel I can no longer hang on to God, I should just let go and let Him hang on to me. I just felt I needed to share that with you."

Tears began to stream down my face. I knew that wasn't a message from Faye or even from her pastor, but a message from God to me. God was letting me know He was hanging onto me at one of the weakest moments of my life.

I was able to release my struggling as I pictured God's mighty hands holding me. In a little while I fell asleep, knowing I was in good hands. I am convinced that nothing happens outside of God's will. I will always remember that although it's good to try to hang on to God, sometimes letting God hang on to us is the best way to live through the trials in our lives. When I asked God for someone to come into my room and bring hope to me, He didn't waste any time. Hope entered my door through an angel named Faye.

Have Your Tickets Ready

Heather Down

I NEVER TURN DOWN A CHANCE TO TRAVEL. THIS TIME I was off to sunny Southern California for a job interview. A nice change from wintry Ontario, I figured. But after a few days in the sprawling Los Angeles area, all I wanted to do was get back home. My city had parks, places for people to meet and greet, life on the streets, no matter how cold. I was used to daily visits with my neighbors and local shopkeepers. LA seemed impersonal to me. People were always jumping in and out of cars, hurrying somewhere. How did anyone make friends here? I felt completely isolated and even a little bit afraid.

My anxiety increased with the congestion at Los Angeles International Airport when I arrived for my return flight to Canada. Outside, the streets were jammed with honking cars, and inside it was wall-to-wall people. I'm no stranger to travel, but I felt like one. *You're a grown-up*, I said to myself. *Get a grip*.

There was some kind of commotion in the security line. "Why is that woman shouting?" I asked the man ahead of me. He didn't know. Was there a crisis we hadn't been told about?

The line inched forward. Dutifully I put my wallet, keys and glasses in the tray. My heart raced as I was scanned and scrutinized by unsmiling attendants. I'd never felt so uncomfortable and alone.

I made it through the security check and breathed a sigh of relief. Adjusting my carry-on bag over my shoulder, I headed for the restroom. Splashing cold water on my face made me feel somewhat better, but my uneasiness remained. What to do now? *Shop!* I decided. Strolling through the stores, I sampled new lipsticks, rejected a souvenir T-shirt and finally bought a glossy magazine. I settled into a seat near my gate and lost myself in reading.

After a while I was vaguely aware of an announcement over the speakers. "What did they say?" I asked out loud. No one nearby answered me. Then I glanced at my watch. *Five minutes!* I had five minutes to catch my flight. Frantic, I unzipped my bag and rummaged for my passport and boarding pass. But where were they? *Dear God* . . . I couldn't find my documents anywhere in the bag! What would I do now? My feelings of isolation welled up inside me. *I'll never get home!* There was no one in Southern California I could call for help. My heart pounded. *Breathe!* I told myself, sensing absolute panic taking over. *Think!*

Then I remembered. I'd put my passport and boarding pass on the counter in the restroom when I washed my face. I bolted from my chair and down the corridor. How much time had passed? A half hour? More? Surely my documents would have vanished!

As I neared the restroom, I heard someone calling my name. "Ms. Down? Ms. Down?" A young, stylishly dressed Asian woman stood at the door, waving what looked like my passport and my boarding pass.

"That's me!" I shouted. She smiled and presented me with the documents.

"You really should take better care of these things," she said.

"Thank you!" I said, crying tears of joy as I looked at the precious pieces of paper in my hands. I sighed and closed my eyes for a few seconds.

I started to say thank you once more as I opened my eyes, but the woman was gone, nowhere to be seen in the airport corridor. I hurried into the restroom, but she wasn't there either. Clutching my passport and boarding pass with an iron grip, I ran for the gate.

"Have your tickets ready," the attendant said. I raised my documents like a triumphant banner heralding my passage home. I no longer felt like a stranger. In what I thought was an impersonal city, God had sent someone who called me by name.

Special Delivery

Margaret D. Anderson

———— ❈ ————

B YE-BYE, DADDY," I CALLED FROM THE CURB, ECHOING
four-year-old Peggy Jean. I put my arm around her shoulder, drawing her close, and we waved till my husband drove
out of sight. This was Lee's first day on his new job with
Montgomery Ward, and we'd just moved to a rented home in
Galesburg, Illinois, from Niantic, one hundred thirty miles away.
I looked at the tidy brick houses around us, suddenly feeling
very alone. Until that summer in 1943, we'd lived near family
and friends. This was a city of thousands, and I didn't even
know our neighbors yet. How would I cope? *God will provide*,
I reminded myself, thinking of the expression I'd heard my
mother-in-law use time and time again.

"Can you help Mommy unpack?" I asked, managing a smile
for Peggy Jean. She nodded. Inside I checked on her baby

brother. Gordon was sleeping soundly in his crib, so we went to the back of the house where all the boxes were waiting.

I walked into the kitchen and gasped. A stranger was seated at the table—a rough-looking man with a beard, long hair and worn clothes. I don't know how he got in. It wasn't uncommon in those days for hoboes to knock on the door searching for a hot meal, but I never expected to find one in the house.

"Who are you?" I demanded, trying to keep the fear out of my voice. I stood firm in the doorway, shielding my daughter.

"I'm your egg man," he replied.

"But I don't have an egg man," I declared.

"Oh yes, you do," he answered quietly but firmly, placing a basket on the table filled with large, perfect eggs, the shells the color of ivory. "I will bring you two dozen each week."

"How much are they?" I asked.

"A price you can afford," he said. Sure enough, it was less than the store charged.

"All right," I said, still not certain this was the best thing to do.

True to his word, the man began delivering eggs. Every Wednesday after the breakfast chores were done and the children were tended to, I'd come into the kitchen and find him sitting at the table. His appearance may have been rough, but his manner was gentle. Each week he chatted with us, his friendly eyes crinkling at the corners, and he always asked to say prayers before he left. I began to look forward to his visits. In fact, he helped me feel at home in this strange new place.

Then the widow from whom we were renting returned from her travels, and we had to move again. We found a two-story frame house far on the other side of town, with a large yard where the children could play. I told the egg man we were leaving, but in the hubbub of moving I forgot to give him our new address.

In the new house, my loneliness returned. Lee had been promoted to district manager, which meant he was on the road all week long. Gordon was one year old by that time and a handful, walking and climbing everywhere. I was in the midst of a difficult pregnancy, and on top of that I came down with the flu. It was all I could do to get through the day.

One morning I dragged myself into the kitchen feeling worse than ever. Seated at the table was the egg man. Never had I seen a more welcome sight.

"What's wrong?" he asked.

"I feel terrible," I whispered.

"Then we'd best pray," he said.

The man called for Peggy Jean and Gordon. He lifted Gordon with his big, rough hands and set him down before a chair, where we knelt in prayer. With a child on each side, I listened as he asked God to comfort and heal me, his words warming me. When we stood up, I felt a little better.

"You are a good woman," the egg man said as he left. "God will bless you and your family."

The next morning I was completely recovered. Little Hal soon came into the world, and new friends took care of the children while I rested at home. Later, feeling myself once more, I realized we had not seen the egg man in weeks. Concerned, I telephoned friends in the old neighborhood. They had never heard of anyone who delivered eggs. It was the same when I questioned our new neighbors. Although I never found the egg man sitting at our kitchen table again, he'd been there when I needed him. My mother-in-law's words had proven true. God does provide.

CHAPTER FOUR

MIRACLES OF CHRISTMAS

Jesus said to them, "I did one miracle, and you are all amazed."
—*John 7:21* (NIV)

The Bus-Riding Angel

Robert Strand

<hr/>

TWO THINGS ARE ALWAYS IN SHORT SUPPLY WHEN YOU are a college student: sleep and money to go home with. Margarete was away at college, a hardworking, diligent college sophomore. She was a resident of a dorm where sleep was in short commodity. Girls being girls, and studies being studies and boys being subjects of many late-night conversations, the nights seemed pretty short.

The Christmas holidays were soon approaching, which meant a trip home was almost in sight. But as always, college professors haven't much heart and usually schedule tests during the last three or four days preceding vacation, so again, sleep was hard to come by. Grandma Hendley had sent the funds for Margarete's long bus ride home. As soon as the last class was over, Margarete made her way to the bus depot loaded down with packages and a few presents. She quickly purchased her ticket and boarded the bus. She was thankful that her first choice in seats was available—the very last seat next to the back door—where she could stretch out and sleep without interruption all the way to her destination of Mankato, Minnesota.

Stretching out with no one to bother her with questions or break into her sleep felt like such a luxury. The only sounds that filled the bus were the quiet murmurs of other passengers and the steady hum of the tires on the highway. Such were the comforting, soothing sounds that lulled a tired college sophomore to sleep.

As she slept, the motion of the bus and her tossing pushed her shoulders against the back door. Suddenly, without warning, the back emergency exit door swung open with Margarete wedged against it! Her head and shoulders hung out the open door—awakening her instantly, of course—and she felt herself falling into the blackness of the night toward the hard concrete of the highway. Her first thought was, *I'm going to die!* She frantically grabbed for the door frame to catch herself but missed!

She prayed the most fervent prayer of her short life in just three words: "Jesus, help me!" And to this day, she says she can almost still feel it: a pair of huge hands caught her and pushed her back into the bus. She quickly looked around, but no one was sitting near enough to her to have touched her.

When the warning light of the open door flashed red, the driver brought the bus to a quick stop and came running down the aisle. Stopping short, he took in the sight of Margarete sitting next to the open door and leaned down to ask her, "Are you all right? I can't understand how it happened. Did you lose anything? Are you afraid? Did you get hurt?" As you can imagine, he was more than a bit upset with the problem.

Still in a sort of shock, Margarete answered, "No sir, no problems."

"Well, then, how did you manage to hold on and not fall out?"

She replied, "I believe I had some heavenly help."

Coming Home

Amy Hauser

A MURKY DRIZZLE SATURATED DULUTH'S WEST MICHIGAN Street, darkening the sidewalk my husband Nolan carefully moved along, counting each pace, each solitary division in the pavement, his hands jammed deep in his jean pockets. He paused in front of an empty lot choked with litter and weeds. Pointing to it, he turned slowly toward the car, where I peered at him through a ragged porthole I'd rubbed in the window fog with the palm of my hand. The rain slanted down on his back, and his glasses were streaked. "This was it," he called, nodding for emphasis. "Right here."

Nolan had found it, the spot where the Blomstrom house had stood. We'd traveled here to Minnesota from our Pennsylvania home, following the thread of Nolan's restless search for his past.

I couldn't help thinking what courage he had. My husband is a strong, loving man, but quiet and private. Rarely does he speak of the day in 1960 when his ten-year-old world came apart. Through the years, though, I've pieced together the story. Nolan had run all the way home from the park that blistering July afternoon to his house on West Michigan.

Stunned onlookers stood in the Blomstrom's neat yard. Neighbors craned out of their windows. Angling his way breathlessly to the front of the crowd, Nolan suddenly froze. There on the grass lay his mother, cradled by his older brother Ronnie. Then a family friend was leading Nolan away and trying to explain the terrible truth that would change his life and the lives of his seven brothers and sisters forever: Nolan's mother and father had been the victims of a tragic accident.

As Nolan now stared through the downpour at the forlorn tangle of undergrowth that was once his boyhood home, I imagined the ghosts sweeping through his memory: policemen milling around the house, reporters scribbling furiously and photographers snapping their cameras, the hysterical wail of the ambulance rushing away his dying parents as a neighbor blotted Nolan's tears with her apron and held him back.

I wished I could wipe it all away for him, all that sorrow and pain in his past, push it all out with love. Though I knew this was his own private moment, I couldn't help going over and putting my arm around him, my fingertips barely reaching his far shoulder. He leaned slightly into my embrace.

After the deaths of their parents, the Blomstrom kids were scattered. Initially, two went with relatives; Nolan and five others were taken in by a local minister and his wife, the Hausers. Family pets were given away, possessions sold off, the house closed up. Eventually the Hausers moved to South Dakota and then Minnesota, where they finalized adoption of the four youngest children. Time passed. The kids grew up and moved on, separated by time and distance. Never again would they celebrate Christmases or birthdays together as a family. They had faded apart forever, it seemed, under the shadow of tragedy.

Yet something, some inexplicable thread, bound the children together. Through the decades and across geography, they managed not to lose touch completely. A graduation announcement or word of a wedding or birth was passed around in the course of a year or so. News circled: an unexpected phone call, an impromptu postcard. One sister married her high school sweetheart; the youngest girl married a minister. Nolan and I were teachers. We married in 1977 and lived in Marion, Indiana. The one mystery was Ronnie. He dropped out of sight sometime in the seventies, not to be heard from since.

Nolan took one quick last glance over his shoulder before we climbed in the car and he started the engine for the trip home. The wipers slapped the raindrops off the windshield as we eased down West Michigan. For the first time in our marriage I felt truly connected to Nolan's past. *It must be so hard for him*, I thought as I studied his coppery profile, as handsome to me as ever, his eyes soft and blue. *Thank God for the children, for the school.*

Our coming to the Milton Hershey School in the rolling countryside of Hershey, Pennsylvania, is, we believe, intrinsically tied up with what happened to the Blomstrom family that fateful summer day in Nolan's childhood. In the early eighties, schools began to close in the Midwest. I'd left teaching to stay home with our two kids, Nathan and Sarah. With layoffs imminent, Nolan's search for another position proved futile. Our daily prayers for someone to buy our house seemed to no avail. We needed to sell so we could move to more fertile job-hunting grounds.

"Lord," I pleaded, "what do You want us to do?"

Late one night back in western Pennsylvania in the small country house where I grew up, my mother lay awake in bed. She was anxious about our job situation. She'd prayed and prayed about it. Now she got up out of bed and paced. Suddenly she sat down and wrote a letter to an unusual school she'd heard of in Hershey, asking about a job for us. It was not the type of school that would normally have appealed to us, yet Mom had felt compelled somehow in the middle of the night to get out of bed and write that letter. When she received the applications, she passed them on to us with a sheepish apology. "Being house-parents at a boarding school probably wasn't what you had in mind, but I was at my wit's end for a way to help you."

Houseparents? We read the brochures and applications. *That doesn't sound like us; we're teachers.* But we were in no position to be choosy. We still hadn't had a nibble on the house when we decided to drive the six hundred miles to Hershey for an interview.

Now a wonderful, mysterious thing began happening in those green farming hills of Pennsylvania. Even before we reached Hershey, a feeling overtook us, a growing feeling of calm, a kind of peace we'd been praying for. We hardly spoke the last few miles.

We listened intently during our interview with the residential director of the school, who explained its history to us. When Milton S. Hershey, the chocolate magnate, died in 1945, the beneficiary of his fortune was the school he had established originally for orphaned boys. Spread today across a nine-thousand-acre campus, eighty-nine student homes accommodate eleven hundred boys and girls.

"Everything is provided at no cost to their parents," he said. "They're here because in some way their lives have been disrupted. Maybe it's been the death of a parent or a difficult divorce. Some parents just want their kids away from a bad environment at home. All are here for a solid education. They live in homes with special couples we call houseparents, who provide a stable, nurturing environment where the students can grow and succeed."

It was one of those clear and vibrant moments when you know your life is changing. Nolan's eyes met mine, and we understood right then that we would come here to live with these children. No hesitation, no second thoughts. That calm sense that we'd been led to Hershey was stronger than ever. Yes, Nolan knew these kids. He'd been one of them.

I wished I could wipe it all away for him, all that sorrow and pain in his past.

We drove back to Marion. And like a blessing, the house we couldn't sell had a buyer the day we returned. It was just a matter of packing now.

Today we live at Student Home Stiegel with our children and eleven boys ages ten to fourteen. Our lives have become interlocked with those of our students and the school. We've seen many lives change—but none more amazingly than our own.

One by one Nolan's siblings visited. Hershey became a common ground for the scattered family, a magnet, a place they came back to. The filament that had mysteriously connected them through the years irresistibly pulled them together once more, this time permanently.

First Nolan's youngest brother Terry and his wife moved here from Oklahoma to be houseparents. They now live across the hill at Student Home Moldavia. Then came sister Donna and her husband from Rhode Island. They're not only houseparents; they're also our next-door neighbors. From New Mexico came the eldest brother Keith and his wife and daughters. Then it was Neal and his family from Illinois—all of them drawn by this remarkable school, all of them houseparents to children whose lives in so many ways parallel their own. Sisters Diane from Mississippi and Kay from South Dakota visited this summer. We joked that we wouldn't be surprised if they too show up one day to stay.

This Christmas season Nolan, Nathan, Sarah and I will join with Nolan's brothers and sisters and their families at one of our homes for a traditional family meal. There amid the holiday scents of fresh pine and burning candles and the singing of carols about a silent night, we'll witness once again a miracle of our own. Nathan and Sarah will look around at their aunts and uncles and cousins, nineteen of us in all, together again because that is how families are meant to be. Not even the tragedy on West Michigan Street could destroy the loving force that bound this incredible family together through the years. Only Ronnie is still missing.

More than light or mistletoe, reindeer or candy canes, Christmas is about home, about family. It is most of all the story of a family—Mary, Joseph and Jesus, a family that grew to include all of us.

We'll sit down to Christmas dinner again this year thankful for the slow-motion miracle that drew this family close again, and in our hearts we'll remember Ronnie, wherever he may be, and in our prayers we will bring him home too.

A Simple Assignment

Zibi Davidson

THIS STORY ISN'T REALLY ABOUT ME, AND IT ISN'T REALLY about Christmas. But it is about a little Christmas tree ornament I made. It began with an assignment I had given my seventh-grade English class, requiring them to explain a process. Doug, one of my students, took some joshing for his project—demonstrating how to make ribbon-and-lace angel ornaments—but they were exquisite. An avid angel collector myself, I made them for Christmas gifts that year.

Sometime later, my friend Pat was asked to lead a retreat for our church. I couldn't attend the retreat, but I volunteered to make gifts for the closing party. With Doug's instructions by my side, I fashioned sixty-five angels of satin ribbon, decorator pearls and silk rosebuds to be given out as lapel pins.

I learned later that one of the participants, Kathleen Murphy, got home that evening to find her son very sick. She rushed him to the hospital, where the doctors said he would be fine. But in the next room was a critically ill baby who was not expected to live through the night. The baby's mother, who had to go arrange for a babysitter for her other child, asked if Kathleen would keep an eye on her infant. And Kathleen, who had not even had time to change clothes, removed the angel ornament from her lapel and hung it on a mobile above the crib.

Later that night when the baby's mother saw the angel dangling over the crib, something awoke in her. Though she was not a religious woman, she was moved to pray for her child. In the morning she and the doctors were amazed. The baby had pulled through. And the young mother left the hospital with new faith in God's power and love.

So as I said, this story isn't really about me. It's about how a classroom assignment became part of a child's miraculous recovery, about the mysterious and wondrous link that connects us all in God's plan. This time, with the help of a tiny Christmas-tree angel, I saw my small part in that great plan.

All My Heart, This Night Rejoices

Judy Stanfield Corley

I PARKED IN THE NEARLY DESERTED LOT AND STARTED toward the hospital entrance, my open coat flapping in the freezing wind. I wanted to feel the cold air on my neck, wanted the snow promised by the imposing mass of gray clouds overhead to pour down on me—anything to break through the numbing grief I'd felt for the past two years.

That Christmas Eve I was on my way to comfort my friend Naomi. Her only child, twelve-year-old Jimmy, had slipped into a coma despite a brave fight with cancer. Naomi had been my first friend in Nashville, where my husband Bob and I had moved eight months earlier. Living in Naomi's apartment building, we saw a lot of her. When

I listened to her play her guitar and sing, I felt an inkling of peace.

I walked up the hospital steps, slipping on the icy slush, and took the elevator to the children's floor. A large tree with blinking lights and shiny ornaments stood in the lobby. The nurse's station was lined with food baskets from grateful families. A radio softly played Christmas music. *Why even bother?* I thought to myself. The display seemed pointless in the face of the sadness and suffering all around.

I walked into Jimmy's darkened room. Tubes protruded from all over his body, and his breathing was labored. A heart monitor beeped. Christmas cards decorated the wall opposite his bed. Naomi stood at the window, her guitar resting on the chair behind her. I went over and hugged her.

"Where is everybody?" I asked. Naomi's relatives had been taking turns sitting with Jimmy.

"They're taking a break. Weren't you and Bob going to a Christmas party?"

"I didn't feel like celebrating. And I thought you could use some company."

She smiled at me in the dimness and then closed her eyes. I looked out at the clouds hanging low in the sky, so thick they made the heavens seem impenetrable even to prayer. I doubted God was listening, anyway. Hadn't my pleas for a child of my own gone unanswered? I thought of the crib Bob and I had so carefully picked out, the toys tucked away on the top shelf in our closet, the baby names I had whispered to myself, longing to call them out loud. Two years earlier when I became pregnant, I was thrilled. But then came the spring day when my doctor sadly told me the baby I had carried for eight months was dead. Later, he told me a second pregnancy was unlikely. I didn't think anyone could ease the loneliness I felt every time I looked at that empty crib, waiting for something that would never be.

It seemed a cruel irony that, on this night celebrating the birth of a child, I was still mourning my son and Naomi was losing hers. So much for Christmas miracles. Naomi picked up her guitar from the chair and held it, strumming thoughtfully. Then she began to sing "What Child Is This?" her clear, sweet voice filling the room. I sat beside the bed and held Jimmy's hand in mine. *I wish we could get through to you, Jimmy,* I thought. *Come back to us.*

Looking over at Naomi, I saw the doorway crowded with people listening to her song. A woman stood behind a little boy in a wheelchair, stroking his hair. A man carried a baby girl with IVs attached to her arms and feet. Other children peeked around the edges of the doorway. Naomi got up and walked into the hallway, still singing. I heard her going up and down the corridor, her voice ringing out with warmth and joy even in the midst of her own sorrow. I kept holding tight to Jimmy's hand, wishing I could give so much of myself to others. But I felt hollow, spent. I had nothing to give.

Jimmy stirred a bit, moaning softly. Outside, the night looked dark and brooding. If only something would happen.

I was so tired of waiting for things. For a child of my own, for Jimmy to wake up, for the snow to fall . . .

Naomi came back with a nurse, who checked the machines connected to Jimmy. "His vital signs are steady but weak," she said to Naomi. "If he doesn't wake up soon . . ." Her voice trailed off.

The nurse left, closing the door behind her. Naomi buried her head in the sheets beside Jimmy. I felt her sorrow so deeply it pushed aside my own for a moment.

"God," I whispered, "please help."

The door opened and I looked up, expecting to see the nurse again. Instead, Naomi's family filed into the room. I stepped back toward the window as they circled the bed and reached out to touch Jimmy's frail body. A blanket of hands, young and old, smooth and gnarled, moved over him. His grandmother lay down beside him and whispered into his ear. Naomi began to play her guitar again.

"All my heart this night rejoices," she and her family sang. "As I hear, far and near, sweetest angel voices." I'd never heard the song before. It was beautiful. Naomi's brother turned to me, stretching out his hand. I hesitated, but he nodded and smiled. I grasped his hand and stepped into their circle. When I reached out for their hands, I felt God reaching out to me through my shell of numbness and filling the emptiness inside me with hope.

There was no blinding light, no thunder, no shaking of the earth. But in that moment I felt my wintertime ending. When I glanced out into the night, snow was falling at last.

Everyone except Naomi stopped singing. Blinking back tears, I looked down at Jimmy. All at once, he opened his eyes. "Sing 'O Holy Night,' Mama," he said hoarsely.

Without a pause, as if she had been expecting it all along, Naomi started singing the song. The rest of her family embraced one another, and me. Wrapped in their arms, I listened to the peal of distant church bells. They seemed to be singing in celebration of Jimmy's awakening. And my own.

I went home to celebrate Christmas with my husband, knowing I had already received the gift I really needed. For the first time in two years, I felt part of the world again. God had been waiting for me to come back to Him as we had waited for Jimmy to come back to us. I saw then that whatever the future held, He would be there beside me. Today, twenty-two years later, I'm reminded of that every time I reach out for the hands of my three sons. Through them, God embraces me with His love—as He did that snowy Christmas Eve when my heart learned to rejoice again.

And by the way, Jimmy eventually returned home and his cancer went into remission.

Christmas Miracle

Connie Wilcox

ALL MONTH LONG I HAVE BEEN SAYING, "IT IS TIME FOR miracles." The holiday season always brings surprises, joy and generosity.

Working at Longmont's transitional housing facility called the Inn Between, I have witnessed these miracles for years. Anonymous donors and community support miraculously appear to help the Inn's many residents. I have the honor of watching people's tears of joy and relief when something they are in need of appears. I see their gratefulness for the help, and the instant renewal to their spirit. Donna Lovato, the Inn's executive director, attributes it to the Inn's angels. When a tenant needs something, Donna just asks the angels to bring it to the Inn. Within a few days, sometimes sooner, it appears! I am fortunate to work in a place where I get to see miracles happen every day.

Last week, one of the largest miracles I have seen occurred at the Inn. One of the residents was in desperate need of a thousand dollars to get her car fixed. She was distraught over the high repair quote. An anonymous donor appeared at our door wanting to donate money for this specific tenant. We graciously accepted the donation and worked quickly to pass it on. We called the tenant to the office and presented her with a check for the thousand dollars. She was shocked, amazed, grateful, shaking and full of tears. By the time she left, the entire staff was in tears as well.

This year, I not only witnessed a grand miracle, I also experienced one firsthand. My family has been struggling financially. For the past several months, the bills have exceeded our income to the point where buying groceries was a luxury. My husband and I both work and run a retail Internet business on evenings and weekends. We have been putting in long days trying to keep up with the increasing costs of survival. I am stubborn, proud and self-sufficient. I have always worked and done whatever it took to keep my family going. We don't live extravagantly, but we are happy with what we have. Our house is a thousand square feet, our newest car is twelve years old and our cell phones don't take pictures. I thought I felt gratitude for the things I have, but now I realize I had no idea what being grateful really felt like.

When my neighbor Judy asked me innocently if I had all of my holiday shopping done, I laughed and said, "Well, maybe

I can buy groceries out of my next check and then Christmas presents with the one after that."

We continued our conversation about our health, stress and kids, and I didn't give it another thought until today, when her son came by our house to drop off a Christmas card. I opened the card and two grocery-store gift cards tumbled onto the floor. I picked them up thinking, *Oh, how sweet.* Then I saw they were in the amount of five hundred dollars each. I started crying and shaking and saying "Oh, thank God!" over and over. I didn't know what to do. I think I had a mini panic attack after that. I tried calling her immediately to tell her I couldn't possibly accept such a large gift, but she wasn't home. I tried to think of what to say to her. While my thoughts were reeling, it occurred to me that my own miracle had just occurred. While I was working at the Inn last week, I had asked the angels for a Christmas miracle. I knew I would need one to make it through the holidays.

I did get to talk with Judy a little later. She explained that she had experienced a similar situation in the past and someone had helped her out. Now her family had had a really prosperous year, and they wanted to share it with others. Still overwhelmed, I felt better about accepting the gift. I cried all afternoon, feeling humbled, relieved and grateful. This experience showed me that the pay-it-forward idea really can work.

I never thought I would be in a position where I would have to rely on someone else just to make it. Being on the same side as those I worked to help every day was a new and eye-opening experience. I thought I understood what they were going through, when I really had no idea. What an enlightening experience. It made me realize that if it happened to me, it could happen to anyone. During the five years I have worked at the Inn, I have always said that most people are just one paycheck away from needing to live there. That day I realized how truthful that statement was.

I will never forget the feeling I had that day. I will always remember the deep imprint this experience has made on my soul. I will make a point to share when I can and to think of how much impact anyone can have by helping others. I thank Judy and Terry for their generous spirit and hope they realize how thankful I am. Their generosity not only makes an enormous difference in my life today but will for many years to come. I give thanks to the Inn's angels for bringing me a Christmas miracle.

Conceived by Grace

Diane White

E VER SINCE I CAN REMEMBER, I'VE WANTED SIX CHILDREN. I fell in love with a wheat farmer, and we married and moved onto the farm. It seemed the perfect place to raise a large family.

After two years of marriage, Dave and I decided it was time to start our family. We were ecstatic when our first attempt to become pregnant was a success. The pregnancy, however, lasted only a short time. Alarmed when I started to spot blood, we knew something was seriously wrong. Losing our first baby was devastating to both of us.

Several months after my miscarriage, I still didn't feel well. Two weeks before Christmas I started to experience severe cramping in my lower abdomen. I saw my doctor, but he was unable to determine what was wrong. The discomfort increased, but I thought the pain must be in my head, so I didn't go back to the doctor.

I had planned to sing several solos in the upcoming church Christmas musical. I was losing weight and felt horrible, and it became clear that I could not participate in the program. The night before the musical, I was curled up in a fetal position in my bed in an attempt to endure the abdominal pain. I had difficulty breathing and by morning I couldn't walk.

David went to church the next day without me. When my mom called that afternoon to ask how I was feeling, I told her I couldn't get off the couch. She insisted that I call the doctor. Although he was heading to Spokane, he agreed to see me.

After examining me, he instructed us to go directly to the hospital in Spokane. We headed out in the midst of a blinding snowstorm.

At the hospital we learned I had a tubal pregnancy. My fallopian tube was bursting, and I was bleeding internally. My difficulty in breathing was caused by blood collecting in my esophagus. After undergoing emergency surgery, I learned I had been over three months pregnant. Because the baby was the size of a chicken egg and fallopian tubes are tiny and narrow, it was a serious matter.

As a result of the tubal pregnancy, I lost my right fallopian tube. I was devastated to learn that I had lost twins; one miscarried and the other fetus was stuck in the fallopian tube. This news grieved me because I had always dreamed of having twins.

After several years of trying without success to conceive, I was given tests to determine why I was unable to become pregnant. One of the tests involved the scraping of my uterine lining so the doctor could evaluate whether or not my uterus could carry a pregnancy.

I was told that the procedure had to be performed close to my menstrual cycle to avoid the risk of aborting a possible pregnancy. To ensure that women are not pregnant, doctors routinely order pregnancy tests before the scraping procedure.

Before beginning the sixty-mile trip to Spokane, I was supposed to take ibuprofen to minimize the pain that normally follows the test. I didn't take any medication because I sensed in my spirit that I might be pregnant. Throughout my infertility problems, I claimed God's promises and read the stories of Hannah and Rachel. God opened their wombs and blessed them, and I knew He would do the same for me. I was confident that God was going to bless Dave and me with children.

When we arrived at the doctor's office, my pregnancy test turned out negative. The negative result surprised me because of what I sensed in my heart. The doctor then proceeded with the test.

After the doctor scraped the inside of my uterus, he said he needed more tissue and had to scrape a second time. After the second uterine scraping, he offered me drugs for the pain. I still didn't feel peace about taking any type of pain medication, so I passed on his offer.

Back home, I suffered the usual cramping and spotting from the scraping. Two weeks after the procedure, I was concerned because I still hadn't started my menstrual cycle. I contacted the doctor, who asked me to come to his office right away. After an exam and pregnancy test, I learned that I was six weeks pregnant!

The Lord protected my son from the doctor's scalpel. I often tell Ethan Aaron that God has great plans for him because his life was miraculously spared before he was born.

God has continued to bless David and me with four more children. Even though we suffered the loss of the miscarriage and tubal pregnancy, we are now a family of seven.

Learning Christmas Love

Pat J. Sikora

O<small>F ALL THE</small> C<small>HRISTMAS GIFTS</small> I'<small>VE EVER RECEIVED, A</small> simple doll from more than fifty years ago remains most treasured in my mind. It taught me a lesson I've never forgotten.

My parents, who owned a small, rundown motel in rural Wyoming, counted on the summer tourist season to carry us through the long, isolated winters. But few tourists had visited our area that summer, meaning that even covering necessities was next to impossible. As the eldest of four children, I was old enough to understand my parents' dilemma but young enough to grieve at the thought of a Christmas even more sparse than usual. Although my friends were anticipating sleek bicycles, walking dolls and stylish new clothes, I knew my gifts would be far simpler. Meanwhile, the younger children continued to expect Santa to fill the gap they knew Mom and Dad couldn't.

Across the street from us was a dilapidated two-room shack. The peeling once-white paint barely covered a dwelling so small and inadequate that it was usually vacant. But that winter it housed the Miller family. We were delighted because the four Miller children were each slightly younger than each of us, making for great playmates.

However, we quickly learned that their life was much different from ours. Their father was long gone—where, they didn't know—and their mother worked long hours at the local café. I don't remember ever seeing her. The children were usually alone.

As the days of early December passed, my brother and sisters whispered of what Santa would bring us. Soon even I was excited enough to join in. Our faith in him was firm, even though Mom and Dad kept insisting that Santa had had a rough year too. I think we somehow felt that if we believed hard enough, he would come through.

And in the past, "he" always did. Despite many lean years, our parents had always managed to make Christmas special, filling the holiday with excitement and inexpensive but meaningful gifts to delight our hearts.

Perhaps most important, in the midst of our poverty we had one precious commodity that money couldn't buy: hope.

Not so with the Miller children. When they spoke of Christmas, there was no excitement, no mystery, no expectation.

Flatly, without anticipation, they insisted, "Santa isn't coming to our house this year." At first we didn't believe them. Who ever heard of Santa totally skipping a family? But when we realized they were serious, our skepticism turned to distress. They weren't even sure they would be able to stay in their little home through the winter.

"How can they have no Christmas?" we quizzed our mother at lunch one day. All she could do was shrug sadly in reply. Dad had no answers, either. We children fretted over their dilemma. We wished we could be Santa to the Millers, but of course that was out of the question. We had no money and our parents certainly didn't need another worry. We pondered for days trying to figure out what to do.

Then one night just days before Christmas, Dad came up with the most absurd idea we had ever heard of. Because Santa wouldn't be visiting the Millers, he proposed that maybe we children should.

"If you really care about your friends," he explained quietly, "your giving needs to be a sacrifice rather than something that doesn't cost you anything. Even if Mom and I could afford to help you, it wouldn't mean anything to you. You'll be getting a few gifts from relatives this year. So why not give one to each of your friends?" *He couldn't be serious!* But he was. We didn't know what to say. We considered his idea for a long time—several days as I recall. We'd be receiving so little ourselves that the thought of giving away even one precious gift was heart-wrenching. But we knew the Millers expected nothing at all.

Once we had made our decision, we could barely keep our secret as we anticipated the joy our gifts would bring. But at the same time, we had second—and third—thoughts. The suspense was unbearable. What precious gift would we lose? What if we regretted the decision? What if the cost was too high? Maybe Santa would come to the Millers after all so we didn't really need to do this. Maybe it wasn't too late to change our minds.

But we had committed ourselves to the plan, and our dad saw to it that we carried through. As we opened our gifts that Christmas Eve, a little doll dressed in a bright blue dress and hat was among my small stack of presents—a gift from my favorite uncle. I held it close for a long minute, gave its hair a lingering stroke . . . and then carefully wrapped it in bright paper.

The cold wind whipped our thin coats and bit at our cheeks and noses as we stepped out into the freshly fallen snow that night. Stars twinkled in the clear sky, and the streetlights turned the icy crystals into a carpet of diamonds. Across the street, the Miller house stood in darkness, a forlorn contrast to our mood.

Excitedly we crept across to the Miller's, new snow crunching under each step. At their doorstep we silently deposited a big bag tied with a red bow. Inside were that doll, a fighter plane from my brother and stuffed animals from my sisters. The tag on the ribbon read simply, "Merry Christmas, Love, Santa." Then we walked the short block to church to celebrate the Nativity, which became real to us for perhaps the first time.

As we ushered in Christmas moments later in our simple country church, I couldn't help thinking how surprised and delighted the Miller children would be when they discovered their presents. They would know that someone loved them, someone remembered them.

I don't remember any of the other presents I received that year, but I'll always remember the lessons I learned about giving. Not just giving useless gifts to people who don't need them, but really giving. I learned that true giving is motivated by love and often by sacrifice, just as two thousand years ago love motivated the Father to give His only Son to a needy world. And Christmas giving is as fresh today as it was that star-filled night in Bethlehem.

The Christmas Thief

Jackie Clements-Marenda

〜❦〜

"THANK GOD YOU WEREN'T THERE WHEN IT HAPPENED."
Our mother's hands folded over the telephone receiver.
"You might have been injured, or worse."

My brother Thomas and I exchanged worried glances.
It was just past 9:00 PM on Christmas Eve 1962, and we
were waiting for our dad to come home for the Christmas
holiday. Company downsizing had eliminated his long-held
local job, and at fifty-two years old, Dad had been forced by
financial circumstances to take a position with a firm located
two hours away by car. Dad wouldn't consider relocating his
family. With the job market so uncertain, he wasn't even
sure he would have this current job within a year. He felt
it was best for the family to stay in our familiar Brooklyn
neighborhood.

The commute was hard on Dad, and he and Mom decided he'd only come home on weekends and major holidays. Friday nights became a time of great joy in our home, while Sunday nights were dreaded. Good-byes never got any easier.

"The children will understand," Mom said into the phone. "You just be careful." Mom hung up and took a deep breath before turning to face us. Before she even said a word, Thomas and I sensed that the news wasn't good.

"That was Dad. Someone stole his car, and he's stranded in the town where he works. You both know that without a car Dad needs to take a bus and then three different trains. Because it's already so late, and because some of the depot locations are so desolate, Dad thinks it's best if he waits until tomorrow before attempting the trip."

We understood, but tears sprang to my eyes. I was nine years old, and this was the first year I was considered mature enough to attend Midnight Mass with my family. Thomas, at eleven years old, was a Midnight Mass veteran, and his tales of the grand celebration made me even more eager to attend. But without Dad in our pew, I knew my first Midnight Mass experience would be sadly lacking.

"That's not all." The tensing of Mom's jaw betrayed the feelings she was trying to hide. "You know how much Dad hates having to be away from us all. So this year, to feel like he was still very much a part of our lives, he decided to do all the Christmas shopping."

"Dad must have liked that," Thomas pointed out. "Instead of just sitting in his room at the boarding house every night after work, he had something fun to do."

"Dad had everything wrapped, ready to be placed beneath the tree as soon as he got home." Mom's brows drew together in an agonized expression. "He packed them in the trunk of the car this morning so he could leave for home right from work."

Thomas said the words she couldn't. "But the car was stolen, and all the packages were in it."

"Yes," Mom said as she flicked an imaginary speck of dust from her dress, fighting to keep her fragile control. "Even if the stores were still open, there isn't any money to replace what was lost."

A tumble of confused thoughts and feelings assailed me, and I faltered in the silence that engulfed the room. Thomas and I knew Dad had taken a large pay cut, which had meant sacrifices for all of us. Our Christmas tree was much smaller than in other years, and we were having turkey for Christmas dinner instead of the more costly roast beef. Even our Christmas wish list had contained just a few items. Had Dad gotten the miniature race car for Thomas and the golden-haired Barbie for me? How about the warm bathrobe Mom desperately needed?

"I hate the man who robbed our car!" The words burst from my lips. "He took Christmas away from us and I wish . . . I wish the man would die!"

"Jacquelyn Maria Bernadette Clements! Such a terrible thing for you to say!" Mom glared at me, frowning. "What the man did was wrong, but you must pity him. Lord knows what sort of desperate situation he's in that it drove him to steal, especially on Christmas Eve."

My eyes met Mom's disparagingly, and my lower lip trembled. I wanted to scream at her about our lost car and presents, but my brother's hand on my arm silenced me. He was right. What good would it do?

"When you're in church tonight, Jacquelyn, I think you should thank God for what we do have." Mom spoke quietly but firmly. "Sometimes the most important things in life are those you can't hold in your hand."

I'd lost interest in attending Midnight Mass, but at eleven-thirty Mom helped us bundle up for the four-block walk. I had never been out at that hour. The sound of ice crunching underfoot was a counterpoint to the still night and the black sky, which was illuminated by the high, white moon and a multitude of bright stars.

Our church interior was all my brother had claimed it would be. The bright moon allowed the arched stained-glass windows to flood the house of worship with brilliant light. Ornate candles and flowers filled the altar, while parishioners who were dressed to portray various biblical characters took their places around the stable replica. Even the choir was brightly attired, ready to sing in celebration of our Lord's birth.

While Father Quinn said the mass, I struggled to find something to be thankful for. We had no money, no car, no Christmas. I couldn't recall the last time Thomas and I went to a Saturday matinee with our friends, and Mom didn't even bake our favorite chocolate chip cookies anymore. Food necessities such as milk and bread came first, and there was rarely any money left over for sweets of any kind. Even our yearly summer visit to our grandparents was doubtful with bus fares being what they were.

The sudden cry of the baby portraying the Christ child drew my attention to the stable scene. But my eyes traveled past the infant, lovingly held in the arms of the Mother Mary actress, and came to rest on a figure who had just entered through the side church door. It was Dad!

A joy like I had never known swelled up within me, lifting with it all the shadows that darkened my young heart. I poked Thomas and pointed; he did the same to Mom. Our already crowded pew mates slid over a bit more so Dad could squeeze in with us. Our family clasped hands, and I realized I had found something to be thankful for: Despite all odds, Dad was home with us for Christmas.

"It was more than a coincidence—it was divine intervention," Dad later explained. "A truck driver in the phone booth next to mine overheard my conversation, and he insisted on helping me get home. He used his radio to contact other drivers along the way, and at rest stops I was passed from one truck to another. Each driver took me as far as he could. The last one dropped me off right in front of the church."

The kindness of strangers on a cold winter's night was another thing for me to be thankful for. The third blessing arrived on Christmas Day when our car was found abandoned about one hundred miles from where it had been stolen. It had minor front-end damage but, surprisingly, the trunk was never opened. All our Christmas gifts were safe.

Only hours before, this fact would have mattered more to me than anything else. However, it provided a mere jump on my happiness scale as I sat playing Monopoly with Dad.

How right Mom had been when she told me, "Sometimes the most important things in life are those you can't hold in your hand." The spirit of Christmas dwells within our hearts, and no one, not even the most skilled thief, can ever take it away.

CHAPTER FIVE

MIRACLES & ANIMALS

*"But ask the animals, and they will teach you,
or the birds in the sky, and they will tell you."*
—Job 12:7 (NIV)

His Divine Touch

Nan McKenzie Kosowan

I SMILED AS I UNZIPPED THE TENT FLAP IN THE EARLY morning half-light, stepped out onto the wet ground and headed for the car with the cat leashes in my hand. I could imagine curious Pepper last night with his paws on the car windowsill, looking out as lightning flashed and rain poured, and timid little Salt dashing under the seat as thunder crashed.

On this first night of their first camping trip, we hadn't taken the cats to bed with us in the tent because they might have been tempted to slip out and explore this Serpent Mounds Park wilderness. We reasoned they'd never be able to find their way back to this unfamiliar tent in this unfamiliar territory.

Minutes later I wasn't smiling. The car window, supposedly left slightly cracked to let in the fresh air, was rolled halfway down, certainly far enough to let two inquisitive cats escape for a night of hunting. As I feared, there was no sign of our cats in the car.

I hurried back to the tent to pull on a sweater and tell the family I was heading for the ranger's cabin to ask for help to find our two city cats out here in the wilderness. Before I could reach the cabin, my husband and two kids were pounding along behind me.

The only electric light of the entire campground was just outside the ranger's cabin under the park's sign. There, unbelievably, sitting straight and tall, was Pepper. He looked at us as we approached, his black-and-white head tilted to one side as though to say, "What took you so long?" Smiling in that inimitable way cats have, Pepper, tail held high in appreciation, rubbed our caressing hands with the side of his head as I clipped on his lead and led our errant little friend back to the tent.

There he devoured a dish of cat food, purred and rubbed us all over again to show his joy at being back in the fold. Then he stood still at the tent door, looking at us fixedly with obvious determination.

"Salt!" said daughter Lynda, "He wants to take us to Salt."

Nobody had been able to mention Salt's name up to that point, but we were all thinking, "Where could Salt be?" Pepper, again leashed, dashed out the tent door and led us at a fast pace to a barn just outside the campgrounds. I think we'll all remember that moment when Pepper ran into the barn and leapt onto a mound of hay to stand at attention over the shaking little white cat cringing there.

Salt had a fever and could hardly lift her head to acknowledge our presence. Lynda (it was her cat) picked Salt up carefully and went out the barn door, cooing softly to her little friend. We followed, with Pepper looking up at his little sister in Lynda's arms as though to say, "It's going to be all right now, Salt; the family's here." We didn't even consider continuing our trip or waiting to have breakfast. We packed up our camping gear, climbed into the car and headed straight to our vet back home, three hours away.

"Chicken fever," the vet told us. "Common among cats. Good you got Salt here as quick as you did. So Pepper's the hero, eh?" he said, stroking the black cat who watched the examination table proceedings.

Once we were home, Pepper relaxed his guardian role, looking into Salt's basket periodically as though saying "Just checking." Other than bringing her a mouse caught in a backyard hedge, which she sniffed but declined, he seemed content to leave his little sister in our hands. A few weeks later, huntress Salt was catching her own mice in the backyard hedge.

We've often wondered how far Salt and Pepper got into their park adventure before they had to escape the sudden, violent rainstorm. Knowing well his black cat's inquisitive nature, son Larry surmised he had led the way out of the far-too-open car window and that Salt had, as usual, followed her adventuresome brother without thought.

Sharing this story with friends, we marveled how Pepper had found shelter for them in the storm and then stationed himself at the one place in the park where he would be sure to be noticed.

One friend listened quietly and then put her finger on the heart of the story. "Well, God gave man dominion over the animals, which means caring responsibly for them. You can't call it being responsible when somebody leaves the car window open so wide your domesticated cats could climb out and get lost in the bush. And because nobody was there to help, I have to believe God gave Pepper a recovery plan that surpasses anything I can imagine a city cat coming up with in the wilds."

I agreed with a heartfelt "Amen!" of gratitude. When we cover our family with prayer every night at bedtime, we include the pets God has entrusted to us. He surely answered our prayers that night as He directed Pepper's courage and caring to turn around a danger-ridden adventure.

All right, who was the careless human who left the car window lowered too far? Nobody remembers, and we all agree it's just as well we don't. But certainly we are impressed with what our loving God can do for His creatures, human and animal, when all around us seems to fail. If cats had tombstones, we could have carved this epithet on Pepper's: "Brave feline paramedic and defender, by the grace of God."

The Charge of the Light Brigade!

Karen R. Kilby

<hr />

Boxes were everywhere! As I went from room to room, I began to feel overwhelmed with the task before me. *There is so much to do! I don't even know where to begin to unpack.* We had arrived a few days before from Florida to Michigan with our truckload of four dogs, our carload of kids and the moving van not far behind.

I had never been fond of our family of dogs. They were yard dogs and never allowed in the house—I considered them more of a nuisance. But I tolerated Thor, Brandy, Buck and Ralph for the sake of the kids. Thor was the first stray to be adopted, and then Brandy. Before I knew it, we had a litter of ten puppies! After much cajoling, we gave in to the pleas of the kids to keep Buck and Ralph.

We had moved into a home snuggled in the midst of a state forest, one of the few homes with year-round residents on our side of the lake. The tranquil lake setting was beautiful and the solitude was appealing, especially to me. Gazing out the window at the pristine stillness of the lake below, it occurred to me—*No one will even know I'm here.* Shaking off a feeling of apprehension, I decided to call David at the office before tackling the impossible task of unpacking. Remembering that our phone service would not be connected for another couple of days, I wondered if I could use my neighbor's phone.

I closed the heavy oak door behind me and started down the dirt road toward my neighbor's house. As the road wound its way through the woods, those apprehensive feelings returned. *With the kids at school and David at work, I really am all alone. I hope my neighbor is home. Thank goodness they are not far away.* As I turned to walk up the path to my neighbor's front door, their huge German shepherd charged into the front yard, growling ferociously.

Freezing in my tracks, I was afraid to move a muscle for fear this raging animal would attack me. "Oh, God!" I cried. "I'm afraid to move! Help me!"

Just as suddenly as the snarling German shepherd had appeared, I heard a mighty roar from behind me. Thor, Brandy, Ralph and Buck came charging into the yard, ready, willing and able to conquer my foe! The menacing shepherd took one look at the charging brigade, put his tail between his legs and ran for cover.

Never was I so glad to see those dogs as they jubilantly pranced and danced around me, rejoicing in their victory. "Good dogs!" I exclaimed over and over, patting each one on the head. As my heroes proudly marched me back home to safety, a newly found affection began to replace the tolerance I had felt before.

Thor, Brandy, Ralph and Buck continued their role as the Light Brigade, our sentinels in the midst of the state forest. As soon as one of us stepped outside the door, they stood at attention with wagging tails, ready to accompany us for a walk in the woods or down the road to destinations unknown. For me, their presence was a constant reminder of God's loving protection—that no matter where I was or in what situation, I was never alone.

My Patty Pat

Lisa Russo

M OST KIDS GET THE SNIFFLES, A COUGH OR A SORE throat now and then. But my daughter Tori gets sick a lot, and even a common cold can send her to the hospital. Or worse. Tori has common variable immunodeficiency, or CVID. It's a serious immune disease, a form of *The Boy in the Plastic Bubble* disease. Fortunately, we don't have to keep Tori in a bubble. Our doctor even encourages us to take her out, let her spend time with other kids when she can and lead as normal a life as possible. So that's how she met Patty.

When Tori was five, she had bronchitis ten times in as many months. Each time, we rushed her off to the doctor for antibiotics or the hospital for IVs. One time, driving home, my mind was clouded with worries. I glanced in the rearview mirror at my daughter, terribly thin and tiny as a three-year-old, her fine blonde hair sticking against her pale cheeks. *God, why does this child have to have this horrible disease?* But then I heard soft sounds from the back seat. Tori was singing cheerfully.

If she could bear it, I could be strong too. Several days later, Tori was feeling much better. "Let's take her to Newkirk's," my husband Tom suggested. His friend Newkirk owned a horse farm in Freehold, New York, and it was Tori's favorite place to visit. She loved the miniature horses and knew most of them by name. A day in the country would do her good.

Tori was the first one in the car, wearing her cowboy boots, nearly up to her knees, and her favorite horsey shirt. As we drove up alongside the pastures of Kinghill Miniatures, I watched the little horses kick up their heels in the warm sunshine. Full of spring friskiness, they galloped and cavorted, while Tori clapped her hands. As soon as the car stopped, she opened the door and dashed out to the pasture gate.

Newkirk was there to meet us. "Watch out for Patty. She's a ramrod today."

It wasn't the first time I'd heard about Patty. Newkirk had his hands full with the young silver chestnut mare from the day he got her. "I can't do anything with this horse," he'd complain. "She never listens to me, raises Cain on the farm and runs around like a demon!"

Tori squeezed through the gate. Unfortunately, she had one thing on her mind. "Patty!" she called, clapping loudly.

I caught up and grasped her hand. "Let's go see the other horses." But Tori shook her head firmly. "Patty Pat!" she called.

In the distance, Patty raised her head from grazing. When Tori called again, the horse perked her ears and turned toward us. Then, all of a sudden, she bolted our way like a streak of lightning. *Oh no!* I didn't have time to react; I just threw my arms around Tori as the horse bore down on us.

Tori, however, relaxed in my arms. Her body wriggled excitedly and her little arm stretched out, reaching for the horse.

I saw Tom charge toward us and Newkirk run to catch the horse. But when Patty was only a breath away, something amazing happened. Instead of ramming into us or bucking or any of the wild behavior she usually displayed, she stopped dead in her tracks. She whinnied very softly, as though saying hello. Her deep brown eyes stared right at Tori. Something in the horse's expression told me she sensed she should be gentle with this child.

Tori reached up and touched her silky neck. Newkirk stared, his eyes wide, his mouth hanging open. "That horse never does that for me," he said. "When I call her name, she runs the other way like a rocket shot!"

Patty lowered her nose and sniffed Tori, who giggled. I loosened my grip. What was going on? This horse was usually rough and unmanageable. When Tori reached up and hugged the horse, Patty just stood there, still as a statue. She let Tori walk all around her, kissing her. I wiped a tear, seeing how tender this horse became with my daughter. They wandered around the field together, fast friends, until it was time to go. Then Patty followed Tori to the gate.

"I don't get it," said Newkirk, shaking his head. "She's never done that before. For anyone. You've seen her, wild as the day she was born."

As our car pulled away, Tori wrenched around in her seat, trying to see Patty. And what was Patty doing? Pawing at the pasture gate, as if she wanted to follow us home.

From then on, we brought Tori to the farm to visit Patty as often as we could. Newkirk even let us buy Patty and keep her at his place. Patty was just as wild as ever except when Tori was around. Then she was calm and docile as a kitten. No one could explain it.

Tori's effect on Patty was clear. But just as amazing was Patty's effect on Tori. When Tori started school, she missed so many days due to illness we eventually had to have her home-tutored. She couldn't play contact sports or join in with other kids her age the way she wanted. Going out was awkward; sometimes she had to wear a mask to protect her from germs. I worried about her missing out on a social life that is so important to young girls. Few moms felt comfortable including her on sleepovers, considering her medical issues.

Every time she got sick, a scary thought lurked in the back of my mind. What if this time she didn't respond to the treatments? What if she didn't get better? She didn't have the kind of life other little girls had. Every two weeks she had to endure

IVs of immune globulins. The side effects left her sick and exhausted for days after. It crushed me to see her like that.

I sobbed into my pillow, *God, I know she is Your child and You know what's best. But my daughter is so weak. Sometimes we feel so hopeless.*

When she curled up in a ball on the couch, quiet and motionless, I worried—did she lose the will to go on? But when she saw Patty, everything was different. We'd pull up the drive and she'd head right to the pasture. "Where's my Patty Pat?" Every time, the horse came galloping.

When Tori felt well, they ran together in the field. When she didn't feel well, Tori sat on the ground, and Patty just stood over her like a sentry. One time Tori was too weak to play outside, so I pulled up a chair and sat her in front of the stall. Patty pushed her nose over the door. I left them together for a while to go talk with Newkirk. When I returned, Tori's school books lay open on her lap and she was reading out loud to Patty.

"Mom, she's going to be the smartest horse in the world," Tori beamed. I laughed and hugged her tight.

One day Patty suffered a devastating injury: she cut the tendon sheath on the back of her leg. No one could change her bandages. "She hates people messing with her legs," said Newkirk. The horse would thrash and kick, her nostrils flaring and eyes bulging. But when we brought Tori to the stable, Patty's eyes softened. Her gaze glued to Tori, she let us change her bandages. Patty stood stock still as Tori talked and sang to her.

Tori is eleven now. She still struggles with her illness, but whenever she gets down, she thinks about Patty and smiles. Illness after illness, treatment after treatment, somehow she gets through, and the first thing she asks is to go to the farm. Clearly she found the will to endure everything she is faced with so she can spend more time with her Patty.

There's no way we can know why Patty is calm only for Tori. Or how Tori draws strength and hope from the little horse. I just know God put Patty in our little girl's life for a reason.

"Where's my Patty Pat?" calls Tori. And I know the answer. *She's by your side and in your heart, the answer to a mother's prayers.* For God can send miracles of hope in many ways, even in the form of a rebellious little horse.

Feline Security Guard

Melody Rain

I WAS ALL THE WAY TO KINGMAN, ARIZONA, ON ROUTE I-40, when I realized I had made the biggest mistake of my life. Because my favorite catsitter was not available at the last minute, I made a quick decision to take Chloe with me on the three-week jaunt across country, from California to Tennessee, to record my second song in Nashville.

Her wails could be heard all the way to Nashville. As soon as Chloe figured out this was not a short ride to the vet but days and nights of driving, she went bananas! *I'm a fool*, I told myself to the tune of piercing cat cries, moans, groans, whines and whimpers. By Flagstaff I knew Chloe was not going to settle down and accept her fate.

In Albuquerque the car quit. It was a blessing. A reprieve! For two days Chloe and I camped out in a parking lot. When the temperature dropped to eighteen degrees the second night and the car felt like a refrigerator, my little sweet Chloe looked at me with perplexed eyes, her mouth turned downward, her expression sour! Very sour!

Nevertheless, I could not have had a better guard cat. By day she squeezed under my hanging clothes and pretended she was somewhere else. By night, while I nestled on a thin mattress covered with two comforters, Chloe sat on sentry duty above the back seat, where she had a clear, panoramic view out the car's windows. The guilt I was experiencing over putting my tiny one through this trauma was equaled only by the companionship and her amazingly watchful eye during her night vigil. She perched a few feet from me, turning her head this way and that like a wise old owl, surveying 360 degrees of parking lot. She noticed every sound or movement, determined to warn me of danger. When someone came near the car, Chloe would jump on me and cry out. She repeated this in Oklahoma City and Memphis on the trip to Nashville, and in Little Rock, Amarillo and Flagstaff on the way home.

When we finally arrived in Nashville, we stayed in the home of a Star Records secretary. I spared nothing in gourmet foods and cuddling, fearful that Chloe might decide to leave me. In spite of everything, the recording session went well. This time I felt more relaxed. The same group of great guys was there to play back-up. We congratulated each other on how well the last song had fared. I sipped my peppermint mocha coffee as I waited to do the first cut of "Wonderful You." Before returning home, I attended the Country Music Awards with Ed Rowe. I shook hands with Alan Jackson and Keith Urban. Reba McEntire came right up to me and congratulated me on my first song and wished me well on my second. *A great lady*, I thought to myself.

On the way home, Chloe escalated to paranoia. She jumped on the dashboard, clawed my clothes and refused to be consoled. Her heart raced, her stools ran, she trembled. If I could only get us home in one piece, I would never put her or me through this again!

Then what I feared most happened! The car began to wobble. I pulled over to the shoulder of I-40, just shy of Needles, to check my tires. When I opened the car door, thinking only of the safety of the car, Chloe sprang. I turned to glimpse her crossing lanes of surging traffic traveling at seventy-five miles an hour. Horns blared and brakes screeched as I screamed. When an eighteen-wheeler zipped by like a rocket entering space, I was sure my sixteen-by-seven-inch cat must have been run over.

I strained my eyes but could see no cat between the flying vehicles. Then, for a moment, I thought I saw her on the twenty-foot-wide grassy divider. Hoping I could cross over, too, I shot up a prayer that Chloe wouldn't try to cross back. I didn't think to pray that she wouldn't keep going. Functioning on fear and instinct, the feline started across the two lanes of eastbound traffic. Without pausing to look both ways as every school kid is taught, my traumatized cat rushed madly into the oncoming stampede.

I jumped in the car and sped for the nearest off-ramp, which happened to be several miles down the road. I re-entered I-40 going west, pulled the car to the side of the road where I last saw her, and searched the street to see if she had been hit. I pictured her glued to the front of a truck or careening around endlessly, stamped to the tread of a tire. Not finding anything and ignoring the arid atmosphere and burning sun, I moved quickly into the prairie wasteland, calling for Chloe and combing the area like a rescue team. Yucca plants rubbed against me as I stubbed my toes on jutting rocks while moving deeper and deeper into the brush.

Soon two sheriffs joined me, seeking the owner of the car parked on the shoulder of the Interstate. I thanked them for not ticketing me and convinced them that their presence was probably not helpful, as Chloe would distance herself. I wandered through the shrubs for well over two hours, calling for my cat until I was vexed. Spent! Where could she be? I had not had time yet to despair completely, but plenty of time to feel the stab of anxiety.

Dread felt like a tight rope around my chest. No tears—raw terror had dried them up. Finally I sat down on a rock, first looking carefully for rattlesnakes. I had already passed a tarantula. I tried to think, to reason like a cat. But after another hour of searching, dread drenched me like a tidal wave. *I won't leave her*, I told myself. *Dead or alive, I will find her. I will not lose her. I will not! So help me!*

I prayed. I pleaded. I screamed at the cloudless and scorching sky. I wandered back to the car to get a drink of water.

Bringing Chloe's water bowl back with me, I sat it down near the rock and closed my eyes for a moment of rest. I was so tired. When I opened my eyes slowly, there sat the cutest little cat, lapping up her water. She didn't even look harassed. I didn't move; I didn't know what state her nerves were in. When she finished drinking, she looked at me. Then, without taking her eyes off me, she crossed the ten or so feet from the water bowl and rubbed up against my leg.

Slowly I reached down, placed my fingers around her neck and carried her to the car. When we finally pulled up to our mountain cabin, our nerves were shot. As we went to sleep that night, Chloe buried under the covers, I couldn't help but think of the incredible vigilance of my security guard. Somehow I knew that anyone who ever attacked me would be clawed to death.

Contemplating my priceless, rare gem, I loved Chloe all the more. Then the reality of the near-death possibilities in the desert hit me. I knew Chloe and I had had help! *Thank you*, I whispered. *Thank you.*

If God Whistles

Laurie Klein

———————— ❈ ————————

SOULFUL EYES LIKE A COW'S, BAT-WING EARS, HIS PALE
hide randomly splotched with brown like Christmas *lefse*—
Charley the Mutt was hardly a looker. Think recycling gone
wrong in the animal kingdom: a 3-D collage of spare parts.
Even our veterinarian paused over the word *breed* on Charley's
initial paperwork. "Anyone's guess," he said with a chuckle.

From our love-at-first-lick meeting at the local pound,
I'd been smitten. My husband Will and I had owned a lot
of dogs; this one soon became *my* dog. Despite his dubi-
ous personal hygiene (he craved close encounters with mud,
manure, dead fish and porcupines), I loved that mutt. Charley
came at a single snap of my fingers, greeted me with joyous
abandon and comforted me over the grueling course of a
long illness.

Then the accident: After eight years together, Charley survived a warp-speed, nighttime collision—with what, we never knew—resulting in anguished cries and dozens of stitches. They crisscrossed his shaved side and belly like zippers put in by a tailor crazed on bad drugs.

In the coming days, as if I didn't have enough to worry about with Charley's recovery, Will asked if I'd volunteer for several months with him on a missions project out-of-state. A reluctant evangelist and even more reluctant traveler, I finally (reluctantly) agreed. Pets, however, weren't welcome. Who would care for my ailing dog? What if we ended up permanently moving there? Would it be kinder to give Charley to some lonely child or widow who would tend him? No. Would you adopt an overactive, half-shaved, cone-headed mutt with all his seams showing?

Days passed, each of them filled with my worries. Irrepressible, Charley was soon trotting alongside me again on morning walks as I prayed for guidance. With every roadside sniff, his plastic buster collar scraped up snow and gravel like a megaphone, the sound producing a contagious rhythm. A person could hip-hop to it—if not already weighed down with dread at leaving her dog (not to mention her home and comfortable life) for mission work that could entail . . . well, almost anything. *Please, God, show me what to do.*

Every morning I tended Charley's crazy-quilt backside, dabbing on salve. His skin was mending, but for some unexplainable reason, his appetite dwindled. Soon he stopped eating, even ignoring soup bones and boxed bowzer treats.

Back to the vet we went, where a new intern puzzled over Charley's symptoms. A heap of bones and fluff slumped on the steel table. The intern ran numerous tests on a dog grown strangely patient. In praying for the young man as he examined my dog, I remembered a pledge I'd made to God months ago. At church, our minister had passed out squares of paper, asking each of us to offer something to God that year as a Christmas gift.

Two things had leapt to my mind. I'd scribbled down both and tucked my paper into the offering bag—never suspecting the possible future cost. I had offered God my chronic fear of traveling, and then, half-heartedly—and only after feeling nudged several times to do it—I'd offered Him Charley, as well. But why would God want a dog? I had shrugged it off.

Well, that's that, I'd thought as we drove home. God knew I was responsive and willing, which was probably all He really wanted. Besides, I rationalized, how could one gift-wrap something as abstract as reluctance or as active as forty long-haired pounds of mischievous mutt?

Now, called back to the present by the intern's touch on my arm, I numbly scooped Charley into my arms, purchased his medicine and headed home. I kept thinking my pledge might now be required of me. Then I'd wonder if the young intern knew what he was doing. *Why should I trust a kid? Shouldn't I demand to see the vet for a second opinion?*

Once home again, I settled my pal on a flannel blanket and went out to the garage to smash a few yard-sale dishes. Crash.

What's going on here, Lord? Clang. *Charley's dying! Is this what You wanted?* I crouched among the broken pottery. *How can I leave him when he's so sick?* Then a worse thought struck: Was Charley's mysterious sickness somehow my fault? I heard no answer, but expressing my fear and frustration had helped me feel a little better. I swept up and went back inside.

By the next day, Charley could barely lick water from my fingers. I could count his bones. Maybe God would miraculously heal him. Yes, He was allowing my dog to inch up on death so that when He healed him dramatically, the young intern would be inspired toward faith. I had certainly dropped enough hints about the Christian life. I would stick with the intern and trust his judgment. Back we went. This time, I was excited.

With our mission departure date now only a week away, I okayed exploratory surgery, a last resort. There was no room in my head for trivial worries about the rigors of travel and mission work now; my prayers centered on Charley, with a passionate P.S. for the young intern. *Spare Charley's life, God, and I'll find him the perfect home. And save the intern too!*

Early the next morning, a Friday, I gently salved Charley's wounds and blotted his runny eyes. "Good boy," I murmured. "What a *good* dog." The seconds clicked by on our plastic wall clock, but I took my time, brushing what remained of his once-silky coat. It flowed over his heaving chest, sleek and baby fine, like the angel hair that festooned our Christmas trees back home when I was a child.

I carried Charley into the clinic alone that day, grateful to be the only client, because I couldn't stop crying—despite my stubborn hope for a wondrous recovery and the intern's salvation. After I set my dog down, he wobbled about, delicately sniffing that telltale aroma common to waiting rooms: part fear, part ammonia, part pine-scented cleaning products.

The intern outlined the procedure, adding, "You can still cancel, you know." Was he having second thoughts? "I trust you," I said with a shaky smile. *And You most of all, Lord,* I silently added. Miracles still seemed possible.

Later, when my phone rang, the intern was excited. "We did the right thing. He's come through beautifully."

"God's answered my prayers!" I cried.

"I hope so," he said. "I really do." He promised the lab report by Monday and invited me to visit Charley late that afternoon before the clinic closed for the weekend. How to pass the time? I busied myself baking bread for the entire staff. I had shared my faith in quiet ways during Charley's appointments. Maybe his recovery would convince them all how real and compassionate God was, that He cares about even the humblest details of our lives—including our animals. No wonder God had asked for my dog all those months ago. I could hardly wait for my visit.

When I walked into the clinic, the yeasty warmth of fresh bread delighted the front-desk workers at week's end. The intern, however, declined a slice. His face looked drawn. "Charley's failing," he said. "And I don't know why. I've had the other vets check him over. Fresh plasma might help, but it's costly."

I sank into a chair. Head bowed, I stared at the speckled squares of linoleum, counted the seams. With God, all things were possible; Charley still might rally . . .

The intern cleared his throat and gently repeated, "We could try the plasma."

I shook my head, suspecting my earlier pledge to God might now be required. The effort of standing up again made me feel old.

"No," I said. "But thank you. Thank you for all you've done. I know you were the right one to care for him. God chose you for us." And I shook his hand. He was so young, so new to the business; I didn't want him to lose heart before his career began.

For the next hour I knelt beside Charley's cage, stroking him, singing to him. Beneath a blue-flannel heating pad, the big ears drooped, the shrunken body shivered. Soulful eyes locked with mine, still devoted, seemingly determined to hang on for my sake.

"You were too weak for this," I whispered. "But we had to try." And then I thanked him for all the times he'd comforted me, protected me, made me laugh, made me know I was loved, without reservation, without condition. A love not unlike God's.

I didn't see the intern again that day. He was leaving, I knew, for the weekend, en route to his hometown to celebrate his wedding anniversary. I truly hoped Charley's decline wouldn't ruin his celebration and was surprised I could care that much about him.

At closing time I drove home fast, no music playing, all the windows rolled down. Later that night, during an informal church service, a praying friend laid her hands on my shoulders. I closed my eyes and a spurt of hope flared. Then, as clearly as I had sensed God requesting my dog all those months ago, I heard someone whistle, just once, with authority and boundless joy. And in my mind's eye, I saw Charley—those shaggy pantaloons like spotted boxer shorts, the huge ears flapping, the long, plumy tail—saw him sprinting—no, *barreling*—straight toward the One who had called.

Early Saturday morning the intern phoned to say Charley was gone. He'd called in from home to check on his progress. He'd wanted to tell me himself. He was so very sorry. Because God had already prepared me, I could assemble my thoughts enough to describe my experience the night before. I told him I believed God speaks to each of us in ways only we understand. I wished him well in his new career. The intern didn't brush me off, didn't say I was crazy. Neither did he say, "I want to know this God of yours." But he listened. Maybe he thought about it afterward.

That wasn't the miracle, though. It was this: I was given an indelible moment of illumination that still lights my way: When God whistled, Charley ran. I went on that mission trip empowered to move ahead with whatever God asked of me. Charley showed me the way.

"Yes, Lord," I continue to say. "When You whistle, I will run."

A Froggy Prayer

Kathryn Lay

⁓⁓⁓⁓⟡⟡⟡⁓⁓⁓⁓

IT HAD BEEN A LONG DAY AS I READ A FINAL STORY TO MY daughter at bedtime. I'd spent hours trying to figure out how to pay all our bills, knowing my husband was working a job he hated. But it was better than no job at all, which was where we'd been not long ago. We'd prayed and prayed for him to get back into teaching and out of the paper-buying business he'd been stuck in the past few years.

I'd prayed that day for a reconciliation with someone in our family we'd been having a conflict with. I'd worked on my children's novel, knowing that one book sale could help our finances a lot. But I'd been praying for these things for a while and we were still in the same situation.

"Please let me see a frog tonight, in Jesus' name, amen."

I hugged my four-year-old daughter good-night and tucked her into bed with her favorite stuffed animal. *A frog?* Her prayer was simple and cute, something from a book of children's prayers. We had been talking about frogs and lizards and turtles that day, three of her favorite creatures.

"When will the frog come?" she asked.

I smiled. "Well, Michelle, I haven't seen any frogs yet this year; we'll just have to wait and see." I felt bad that she would be disappointed.

"God can do anything," she announced. "Just like Daddy."

A lump filled my throat. She trusted in her father *and* her heavenly Father. Difficult times had made me doubt God's love for me.

I wanted to give her my own reassurance that God loves her even if she doesn't see a frog. But somehow it wasn't easy to give her the hope I wasn't feeling. I'd prayed for my own frogs lately: for that better-paying job for my husband, for my writing career to take off, for a more dependable car, for the strained family relationship to be repaired, for other things. But I was still struggling to find those frogs, those answers to prayers.

I went into the kitchen to do the dishes. With hands sunk in hot, soapy water, I closed my eyes. "I know it's a silly request, God. But, there's something about the way she truly believes You'll answer her prayer. Do You hear her? Do You hear me?"

When had I lost that complete trust in God that my daughter now had? It was a simple prayer to see a frog but just as important to her as the bigger things were to me. Somewhere deep inside I knew God still loved me, still loved our family. But it seemed my prayers were stopping at the ceiling. Did God still answer prayers?

My husband returned home late from his volunteer work at church with the English as a Second Language classes for refugees. Michelle had been asleep an hour. Richard and I talked over our day and how the classes went that night. He told me how God was blessing them with new students from all over the world and how it was a great opportunity to minister to them both physically and spiritually. I wondered how I could minister to anyone when I spent so much time worrying about my own problems. Could I honestly tell these people from faraway lands that God would provide for them here, that there was hope?

I wanted to tell my husband I'd quit praying, afraid to be disappointed anymore. Would he understand? Would he be disappointed in me? Had he given up on praying for our needs and not told me as I hadn't told him?

"Oops, laundry," I said, jumping up to move the wet clothes from the washer to the dryer. I turned on the garage light, startled by movement near the open door that led to the backyard. Our dog followed us into the garage and then ran and barked at the corner, stopping to sniff at something I couldn't see. He whined and wagged his tail and began to growl.

"Stop it, Tippy!" I shouted, worried he'd wake up Michelle. I took a careful step forward, ready to run if one of our giant, fast-moving water bugs should suddenly head my way.

It wasn't a water bug. Near the back door sat a large bug-eyed brown frog. "Outside," I ordered the dog. After a momentary chase, with the frog keeping two hops ahead, I held the bulging, squirming creature in my hands and carried my prize into the house.

"Hey, look," I said, holding it out to my husband. "I think Tippy was about to have a late-night snack of frog legs."

"Wow, it's too bad Michelle's not awake," Richard said, touching the frog's bumpy head. "You know how she loves frogs and lizards and turtles."

My mouth nearly hit the floor as I remembered her prayer. "Quick," I shouted, "wake her up!" My surprised husband stared at me as if I'd done one too many loads of laundry. Under most circumstances, after a very long day with our active child and an even longer evening of convincing her to go to bed, I rarely encouraged awakening our little sleeping beauty. But this was different. This was important. She *needed* to see this frog.

I hurried down the hall, quickly explaining to my husband about our daughter's prayer. I didn't tell him I hadn't believed it would be answered or that a froggy prayer was tied to my own fear that God might not care about us. I just told him it was important that she see the frog that night.

"Michelle, wake up. Look what I have," I said, holding the frog close to her. "God really answered your prayer." My heart beat faster as I expected her to leap out of bed with excitement.

She held the frog and petted it, more sleepy than interested and not the least bit surprised her prayer had been answered. "I knew He would," she said as she fell back onto her pillow and closed her eyes.

But I was overwhelmed at the quick response to her simple prayer. What a loving Father, to see how important such a small child's request was, a chance for her to see the power of an earnest prayer.

I carefully took the frog out into the front yard and put him into the bushes. He hopped away and I grinned, wondering if he was off to answer someone else's prayer. My faith took a leap that night as I watched the frog go. Sometimes my daughter teaches me more than I teach her. And sometimes a frog is more than just a frog. This time, it was a small way for God to show me in a huge way how much He loves our family, even when it doesn't seem He is listening.

A Sheep in Wolf's Clothing

Dorothy Faye Higbee

<hr/>

LEARNING TO LOVE IN DEED AND TRUTH IS MUCH HARDER than most people realize. In my case, God's rich sense of humor and classroom instruction showed up with four paws, a tail and lots of fur.

Leushen was a pound puppy. Part wolf, part malamute, he was abandoned at the Moscow, Idaho, animal shelter and destined for euthanization. After all, who in their right mind would want a young wolf-mix? Our son Jerry, that's who. He fell in love with the gray-and-black puppy with a white stripe down its nose and brought it home.

He brought it home all right—to our house, not his. And we already had one big dog that was quite protective of his territory. We were a little apprehensive but took in the cute creature because his soft eyes and happy smile tugged at our hearts. Then he started tugging on everything else.

"But let patience have its perfect work, that you may be perfect and complete, lacking nothing" (James 1:4, NKJV). I'm not one to give up on people or animals, but this one proved to be a real test of our fortitude. His first few months in our home were wrought with disasters. He ate our couch (a queen-sized sleeper) all the way to the frame. He ate my husband's metal-detector earphones. He ate two television remotes.

His life expectancy waned as we tried every method of attack known to man, from Tabasco sauce on the furniture to big rawhide bones. He didn't care for rawhide and really loved the flavor of Tabasco.

Leushen cowered when we tried to pet him, which meant he had been abused, so we set about to alter his destructive behavior. That wasn't counting the deep layers of fur that came off that dog's body at certain times of the year. His fur killed at least two vacuums. So the first step was to ban him from the house when we were not inside.

That went over well. Leushen and our big Newfoundland named Joshua became partners in crime. One week, Joshua stuffed his big head under the fence and held it up so Leushen could escape, and they sauntered off together for a walk around the neighborhood. We lived on one of the busiest streets in our town. My husband was at work and wouldn't be able to fix the fence until the weekend. I was beside myself with worry that entire week, knowing that while we were at work, the dogs were probably out and I'd have to hunt them down. I prayed hard that the dogcatcher would be snoozing in his office instead of out chasing our dogs, and that all the cars would miss them.

On the last day of the week, the dogs were actually in the yard when I came home, and I noticed that the back gate had new boards nailed horizontally over it. Hmmm . . . either my husband had lost it or someone got fed up with a wandering bear and wolf in the neighborhood. Turned out to be exactly that; a frustrated neighbor did the "honey do" task before my honey got to it.

Something dawned on me about Leushen's rather annoying behavior: People who have been abused often act according to their own feelings rather than an acceptable set of guidelines. They also require heaps of patience and a lot of extra cleanup. Although I think running a vacuum is easier than cleaning up after some people, I could almost hear the Lord snicker. *What took you so long?*

Armed with a new view of our situation, we began to treat Leushen as part of our family, or pack. As the months passed, he stopped eating all the plastic in the house and learned that rawhide wasn't so bad after all. As soon as the fence was permanently fixed, he even stayed in the yard with his pal and softened to become a very real blessing in our family. He slept by the bed at night, right beside his brother, and rarely exhibited the wacky behavior of his arrival.

We learned to apply the dog-loving principles to people and found that if the love is consistent and available, people can grow beyond their bad pasts. Leushen was an excellent example of success with love.

Then came the day his pal Joshua passed away. A bout with bone cancer took the big Newfoundland and left Leushen alone. He was devastated, as most people are who lose a loved one. He sat by my bed with his head on my covers and whimpered through the night. I take that back. He and I both whimpered through the night. We were complete wrecks; it was time to find a new puppy.

An investigation through the local newspaper revealed a Newfoundland breeder with one pup left. Ezekiel the puppy came to live with us, a fluffy black brother for Leushen. Although Leushen wasn't happy about having to share Mom and Dad, Zeke grew on him. They got along famously—or infamously, as the case may be—and Leushen was now big brother of the family. Whether teased by a local rabbit, sprayed by a skunk or examined as possible food by a roaming cougar, the boys (as I called them) grew into adventurous and always humorous creatures. (Well, except perhaps for the two weeks it took to get the skunk smell out of their fur.) Even our granddaughter fell in love with the wolf puppy with a soft heart and even softer fur.

On a crisp September afternoon in 2002, the boys began to bark excitedly. I opened the door just in time to see Leushen launch himself off the back porch and fly through the air, trying to catch up with whatever had him excited. He yelped and fell to the ground, unable to walk on just three legs.

Zeke walked back to sniff his brother and looked up at me with worry in his eyes. My husband and I loaded Leushen into the car and sped off to the vet clinic. The vet told us the dog had done exactly what Joe Montana, the football star, did: He tore the ligaments in his back leg. Dr. Erickson told us that in an animal his size, the best treatment would be surgery to repair the damage. Otherwise, the dog would more than likely be lame. The surgery would cost around $750, which was not in our household budget at that time.

We loaded Leushen back into the car and took him home. We simply didn't have that kind of extra money. Sadness gripped me as I wept over the dog. I stroked his wolf coat and looked deep into his golden eyes. We couldn't put him down, so I started praying. Then the Holy Spirit nudged my heart. *Do you do this for people? What's your response to people who damage themselves? Do you care enough to believe for them and pray for God's mercy? Or do you run from them?*

My heart broke. I'd rather not deal with difficult people. I needed true love that persevered. If God could do it for me, I should be able to do it for others. A few days later, Leushen had learned to hobble on three legs. But another yelp, another porch launch, and Leushen had damaged the other leg. (We needed desperately to fix the back porch, which we did.) You could tell he was in serious pain, as he could not move without severe yelping.

I prayed even harder; oh yes, and did a little hollering at God too. Not only didn't we have enough money to spend on two legs; this time I was madder than ever that my dog was hurt. I prayed strongly and gave him baby aspirin daily. I wasn't going to disappoint the Lord again. If I could hang in there with the dog, I could hang in there with people.

Although Leushen didn't move much for a few days, one afternoon I opened the back door to find him running—yes, running—across the back yard! No limping, no yelping, no whimpering, just running and fully able to keep up with his buddy Zeke. It was a true miracle, one of God's compassions that carried a lesson for people and animals alike.

The vet was surprised, but because he is a Christian, he just smiled when he saw the dog again. God is love. Leushen made me wonder if we would ever love people as well as dogs love us. Rescued from death and loved back to peace, amid prolific lessons for humans. Dog is just God spelled backward, you know. I'm pretty sure the Lord gets a kick out of that, because there is a love lesson in there if we will listen.

Leushen passed away of old age in the fall of 2006. He turned out to be a sheep in wolf's fur, a part of our family flock we will never forget. He taught us how to love in spite of bad behavior and that love truly does cover a multitude of sins.

In true heavenly humor, the Lord had us start a home church in 2003, which allowed us to put into practice the lessons we had learned. We will miss Leushen, but we will never forget the truths hidden in his life.

The Gift of
the Hummingbird

Marilyn A. Kinsella

HUMMINGBIRDS ARE FASCINATING LITTLE CREATURES. They whirl around with flashes of iridescent colors. Their elongated beaks swish the air like miniature swords. They maneuver the skies with the ease of stealth bombers. Sometimes you see them out of the corner of your eye, and then they disappear in a radiant arc.

My mother believed in pixies and fairy dust. She had an imagination that made shadows dance on the wall at night. During the day she could make petunias twirl around in their ball gowns. Her mother had beautiful gardens around the house and, when not helping with chores, Mom spent many an hour playing in them. It was her magical place.

Her favorite spot was under the front porch, where she and her brother Les would hide and wait for the hummingbirds. The tiny birds were attracted by the big bright-red flowers along the side of the house. She and Les, under the porch in a perfect hideaway, could see out, but the hummingbirds couldn't see in. A lattice border was all that separated them from the little hummers.

Their chubby faces shining in anticipation, she and Les looked out anxiously and became very quiet. About four o'clock, a faint distant hum began. Then they came: a squadron of green winged leprechauns dive-bombing out of the sky and into the hearts of the red flowers. Invariably, the children felt giggles bubbling up and put their hands over their mouths. Now the giggles came out in a series of chortles and chuffs. Sometimes a curious hummer peered inside with its black beady eyes. Then, in a wink . . . it would be gone. I guess that's why my mom was always fascinated by hummingbirds.

When they became fashionable as gifts in the early eighties, Mom and I gave each other hummingbirds. Some were rather silly: thermometers and potholders; others more sublime: sun catchers and delicate crystalline sculptures. Candleholders, plates, music boxes, scarves, paintings—if it had a humming-bird on it, we bought it for each other.

Our birthdays were only four hours apart, and we often shared our birthday celebrations. We laughed hysterically one year when we gave each other the same gold humming-bird pin. Mom especially liked the "anything" cards with our favorite bird on it. Inside I'd write some trite poetry that made her laugh.

That's why I asked her to send me a hummingbird after she died in October 1997. I carried a guilty feeling for having to move her to a nursing home. Looking back, I think it was the best solution to a very difficult situation, but that didn't make my decision any easier, especially when she didn't want to be there.

So that November, crying alone in my bedroom, I said out loud, "Mom, I want you to send me a hummingbird. It will be a sign of forgiveness and that you are in a much happier place. And, by the way, hummingbirds are hard to find this time of year, so if I get one, I'll know it will be from you."

Well, days and weeks went by and no hummingbird. I even remember thinking on Christmas Eve, "I guess she's still angry."

Then on Christmas morning I must have had twenty gifts at my feet. As per our family tradition, we each selected one to open first. At the appointed moment, we all opened the first gift of Christmas, and there it was: a beautiful crystal hummingbird on a flowered stem. At first I was speechless; then I started to cry. My family was a bit puzzled. Why was I getting so emotional over a hummingbird?

Finally I blubbered out, "You don't understand. It's from my mom. I asked her to send me a hummingbird." My husband Larry actually purchased the gift. He believes a coincidence is a coincidence is a coincidence. That's why they coined the word *coincidence*. But he said, "I don't mean to lend credence to what you're thinking, but it was a bit odd. I already bought your toaster and showerhead and thought I should buy you something pretty. Suddenly, I thought of a hummingbird."

"See," I said, "you were listening!"

"No, I was desperate."

Then he added, "But the really odd thing was, I had a hard time finding a hummingbird. I went to four or five stores before I found one on a kiosk."

"I know, because hummingbirds are hard to find this time of year." If I needed another sign that the hummingbird was from Mom, that was it.

CHAPTER SIX

MIRACLES IN DIFFICULT TIMES

Through whom we have gained access by faith into this grace in which we now stand. And we boast in the hope of the glory of God. Not only so, but we also glory in our sufferings, because we know that suffering produces perseverance; perseverance, character; and character, hope.
—Romans 5:2–4 (NIV)

The Mystery of the Missing Shepherd

W. Jean Greeley

T HE GAME OF CLUE IS A GREELEY FAMILY FAVORITE. We've spent countless holidays trying to find out "who done it." Was it Miss Scarlet in the kitchen with the knife? Or Colonel Mustard in the library with the candlestick?

I married into this Greeley tradition and struggled to match wits with the "expert" detectives in the family. Maybe that's why I had so much trouble the evening I had to solve the mystery of the missing shepherd.

As I look back on it now, it seems rather comical: having two sheriffs' departments out looking for someone who wasn't actually missing. But at the time, I didn't know that; I was sure I'd never see my husband alive again.

Late on a Thursday afternoon in January, I arrived home from Cherokee, where I teach seventh-grade language arts. As I drove the little blue Fiesta into the garage, something seemed wrong. Ken's car was not in the driveway. *Maybe he's out checking his sheep*, I thought as I went into the house.

"How was school?" I called to Jan, our fourteen-year-old.

"Fine."

"Dad wasn't here when you came home?" I questioned.

"Nope."

We visited for a while, catching up on the day. Diana, my older daughter, arrived home and we started to get supper ready. While I started fixing the meal, the girls cleared the table of mail and income tax forms Ken had left there.

Ken is always here on the dot of six-thirty, I fretted. When six-thirty came and went and no Ken, I really began to worry. He always had let me know if he was going to be late or away.

It's not unusual for Ken, being the minister of our church here in the small town of Sutherland, Iowa, to be called away on an emergency. So after the girls and I had supper, I searched the papers we'd moved off the table. Perhaps Ken had left a note there after all. Income tax forms . . . *ouch!* I thought as I looked at the bottom line. Mail . . . a couple of bills, some junk, a card. I stopped my search while I looked at the lovely card sent to us by one of the members of our congregation.

How nice, I thought as I set the card up on the mantel. But that was it. No note from Ken.

I carried on as normally as I could, but my ear kept straining for the sound of Ken's car or the ring of the telephone. As the evening wore on, my nerves worked overtime, and it showed.

"Mom, just look at the way Dad hung up my skirt!" Diana complained.

"Diana!" I snapped, "Most dads wouldn't even think of doing the laundry, let alone hang up your skirt! You should be thankful, not complaining."

We went a few rounds on the subject before Diana gave up and went to bed. I couldn't believe it. Here I was extremely worried about his safety, and all she could do was criticize him.

About eleven o'clock I finally decided to go to bed. I prayed Ken was safe and I'd be able to go to sleep. To my surprise, I dozed right off.

And then, just as if Colonel Mustard had dropped his candlestick beside the bed, I was awake. It was midnight and Ken was not home. Something was wrong! My mind started to explore the possibilities I'd been trying to avoid all evening. I had to talk to someone. I phoned my sister Judy in Cherokee.

"Jean," she said, "I think it's time to call the sheriff."

I wasn't ready to take that step, so I waited another half hour, pacing the floors like a pregnant cat. Then I decided to call one of the church elders. Ken keeps his flock of sheep out at Segelke's, and he and Donnie should have crossed paths at some time during the day.

Ken gets a lot of kidding about his sheep, but he loves them. He's had sheep ever since he was in high school. I learned early

in our marriage how to bottle-feed lambs and not to be surprised if three or four of them were living in our basement.
Both churches we've served have been in rural communities,
making it handy for Ken to keep his favorite hobby thriving.
You might say he actually has two flocks of sheep: the real ones
that go "baaa" and the figurative ones of our congregation. And
it was at this point that those church sheep became involved in
the mystery.

I called Donnie. He said, too, that it was time to call the
sheriff. He also suggested I call Mavis Rehder, another member
of our flock, who had been looking for Ken earlier. So 1 called
the sheriff, I called Mavis, and things began to happen.

The sheriffs' departments from two counties started searching the country roads. Mavis and her husband Wes drove into
town to be with me. We started to call the hospitals in our area
and church people he might have visited that day. I called Ken's
dad in Minnesota, thinking there might have been a family
emergency. Mavis even made one phone call to some poor man
and got him out of bed to answer his phone, only to find out
she had dialed the wrong number! But nobody knew anything
about Ken's whereabouts.

About 2:15 AM, Donnie and his wife Jackie also came into
town to be with me. I was really frightened by this time. In my
mind I knew Ken was in a ditch, either dead or dying. I started
thinking about what his funeral would be like . . .

"There's no dial tone." Mavis' words brought me back to the
present. "It was working just a minute ago."

We knew the reason for the dead phone must be that the "wrong number" Mavis had called earlier had not hung up his receiver.

"Can you remember the number you called?" someone asked. Mavis thought for a moment, and to everyone's surprise she actually remembered it. That sent Donnie to the phone book scanning the numbers till he found the right one. He and Wes then headed across town to the address listed with that number. Was that guy ever annoyed! First the phone call and now two complete strangers knocking on his door in the middle of the night.

I wanted to start the prayer chain. I didn't care anymore who had to get up and get on their knees. Besides, if Ken had visited any church people that day, we could trace his steps and know which roads to hit.

Jackie suggested we check to see what clothing he had with him. I went into a near panic when I noticed that both of his really warm coats were still in the closet. Especially because Judy had called back and said that, with the wind-chill factor, it was thirty-below outside. *If he has car trouble*, I thought, *he'll freeze to death.* Jackie, remaining calm, suggested we try the garage. There we found that a pair of work boots was missing. That meant overalls and work gloves would be gone too. I found comfort in that; at least he'd be warm.

Again I suggested activating the prayer chain.

"I want to try one more quick phone call," Donnie said. "I have a hunch."

We all waited and listened while Donnie dialed. "Denise, sorry to wake you," he said into the phone. "Is there a station wagon sitting in your yard?"

Pause.

"Did Ken go with David?"

Pause.

"Well, praise the Good Lord!"

Relief spread around the room like ray of sunshine. Then we all started talking at once.

Donnie had known that Dave Steffen, one of our young farmers, had left that day to take a load of hay down to Texas. His hunch that Dave had asked Ken to ride along at the last minute had paid off.

"I would have thought of it sooner," Donnie said, "but when I talked to Ken this morning, he never said a thing about it, so he must not have known yet."

Ken returned home on Saturday. We've never laughed or cried as much as we did when I told him of all that had transpired while he was away. I was pretty embarrassed when he showed me the hurriedly scribbled note on the back of that card I had placed so carefully on the mantel. As it turned out, Dave had called at the last minute to see if Ken would ride along. Ken said he wrote me a note on the first thing he got his hands on. What he hadn't counted on was our clearing off the table and flipping over the card before I had a chance to see the note.

Mystery solved!

Besides the obvious need for a more reliable method of communication, I began to wonder if another mystery was hidden here, this one from God. As I relived that evening in my mind, a few clues kept surfacing.

Clue No. 1: Wes and Mavis and then Donnie and Jackie left their warm beds to come out into the cold just so I wouldn't have to be alone.

Clue No. 2: They took over willingly when I was almost too distraught to think clearly. Making phone calls, lending their love and support, letting me cry and voice my fears. Comforting me with actions and words.

Clue No. 3: Even though we never used it, the prayer chain was there, and once activated, the support group would grow.

In the game of Clue, when you have all your clues gathered and you've evaluated them, you are ready to make an accusation. And now, after careful consideration, I am ready to solve the hidden mystery in the Case of the Missing Shepherd . . .

God uses people! He uses them to be an extension of Himself. My friends, wanting to be with me even though the hour was late and the night was cold, showed God's eagerness to be near me anytime and in any situation. Their willingness to help was His willingness to see me through the tough times. Their words of comfort were really His words of care. My comfort in the knowledge that there was a support group of people yet untapped in the prayer chain is symbolic of the vastness of His power, ready but untapped.

I'm glad it turned out well. I am also glad for the friends God has given us. I would have had a hard time making it through that night without the support He gave me through them.

Another mystery solved! I think that with my newfound detective skills I'll be ready for the next family game of Clue!

Our Miracle Journal

Ed Gage

COLD RAIN DRIZZLED STEADILY IN LATE DECEMBER 1984 as my wife Mike and I sat at the dining table and contemplated the new year. It promised to be as dismal as the weather outside. We were in the midst of the holiday season, but we had nothing to celebrate and certainly nothing to look forward to.

Two years earlier, just before Christmas, Mike had been injured in an auto accident. The doctors said the daily pain she felt would last the rest of her life. We had no disability insurance, so between the loss of her income and the large medical bills, our finances were a wreck. Still worse, my university job was on the line due to Louisiana state-government budget cutbacks.

Staring down at the cold dregs in my coffee cup, I racked my brain to think of a way to improve our gloomy circumstances. But it was no use; things were only getting worse.

Out of desperation, lately we had begun praying and meditating after hearing a seminar speaker say that, no matter what the situation, it was possible to change your life by first attuning to God and then watching for changes.

Maybe it gave Mike some hope, but my viewpoint was that it didn't work.

I picked up a handful of the bills littering the table and disgustedly let them drop. "I'm sick and tired of just getting by," I said to Mike. "We have to make something happen!"

From the midst of the bills, Mike picked up the checkbook register and idly thumbed the pages. "At least our money problem is simple," she said, "just a matter of not enough deposits to balance the withdrawals."

Suddenly she was excited and sitting up straight. "You know, that's the real problem we're having with life," she said, waving the checkbook in my direction. "We need more deposits of good events in our lives. The prayer and meditation are good, but we need more neat things happening in an active way."

"Great," I said caustically. "Why don't we start looking for miracles?"

Mike's blue eyes shone with enthusiasm. She had taken my sarcasm for sincerity. "That's perfect!" she said. "We say we believe God can work in our lives. Let's keep a record! We'll mark down anything that makes us feel joyous, that gives us a sense of the miraculous. Then in tough times we'll just take a look at the record." She looked directly at me. "Okay?"

Frankly, to me it sounded a bit crazy. But I already had said something must change, and I had no other suggestions. "Okay. I'll try," I said doubtfully.

And that's how our Miracle Journal came to be—a section in a brown loose-leaf notebook in which we already kept lists of chores to do, errands to run and bills to pay. It was just a few pages with a divider-tab marked "Miracles."

But if we thought we were going to find miracles, far from it! Late the Saturday night before New Year's Day, we were returning home to Shreveport from a trip to Tyler, Texas. There was little traffic on the interstate and we were cozy in the heated car. Then I glanced at the temperature gauge! Disaster! It was entering the red danger zone! *Terrific*, I thought bitterly as images of being stranded at night flashed into mind.

Fortunately, within a mile we reached an exit ramp. Gingerly, I steered the car up it and toward a quick-stop grocery on the outskirts of Kilgore.

"What rotten luck!" I said to Mike. "We may be stuck here till Monday."

"Well, I think we are lucky," Mike said. "You have only one relative in all of East Texas and he lives right here in Kilgore. So stop and go call."

One phone call later we learned that, luckily, my Uncle Ed had returned fifteen minutes earlier from a Christmas trip to Dallas, bringing two of my favorite aunts from Dallas with him. The five of us had a wonderful surprise holiday visit that night and the next day. Sunday afternoon, after refilling the radiator and tightening hoses we had thought were leaking, we drove the sixty-five miles home.

At the repair shop on Monday, the mechanic said the problem was not loose hoses but a blown head gasket on the motor. "You were lucky to make it back to town," he told us, "especially without damaging the engine."

Luck? Or our first miracle?

Back at the house, Mike did not share my uncertainty. "It was all a miracle," she said. "All of it. Write it down."

"It could be just coincidence," I said.

"How many coincidences in a row does it take for you to believe something positive is happening?" she said.

So I got out the Miracle Journal and wrote it down. Reluctantly.

It wasn't that I didn't believe in miracles, just that they always happened to somebody else. For Mike's sake, I tried to keep an open mind about this prayer, meditation and miracle business. But down deep I knew there was no free lunch.

I was able to make that point to Mike one Friday night when our spirits were as low as the balance in the checkbook.

"I sure wish we could go for pizza," Mike mused. "That would cheer us up."

"Great," I said, "but payday is nearly a week away, so no pizza tonight."

After I'd brought Mike down to earth, our spirits sagged lower.

A few minutes later the phone rang. Friends Randy and Judy had just received good news. Would we like to help them celebrate by going out for pizza? Their treat!

Mike was exuberant. "Go write it down!" she said.

"What do you mean?" I asked. "It's just a coincidence."

"Ha!" Mike said, and went to get the Miracle Journal herself.

"Being asked out for pizza is not a miracle," I called after her. "Turning water into wine or something like that—that's a miracle. When something like that happens, we'll know we're really onto something."

Meantime we continued to pray and meditate regularly and to jot down the day-to-day happenings that left us feeling in a more positive frame of mind. Even I had to admit that those little notes on positive happenings in our lives were starting to have a cumulative effect. But miracles? I was still skeptical.

In February it snowed, something of a miracle in Louisiana. The heavy, blowing flakes laid a thick mantle of white over the entire city, closing streets, schools and businesses. I used the day off from work to complete a magazine article, my first freelance writing effort in years.

As the snow continued to fall, Mike and I bundled up for a tramp through the novel weather to drop the finished article in a postal box a few blocks away. The heavy flakes swirled around us as we moved along the center of the snow-covered, deserted street.

Nearing the mailbox, we joked about what a momentous occasion it was, what with the falling snow, the unexpected holiday and the article submission. "All that's missing is something to toast the story on its way," I kidded as I dropped the envelope inside the box.

Turning around, we began the snowy walk home. We had gone barely half a block when the door of a nearby house swung open, spilling out peals of laughter and a jubilant group of adults carrying a sled out into the wintry scene. "Come join our sledding party," they called, offering us sparkling cider from snow-chilled glasses.

We thanked them but declined their party invitation and walked on. Then Mike turned to me, a mischievous gleam in her eye. "It's not exactly water into wine," she laughingly said, "but you have to admit that turning snow into cider is pretty close."

Coincidence again? It had to be, I thought, even though we knew none of the group, and offering drinks to strangers in a snowstorm is not exactly an old Southern tradition. But these coincidences were piling up. Although still doubtful, I was beginning to have doubts about my doubts.

As the weeks passed and our pray, meditate, watch-for-miracles routine continued, a strange thing began to happen. The pages of the Miracle Journal expanded and so did my gradual understanding of how God can work with us in everyday situations if only we make the effort to be receptive to Him. The seminar speaker had spoken of attunement as a two-step process: "To talk to God, pray," he had said. "To listen to God, meditate and pay attention to those inner promptings."

But at income tax time in April, that didn't make much sense as I found myself seated at the dining table facing piles of receipts and bank statements. Finally, after working on the tax sheets for hours, I put down my pencil, turned off the calculator and, with a sigh of relief, prepared to seal the paperwork. Suddenly I had an urge to check the figures one more time.

Ridiculous, I thought. I already had checked over the return three times.

The seminar speaker's words drifted through my mind: "Pay attention to inner promptings."

With a groan I picked up the pencil and calculator. I reworked the tax figures one more time—and found an overlooked deduction that increased our refund by 250 dollars. The Miracle Journal was making a believer of me.

Jubilee!

Lynne Hart

<hr/>

P LE-E-E-EZ, LET'S TALK," I BEGGED FOR THE UMPTEENTH
time.

"Get out of my sight," he snapped and stormed out of the
kitchen.

The now-familiar lump tightened in my throat. Teary-eyed,
I dropped into a kitchen chair, crying, "Lord, what's happening
to us?" How proud I'd been when Dan quit drinking! How perfect life was going to be. Now I laughed at my simple-minded
optimism, my great expectations. Alcohol had been Dan's best
friend; when he was forced to quit drinking he'd sunk into a
stony, severe depression. For six months he'd refused to speak,
stalking past me as if I were invisible. At most he'd snarl, "Get
lost" or "Go away." After twenty-one years of marriage, we were
headed for divorce.

That night, I buried my head under the covers, pleading, "O Lord, help me!" I wanted to sleep forever. Morning found me worn and weary. Before, I'd always prayed for wisdom, insight and healing, but this morning I cried out in full helplessness: "Lord, please show me what to do—I don't want this marriage to end!"

As I went through my Bible, Leviticus 25:10 seemed to leap from the page: "And ye shall hallow the fiftieth year, and proclaim liberty throughout all the land unto all the inhabitants thereof: it shall be a jubilee unto you."

That Scripture haunted me all day. Dan's fiftieth birthday was only three weeks away. Was the Lord telling me I should honor his fiftieth year? And if so, in what way? Maybe a birthday party. No, that would be ridiculous. How could I throw Dan a party? We weren't even speaking.

A week passed and that Bible verse still sat in my mind. Even the crazy idea of a party. Finally I thought, *Okay, I'll invite our friends Jane and George for a cookout the Sunday before Dan's birthday. After all, fifty years of life is special.*

I called, half hoping they couldn't make it, but Jane accepted. "It's a surprise," I said just before hanging up. I couldn't believe I'd done it.

Four days before the cookout, Dan and I sat on the patio, each pretending to be alone. After weeks of near-total silence, we had started a tense conversation that soon blazed into an argument. Through gritted teeth, Dan snarled, "This isn't working anymore; I want out," and he left.

"Get out, then," I hissed at his departing back. Alone with my whirling thoughts, I cried, "Lord, how wrong I was! You didn't want a jubilee; I just imagined it. I'm sorry, but I hate him." What a foolish idea, planning a party under circumstances like these. It was like arranging deck chairs on the Titanic. *I'm calling Jane to cancel*, I thought. *I want out too.*

Just then Dan came back. He must have felt bad, for he said in a surprisingly casual tone, "We have such nice neighbors. It's too bad they haven't been over more often."

Suddenly, my depression lifted and my spirit soared as a voice sounded inside: *Jubilee—a celebration!*

I held my breath. I wanted to laugh or shout. Instead, I jumped out of my lawn chair and into the house to make phone calls—not to cancel the cookout but to invite all our other neighbors and friends! Amazingly, all the people I called said they'd be delighted to come and offered to bring something. I happily accepted.

Next afternoon, as I stood contemplating an unmade bed, I overheard Dan on the phone with our family doctor. He'd badly pulled a muscle in his back. The prescription was hot half-hour-long baths, four times a day. What a fix! Now I had thirty-two people coming for a surprise party, and I had a dirty house and a bedridden husband who "wanted out"—yet somehow I knew everything would be fine. I can't explain how, but I knew this party was the right thing to do. Was I crazy, doing all this for a man who wouldn't speak to me? No, for the first time in my life I felt mysteriously, truly inspired.

That night I slept like a baby, certain I was doing what God wanted me to do.

Saturday, the day before the party, I wanted to make Dan's favorite potato salad. I boiled a party-size pot of potatoes without his noticing. But where would I cool them? I put them in a grocery bag and hid them in the trash. A stroke of genius! When Dan took his next therapeutic bath, I retrieved my potatoes, made the world's fastest potato salad and hid it safely, way in the back of the refrigerator.

A little later our former neighbors the Bakers phoned. They'd be in town for a three-day convention—could their daughter Nancy (our fifteen-year-old daughter Trish's friend) bunk in with us? The last thing I needed was an overnight guest, but on second thought it gave me the perfect excuse for some frantic housecleaning. Trish, who was in on my plans, whirled into action, scrubbing and dusting and vacuuming and polishing.

By this time I was in a trance. Floating out the door toward the supermarket, I saw a party-supply store. Decorations! I'd almost forgotten! I bought balloons, crepe-paper streamers, a Happy 50th Birthday banner, matching plates and napkins and lots of candles. While Dan soaked, I hid in the guest room and inflated twenty-five balloons. It was a blessing he was ignoring me, or he might have wondered why my face was blue. All day long Trish sneaked to and from my neighbor Jane's, carrying ground meat, cheese, pickles, hamburger buns, ice cream. "Take this to Jane's," I barked like a drill sergeant. "Buy this! Borrow that from Jane."

Sunday! Party day was here! Everything was all set except how to get Dan out of the house. The guests were coming at six. During church I prayed for a solution. As we were leaving, Trish's boyfriend Eric asked if I needed help. I told him about getting Dan away from home.

"I'll take care of it," Eric said. Who'd have guessed Eric would be the answer to a prayer?

At 5:20 PM the Bakers arrived, depositing Nancy and her luggage. Still no word from Eric. What did he have planned?

By 5:30 PM my stomach was churning at high speed. At 5:35 PM the phone rang and I jumped, spilling my iced tea.

"Hi, Lynne, is Dan there? It's Jim." Eric's father! So that's who Eric had enlisted!

"Dan, telephone!" I called, with a silent thank-you. Dan fell for Jim's crazy story—that he needed a lift home—and made a quick exit.

When he left, I resumed my sergeant's role: "Hang the balloons and crepe streamers! Hang the birthday banner! Bring all the chairs from the basement!" Jane hurried in through the kitchen with the food.

At six o'clock sharp, in came the guests, carrying beautiful salads, pies, cakes. Instantly my picnic table was a marvelous crammed display suitable for the cover of *Better Homes and Gardens*. Trish had baked a big lovely birthday cake at Jane's. With its few errors camouflaged by fifty strategically placed candles, the cake had a warmth and charm only youth could create. It was the perfect centerpiece.

"We're ready," I breathed—just as our sentry shouted, "He's here!" Everyone hurried to the front door, and as Dan entered, we shouted, "SURPRISE!" He gazed in astonishment at the people and at the brightly decorated rooms and staggered backward against the door.

"You got me!" he exclaimed. "You really got me!"

Dan stood leaning against the door, totally shocked. Running to him, Trish gave him a big kiss, saying, "Happy birthday, Daddy!"

I followed, kissing him and squeaking, through the catch in my throat, "Happy birthday, dear."

After eating, and before opening his presents, Dan asked for our attention. He thanked God for Trish and me, for helping us stick together through the tough times and for such wonderful friends. My heart leapt as his eyes sought mine while he spoke. Tears of joy, not pain, welled up inside me. He said this party was the most wonderful thing that had ever happened to him.

My tears finally flowed when Dan wrapped me in his arms and kissed me, the first kiss in a long, long time. "This is fantastic. I can't thank you enough, Lynne," he whispered in my ear. His warm, muscular body felt so comfortable and right as I hugged him. I wanted to hold on forever.

A friend provided a big Roman candle, which we lit at dusk. The spectacular dancing gold jets, shooting up into the night sky to our oohs and ahhs, made the perfect ending to a jubilant day.

From that night on, Dan and I were on the road back. Sure, we needed help, mostly from a chemical-dependency counselor who helped us as Dan and I strove for understanding on our often difficult path to recovery. But the worst was over. We'd won.

One evening a year after Dan's jubilee party, I heard him say to our minister, "You know, there was a time when I was deeply depressed and God showed me love in an overwhelming way. That was a watershed moment for me." As we drove home, I asked Dan what he'd meant.

He looked at me, his eyebrows lifted in astonishment, and said, "Why, the birthday party, of course. It showed me what I'd been too blind to see—that you still loved me and what we had was worth saving. Lynne, that birthday party saved our marriage, and maybe it saved my life."

The Last Ten Seconds

Ed Turner

IT'S A PERFECT DAY FOR SKYDIVING, I MARVELED AS I SQUINTED up at the brilliant Florida sky. Some friends and I were driving down to Clewiston, near Lake Okeechobee, to practice a star-formation jump we planned to perform in an upcoming competition. The jump required extraordinary timing and precision, and we'd come up with some ideas on how we could link up and form the star faster in midair. A quicker formation meant we could maintain it longer and score points with the judges. The twelve of us wanted to do some fine-tuning on our teamwork. In this sort of skydiving, you put your life in the hands of your partners.

I had no problem with that. My partners were all seasoned jumpers. My good friend Frank Farnan, for instance, had twenty-five years of experience. With Bob, Mike and the others, between us we had thousands of jumps to our credit.

Hurling yourself out of an airplane at thirteen thousand feet may not be everyone's idea of a relaxing good time, but for me it was the perfect way to spend the day. I've always been the adventurous sort. I learned to fly when I was fourteen. I was a fighter pilot in the Air Force and went on to a career in commercial aviation. The open sky offered me the perfect stage to test myself. I never doubted my ability to meet a challenge and conquer it, to act quickly and decisively. Maybe I had a streak of daredevil in me, but proving myself made me feel in control, invincible.

We did a lot of joking and horsing around at the airstrip as we climbed into our gear and checked out our equipment. But once airborne in the cramped Twin Beech, the mood grew serious. As we attained jump altitude, I secured my chute straps and double-checked the warning buzzer in my helmet. During the jump, the buzzer would automatically alert me when I had ten seconds left to safely yank the rip cord. Once that ten seconds passed, I'd be in real trouble if my chute wasn't out. There was no room for mistakes.

I was the fourth one out of the plane. I had just an instant to enjoy that first breathless rush of exhilaration before linking up with the three other divers. It is a feeling of both weightlessness and tremendous speed, of silence and the roar of the wind. Below, the earth looked like a painted set piece. I linked hands in the formation. Two more men hooked up. Then Mike. Then

Frank. Then two others. Things were going smoothly. We were actually slightly ahead of schedule in forming the star.

Suddenly I noticed a disturbance to my right. The eleventh man out of the plane had hit the star too rapidly and collided with Frank. The jolt instantly knocked Frank out of formation. A second later he fell away from the star and began plunging limply toward the earth.

He's out cold! I realized with a twinge of panic.

Instinctively I glanced above me to see about Bob, the twelfth diver. Bob swooped past the formation headfirst in desperate pursuit of Frank.

I'm not doing any good sticking with the formation, I thought quickly. I wasn't even sure the others grasped what was taking place. It was all happening so fast. I released and went into a head dive after Bob. We had to catch up to Frank before it was too late.

I plummeted toward the two men at two hundred miles an hour, tucking in my arms to streamline my body for minimal wind resistance. The force of the dive tore at my goggles. When I got to within fifty feet or so of Frank, I was able to slow down and get a good look at him. A knot twisted in my stomach. He was on his back, unconscious, completely helpless.

Below me I saw Bob making a pass at Frank, trying to reach his rip cord. He missed. To my left I spotted Mike. Apparently he too had seen what was happening and had rocketed after me. Bob made another lunge at Frank. Then Mike moved in. Both missed.

Frank had been knocked out at about eleven thousand feet. I knew we were still pretty high up, but I also realized how fast

Frank was slicing through the air. We had less than a minute to save him.

I veered down toward Frank. Every time I got close, he drifted away. He was beginning to spin, his arms and legs swinging wildly. I was running out of time. The only thing to do was dive down past him, make a lunge as I went by and try to grab him in a bear hug. With any luck I'd be able to jerk his rip cord and then get out of the way.

I braced myself. *Okay, Ed, you're an old fighter pilot. Use your instincts. React to his movements.* I adjusted my goggles and made the final pass. I drew close. Frank was upside down. I was just a few feet above him. Suddenly I noticed movement; Frank's left hand appeared to be hitting groggily at his rip cord as though he was getting ready to pull. *Oh no,* I thought, a burst of fear gripping me. *He's coming to.* I was in danger of becoming tangled in his chute. I had to make a split-second decision: make a grab for him now or get clear. Everything I knew and was trained to do screamed at me to roll over to the side and get out of the way before he pulled his cord, or we'd both be killed.

I backed off and fell below. I looked up, expecting to see his chute blossoming above. Instead, Frank continued to plummet haplessly. I saw now that the movement I'd detected was nothing more than Frank's arm flapping uselessly in the wind. In that one terrible instant, I'd made the wrong decision. I should have grabbed at him while I could, but my nerve had failed me. My mistake would cost my friend his life.

I glanced wildly at my altimeter ... forty-five-hundred feet. We had maybe thirty seconds left. I was doing everything I could to create as much drag as possible so I could climb back up to him, but nothing was working. On his back, Frank was creating more wind resistance than I could equal. The distance between us lengthened. For the first time in my life I felt utterly out of control. The seconds were ticking off in my mind. *Twenty-four ... twenty-three ...*

Then, unexpectedly, inexplicably, I heard myself calling out, *God! God, please help me!*

I was not a religious man. To me, God had always been distant, impersonal. In tough times, I'd learned to count on myself. I didn't believe in asking for help; only the weak begged. But now all of my toughness and self-reliance availed me nothing. I only knew I couldn't get out of this mess alone.

Bob and Mike came in for one last desperate approach from the side. Frank was like a football during a fumble as the wind buffeted him first one way and then the other. The angle of their approach caused a draft that pushed Frank away.

But it also caused a small vacuum directly below him. Suddenly Frank dropped. In an instant he was directly in front of me and perfectly level! Only a few feet separated us.

I straightened my legs to swoop in on him before he fell out of my grasp. Just as I leaned my body in his direction and reached out—

BUUUUZZZZZZZZZZ!

I flinched. It was the altitude alarm in my helmet blasting a warning. *Ten seconds left ... nine ... eight ...* I didn't dare hesitate now.

I was so close! One peek at the up-rushing ground would shatter my concentration. I inched closer to Frank. *Five seconds . . . four . . .*

I shot forward and grabbed hold of Frank's leg with my right hand. The fingers on my left hand twitched just inches from Frank's cord. *Two . . . one . . .*

With a final lunge I grasped his cord and pulled. In almost the same movement I shoved him away with all my strength and yanked my own chute.

Only when I felt the familiar tug of my parachute clutching the air and slowing my descent did I finally allow myself a glimpse of the ground. It was a beautiful sight as I drifted lazily back to earth. But most beautiful of all was the sight of my friends' parachutes billowing in the breeze: Bob's, Mike's . . . and Frank's.

A month later we were all back at Zephyrhills for the competition, including Frank. He'd suffered only a mild concussion in the accident and a bruised elbow when he landed. But to this day Frank has no recollection of the jump.

It's a jump I'll not likely forget. My life has not been quite the same since. I still love the excitement of challenging myself, but I no longer think of it as something I do alone. People said I was a hero for rescuing Frank, but when I hit the ground that day I felt as if I'd been the one rescued.

In a moment of fear and trouble I discovered a very present help. It is a help I ask for now before I jump. In the longest—and shortest—sixty seconds of my life, God showed me that real men aren't afraid to ask for help. True courage comes from believing that God's strength is always your strength.

The Mother I Had Always Known

Barbara Wernecke Durkin

❧

I'D ALWAYS WELCOMED THE FRIENDLY SOUND OF MY BROTHER'S voice calling from Maryland, but this time his words jolted me as I stood with the kitchen phone to my ear. "Bar," said Dick somberly, "we have to make a decision tonight. The nursing home we found down here can only hold a place for Mom until the morning, and she'll have to be in the room within a few days. They want to know right away. Call me back in an hour."

After I hung up, I stared at the phone for a long time before moving. *One hour.* One hour to decide whether to send our Alzheimer's-stricken mother from upstate New York all the way down to southern Maryland, where I wouldn't be able see her regularly, couldn't supervise her care or oversee her daily routine ...

One hour versus three years. That's how long my husband Bill and I would have to wait to get Mom into an acceptable facility near us. We were not sure we could handle another three years of caring for Mom. Now Dick and his wife had found a good home that could take Mom immediately.

I went into the living room and told Bill. We talked together quietly and agreed: Dick's plan was best for Mom. We'd known all along it might come to this.

I was tormented by the crushing prospect of being separated from Mom now that she needed me most. We'd always been a great team, Mom and I. Dad died when I was a teenager, and Mom raised me on her own. We'd braved many tough times together. Mom showed me how to face life's worst moments with courage, grit and—most of all—good humor. She always laughed her way through hard jobs and sang through bad days.

"Everyone is my friend," she'd say, and because she believed it, it was true. My mother had always been there for me, giving me strength when I needed it most.

But Mom had not really been there for me in recent years. I was the one who was giving strength now. Except for increasingly rare moments of lucidity, she'd become lost in her own private world of memory and fantasy. Television no longer interested her because she couldn't follow the plots. Reading was hopeless for the same reason. Once we would sit for hours laughing and gossiping; now after a few sentences, her interest waned and she'd fix her gaze on some distant spot in some distant twilight world I was not a part of. I was powerless against the thief that was stealing her mind.

"Where are we now?" she'd demand as she sat gazing out our dining room window at the birds. "Whose house is this, anyway?"

Mom could be difficult and stubborn, even irrational. Sometimes she was impossible. The strain wore me down day by day. After listening to her sing the same repetitious song or poem perhaps a hundred times in one afternoon, my nerves were shot by the time Bill and the boys came home. Everyone was affected.

At night, though, when I tucked her into bed, Mom would invariably remember to say her prayers. Like a little child, she would recite the old familiar "Now I lay me down to sleep," the first prayer she taught me when I was a girl. Then she would bless her sisters and all of us, because she did, indeed, still know who we were and how she was connected to us. That was the one foundation her sickness couldn't erode.

I too would say my prayers at bedtime, asking God to give me strength to help Mom. But I was helpless to halt Mom's deterioration. Each day her lustrous emerald eyes grew more muddied. I wondered how long it would be before they looked at me blankly and saw only a stranger.

After two days of sorting, packing and complicated paperwork, we left for Maryland. They were the saddest days of my life, a life I had spent never very far from my mother.

"Who'll make sure she has everything she needs?" I worried out loud to Bill. I asked God to give me more strength, but I didn't feel it. I knew Mom required professional supervision, yet the thought of a stranger coming to her in the night when she would ramble and wander around like a sleepwalking child seared me with guilt.

I packed what I thought Mom would need in her tiny half-room at the home. The trip down was a blur. In my mind I kept trying to slow time, to stretch out those final hours before I faced what I wasn't sure I could handle. But everything seemed to be moving so fast.

Before I knew it, I was signing the documents at the nursing home, while Mom looked on with a sort of dull curiosity. It was an excellent, well-staffed nursing home, where Mom would get the best of care, but she didn't seem to grasp what was happening. I took her arm and we walked to the room marked 107-A. There was a bed with Mom's name over it. Mom was dressed in her usual slacks and colorful top and her favorite shoes, red high-top Reeboks. She sat on the narrow bed swinging her feet like a little kid.

Dick and Marge left quickly—they'd look in on Mom daily. Bill and the boys kissed her and headed for the parking lot. They promised we'd be back to visit. But I couldn't bring myself to say good-bye. I kept asking her every foolish little question that popped into my head: Did she remember where the bathroom was? Did she remember her roommate's name? Did she know where I put her hairbrush and mirror? All sorts of silly things.

Finally there was nothing more to ask or say. I stared at Mom, sitting on her new bed. I wondered if she completely understood what was happening or what I was feeling. Then I wrapped my arms around her and held on for dear life. I hugged and hugged and kissed and kissed her. I stained her bright sweater with angry tears. *Why does it have to end like this, God?* I demanded. These were supposed to be the golden years for Mom, years when I could make her happy. I'd always planned the best for Mom in her old age. Now I was saying good-bye.

Abruptly she pulled away. I saw a sudden spark in her eyes, a piercing look of recognition and the old fire. She sat up straight and tall.

"Stop crying now," she said firmly. "Say good-bye and get going. Don't worry about me. Everyone here is my friend. I will be well taken care of."

She looked hard at me for about five seconds as I stood still with amazement and stared into the face of the mother I had always known, that familiar mom who knew and understood, who laughed and sang and was strong for me when I needed her.

"Mom!" I cried, and reached out for her. But it was like reaching for a phantom. As quickly as my "real" mom had appeared, she dissolved again into the little child swinging her feet in their bright red sneakers.

My mother let go of me when I could not let go of her. For one last brave time she was strong for me. And for a moment, God showed me His love in a small miracle I knew was a sign that He would watch over Mom now that I no longer could, the way He watches over mothers everywhere.

Angel in Our Backyard

Denise Brumbach

I WAS WORKING IN THE BEAUTY SHOP I OPERATE OUT OF OUR home when my husband Den came in, a troubled expression on his face. "Look what I found in the girls' tree house," he said. He held out some jeans and a T-shirt. "It looks as if someone's living in our backyard."

"It's those kids," I said, aghast. "Den, you're on the borough council. We've got to do something!"

Lately there had been several acts of vandalism—a shock for our small town—and teenage boys from out of the area had been seen roaming the streets. It was the fall of 1991, and crime had become frighteningly real in the nearby city of Lancaster. Our town was determined to keep the problem from spreading to Manheim.

"I'll report this to the police," Den said.

A few days later I looked out the window and saw a group of teenage boys sauntering out from between our house and the neighbors', heading up the street. I ran out the door and, putting two fingers in my mouth, gave a piercing whistle.

The boys turned around. There were four of them, wearing relatively clean jeans and T-shirts, no gang colors that I could see.

"Hi," I said. "What were you guys doing in our backyard?"

"Just cutting through," one said.

"Why aren't you in school?" I asked.

"Don't need that garbage," said another.

But then a tall young man stepped forward. Unlike the others, he looked right at me.

"I'd like to be in school," he said. "But not in the neighborhood I'm from." He had a Hispanic accent and was slender and clean-shaven, with cinnamon-brown eyes.

As they headed down the street, I turned back to the beauty shop. At least they didn't seem like gang members or hardened criminals. And there was something compelling about that kid who wished he was in school.

Somehow I wasn't surprised when he reappeared a day or so later as I was raking leaves in our backyard.

"Hi," he said. "Can I give you a hand?"

I studied him for a moment, trying to read what was behind those eyes. I handed him the rake.

"What's your name?" I asked. "Where are you from?"

"Angel Melendez," he said. "I'm from Lancaster. But things there are getting kind of rough."

"So where are you living now?"

"Sometimes I crash with a friend," he said. "I stashed some clothes in your tree house. Sorry. I didn't mean to cause any trouble."

"You want them back?" I asked. He nodded.

I went inside, leaving Angel working industriously. After gathering his clothes, I watched him from the upper deck. He was so thin. Lunch seemed a fair exchange for raking a huge pile of leaves. The lawn looked good. Angel sat at the kitchen table and wolfed down the sandwiches as if he could have eaten half a dozen more.

Over the following days, Angel continued to stop by to chat. Sometimes he talked about his dream of becoming a Navy pilot. He started coming around in the evening when Den and I and our teenage daughters Haley and Amanda were watching TV. Whenever I put out snacks, he ate ravenously. As he cheerfully said good-night, we knew we were sending him out—to where? Nowhere.

Then one night Den said, "Angel, if you have nowhere else to go, you can sleep out in my workshop."

"Thanks," Angel said, smiling. He turned at the door, a bit nervously.

"Mr. and Mrs. Brumbach," he said, "I would really like to finish high school. I was wondering if you could help me get in."

As we prepared for bed, Den and I turned to each other with the same questions. What were we going to do about Angel? He seemed like a nice kid. But did we want to get involved?

"Before this goes any further," Den said, "I'll have the police run a background check on him, to make sure he is who he says he is."

In the meantime, Angel informed us of what he had found out: To enroll at our high school, he needed a permanent local address as well as a parent or legal guardian who was a district resident.

That night when Den came home he summoned Haley, Amanda and me to the kitchen table.

"I talked to the Manheim police," he said. "Officer David Carpenter called Lancaster and spoke with a Sergeant Wilson. It seems the kid's been on his own since he was eight years old. He's seventeen now. But what impressed Sergeant Wilson is that, for a kid who's had to raise himself, Angel's never been in trouble."

"All he wants to do is to go to school," Haley whispered. "How can we not help him?"

It turned out Officer Carpenter had been impressed by Angel as well. Several nights later he called.

"I know a police officer isn't supposed to get personally involved in his work," Carpenter said, "but sometimes you have to. I don't have room for Angel to move in, but I'm willing to become his legal guardian."

The rest of our community was harder to convince. We started to receive phone calls—many of them anonymous— that made it clear Angel was not welcome in our town.

The school didn't seem to want him, either. Weeks turned into months as red tape continued to block his admission. In the meantime, Angel got a job at the local McDonald's. He had breakfast and dinner with us and then spent the evenings doing odd jobs around the house or watching TV.

The weather turned frosty; Den's workshop where Angel slept was unheated. We called another family meeting. As fond as we'd all become of Angel, letting him move into our house was a big step. Maybe too big.

"What else can we do?" asked Haley.

"It's getting really cold," Amanda added.

It was brave of them. I knew they were being questioned at school by kids who didn't understand the situation. They only saw that Angel was Hispanic and a "city boy."

"If he becomes a member of the family, he'll be treated like one," I said. "He'll have chores and a curfew; he'll have to work hard and obey our rules."

We all agreed that Angel could move in. He was ecstatic at being invited to sleep on the living-room sofa.

"The doors lock at ten," I warned. "You've got to be in by then."

"Yes, Mom," he said.

That kid had really gotten to me.

"Angel," I said, "you've been through some tough times in your life. How have you managed?"

"God kept me going," he answered. "When I was about seven, I started going to this place called Teen Haven. It was kind of a youth center where they told me about Jesus. As I've grown older, I know he's still with me. He's kept me safe and led me to people who care, people like . . . you."

Finally, six months after we had started the process, Angel had a legal guardian and a permanent address. I'd never seen anyone as excited as Angel was on the morning Officer Carpenter and Den took him to enroll in school. He wore his best clothes and held his notebooks as if they were winning lottery tickets.

It was a wonderful victory, but it had taken a toll. Den and I saw our social life starting to slip away except for a few close friends. Business had fallen off at my beauty shop. People who normally offered a friendly hello while passing by now ignored us. Sometimes Den and I snapped at each other in misplaced frustration. I began losing sleep. Many nights I paced, crying and praying. Was it all worth it? Should I just ask Angel to go?

One night, depressed and confused, I sank to the kitchen floor in the darkness, and my tears poured forth.

"What's the answer, Lord?" I asked. "It would make it easier on the rest of the family to ask Angel to leave. But he's your child—and he's trying so hard. What should I do?"

As the cry for help left my lips, the far side of the kitchen began to glow with a hazy yet bright light. Blinded by the increasing brilliance, I sensed a loving warm presence in that kitchen with me. Somehow I knew it was an angel. It delivered a message silently but clearly: *Deni, let him stay. It will be all right.*

More amazing than the unearthly glow was how, in the twinkling of an eye, I was enveloped by a blanket of peace. No matter what hardships lay ahead, I knew God would be faithful to us if we were faithful to him.

When I looked up again, the kitchen was dark and I was sitting alone by the radiator.

That was three years ago. The people at the school got to know Angel. Teachers found an eager pupil; coaches found a first-class athlete; the other kids found a loyal friend. And my anxiety and frustration were replaced by love and understanding for those who had reacted negatively toward a kid who was different. When I was ready to forgive and reach out once again to those who had dropped us, many were more than ready to renew our friendship. People who had been wary of Angel started to help him, providing money for glasses, clothes, shoes. He was even offered a part-time job at a local lumberyard.

Angel worked so hard to catch up in school that he's earned mostly A's and Bs. He played on the school teams until he turned eighteen; now he helps manage them. When he discovered his poor vision would keep him from becoming a Navy pilot, he set his sights on college; he talks of someday studying marine biology.

The Bible says some have "entertained angels without knowing it" (Hebrews 13:2, NIV). We're lucky—we do know it. I thank God for the day our Angel left his clothes in our tree house and for the angel in the kitchen who told me to let him stay.

One Potato, Two Potato

Roy Davis

J UST AFTER WE RELOCATED TO A NEW TOWN, MY FATHER WAS let go from his job as a welder. Dad diligently searched for work, and Mom tried to scrape together meals for my brother, sister and me. Soon my parents had spent all their savings. When things grew desperate, a nearby farmer offered us potatoes from his field. We ate potatoes three times a day: fried for breakfast, baked for lunch and mashed for dinner. Several weeks passed and Dad was still unemployed. Mealtimes grew quiet and morose.

After breakfast one morning, Dad pushed his chair away from the table and headed outside. I followed and saw him rummaging under the seats in the car. He found some coins, pocketed them and said, "Tell your mother I'm going to town. I'll be back before supper."

What is he doing? I wondered.

When he returned he was clutching a small brown bag. He whispered to Mother, who shooed us out of the kitchen.

"We're going to have a special meal to celebrate," Dad announced.

"Celebrate what?" I asked. We didn't seem to have much to be happy about. And surely Dad would have told us if he had found work.

"Life, Roy. We're celebrating life. Things may be tough for us right now, but I know that with God's help we will get through this. He has truly blessed us."

Then Mom brought out dinner. Mounds of pink, green, blue and orange were piled on our plates!

What's this? After devouring the first bite, I knew: mashed potatoes. But because of all the colors, they were fun to eat. My brother, sister and I giggled as we ate, and the cloud that had been hanging over us at mealtimes was lifted.

A couple of weeks later Dad found a job, and we happily quit our potato diet. My father had bought food coloring with those coins. His purchase brightened our meals that night, and his philosophy continues to color my life. Now, when my family experiences tough times, I make rainbow mashed potatoes as a reminder of how fortunate we are.

CHAPTER SEVEN

MIRACLES OF HOPE

Guide me in your truth and teach me,
for you are God my Savior,
and my hope is in you all day long.
—Psalm 25:5 (NIV)

In the Courtyard

Barbara Brueski

W HILE FINISHING MY ERRANDS ONE DAY, I NOTICED AN older couple briskly walking away from the bench area outside the bank. I continued toward my car, wondering why they were hurrying. My heart sank when I saw the reason for their quick departure. A homeless woman was slowly sitting down on the bench. She didn't look like much of a threat, yet the couple's faces had been filled with fear and mistrust.

I felt a familiar guilt from having shown the same fear and contempt myself. I remembered a time not so long ago when I was stopped at a red light. An exhausted-looking man stood right outside my car holding a sign that read "Hungry. Please Help." Paralyzed with fear, I looked away. Part of me wanted to pass a few dollars to him. But I wondered if he would try to grab my purse or hurt me or my children. The light turned green.

Whew, I thought as I pulled away. But then I felt disappointed with myself. I had missed an opportunity God had placed in my hands.

Someday I will help, I thought. *Someday.*

This past summer we suffered through a terrible heat wave, with no rain in sight. Every day I drove past a small courtyard after dropping my daughter off at preschool. Homeless people slept and sat on benches, many wearing heavy clothes in the blistering sun. One old man in particular always caught my eye because he looked so miserable. Thousands of people saw this scene every day, yet no one seemed to really notice. On the third day of high temperatures I heard a radio warning to drink plenty of water to avoid heatstroke. Well, that did it: Something snapped inside me. I had passed the same people lying on the same benches too many times. The "someday" I'd planned to do something had arrived.

During my lunch hour, I drove to a nearby store. I bought a Styrofoam cooler, a few bags of ice, bottled water, sports drinks and some small hand towels. I said a prayer as I packed the cooler and placed the hand towels among the bags of ice.

My hands started to shake as I approached the courtyard. My heart was practically beating out of my chest! As I parked, climbed out of the car and walked around to the passenger side, I nervously felt dozens of eyes on me. I had never been so afraid.

I picked up the cooler and casually brought it over to the old man. He lifted his head and slowly sat up. What happened next caught me completely off guard: The man cowered away from me. I looked into his eyes for the first time—really looked. And I saw fear behind them. It made my heart sink.

Smiling, I softly asked if he was thirsty. The man noticed the cooler for the first time, and his fear changed to confusion. He looked inside the cooler as I lifted the lid. Then he smiled and his face relaxed. I handed the man a drink, which he shyly accepted.

Explaining that the hand towels were to cool his head, I asked him to make sure everyone in the courtyard got something to drink. With a hoarse voice, he said, "Thank you."

Another gentleman approached us when he saw the cooler and smiled as he opened a drink. Gradually, more people came over and accepted cold towels and beverages. I had to get back to work, and everyone smiled when I waved good-bye.

As I drove back to the office, I thought about the people in the courtyard. For years, I had viewed homeless people as dark and dangerous strangers to be avoided. But that day I realized they need to be acknowledged and cared for just like everyone else—not treated with fear and mistrust. They need kindness. Because when it comes right down to it, no matter what we do or how we live, all of us are children of God.

The Ringing of the Bells

Marian Webster

RAIN POURED DOWN IN PUDDLE-SPLASHING TORRENTS AS I stepped out into the darkness from under the portico at UCLA Medical Center in Los Angeles. My only protection was a flimsy garbage bag held above my head. Rain mixed with my tears. My knees began to tremble and buckle, pulling me down onto the soaked pavement.

I cried out, "Oh, God, help me. I can't go on."

My husband had been diagnosed in early October 1996 with spindle cell carcinoma and was immediately referred to a top surgeon at UCLA Medical Center. Surgery was scheduled for December 3, 1996. When the surgical team finished, the inner left side of my husband's face was a shell, nothing but emptiness from eyeless socket to roofless mouth. The neurological surgeon on the team had gone even further, cutting along the hairline to determine how close to the brain the cancer had spread.

The surgery was more than we could ever have imagined. The surgeon's question to my husband at the initial interview seemed so minor.

"I only have one question," he had said. "Do you mind if you have to lose your eye?"

My father lived his entire adult life with an artificial eyeball, which hadn't kept him from living a normal life. If my husband faced the loss of an eye like my father, it would be a small price to pay. The first sight of my husband after the thirteen hours of surgery was with his head totally swathed in bandages that also covered his left eye. Reality hit when I saw the large empty socket where his eye had been and nothing but emptiness from socket to mouth.

The days and nights became an endless vigil at his bedside, letting him feel my touch, trying to ease his pain. The walk to my hotel on Tiverton Avenue almost two blocks from the hospital was mainly to shower and change clothes. Sleeping was difficult—I wanted only to rush back to my husband's bedside.

A week after the surgery my husband had an especially difficult day. My weariness, my despair at watching my husband suffer was overwhelming. I badly needed to shower and change clothes before spending another night at his bedside. Finally, around 8:00 PM, I left. As I stepped out into the darkness and the rain, the weight of it all was suddenly more than my body and mind could bear, more than my legs could hold. My knees trembled and buckled beneath me. My cry to God came from the depths of despair.

At that moment, church bells began ringing: *What a friend we have in Jesus, all our sins and grief to bear. What a privilege to carry, everything to God in prayer. . . . Are we weak and heavy laden, cumbered with a load of care? Precious Savior, still our refuge, take it to the Lord in prayer.* The familiar words rolled through my mind as the bells pealed on and on. It was as if God had opened a special slit in heaven to pour anointing, healing oil onto my head. It cascaded down my body as I knelt in the pouring rain.

Finally the bells fell silent. I rose to my feet and continued my walk to the hotel, arriving with clothes and shoes only slightly damp, not soaked as they should have been. My soul, mind and body filled with God's love. God had given me strength to push on when all my strength was gone. In the months that followed, I needed that strength as never before.

My husband was in the hospital almost two weeks that time. Daily I trekked back and forth for brief periods at my hotel. I ate in the hospital's cafeteria. Occasionally, when he was asleep or taken for various tests, I took short breaks to walk outside the hospital for fresh air and to stretch my legs after long hours of sitting.

After his discharge came many days of painful follow-up testing and treatment. Appointments required frequent trips back to UCLA Medical Center. The dental and prosthesis laboratory spent hours fitting my husband for a large mouthpiece and upper plate that would provide a roof for his mouth so he could eat and speak better. Our final visit to UCLA Medical Center turned into five days of continuous hospitalization while more tests were done: CT scans, MRIs, spinal taps, even spinal drainage. On a Saturday morning in mid-August, the neurological surgeon came to his bedside with the final results, and then he led me outside into the hallway. "Take him home and let him die. It won't be very long."

Six weeks later, on October 2, 1997, my husband passed away at our home in Arizona. God's love reaches out to us in miraculous ways. You see, that dark rainy night sometime around 8:00 PM is the only time I heard the ringing of the bells.

The tears still fall every time I hear the hymn "What a Friend We Have in Jesus." Often I must leave a church service until the song is finished. It is a reminder of the most difficult time in our lives. It is also a reminder of the anointing, healing oil God poured over me as I fell to my knees onto the rain-soaked pavement and cried out to Him for help.

Recently I began searching the Internet to find out if a church actually existed in the vicinity of UCLA Medical Center—a church that, eleven years ago, played the bells. After several phone calls to other churches, my search finally led me to Westwood Hills Christian Church at 10808 Le Conte Avenue. I called the church office. Yes, I was told, the church is located across the street from UCLA. Yes, they have a carillon that plays every hour. The bells play a hymn at noon and at

5:00 PM every day. Other than that, the bells play only a short hourly prelude and then chime the hour. They stop after chiming the hour at 8:00 PM.

During all those visits to UCLA Medical Center, through all the hours, days and nights we were there, I never again heard the bells. I never heard them chime the hour. I never heard them play another hymn. I don't question why I heard the church bells ring only on that night. I don't even question why the bells played "What a Friend We Have in Jesus" at that hour when normally a hymn is played at noon and at 5:00 PM. I only know that when I reached my breaking point, when weariness, grief and despair sent me to my knees in the pouring rain on that dark December night around 8:00 PM, the bells played that song for me. God's gentle kindness bathed me in peace and comfort—a miracle moment in my life.

Surprised at the Slopes

Betsey Tinker

AT SEVEN YEARS OLD, MY SON MATTHEW WAS STILL AN only child. This was not by choice. Not by his choice and definitely not by ours. Nor was it for a lack of trying, crying or praying. It was just due to an imperfect world, and our little family of three was making the best of it.

As the mother of an only child, I *may* have tended to overanalyze some of my parenting choices . . . occasionally. Okay, maybe more than occasionally. And maybe "overanalyze" is a bit of an understatement. I wasn't overprotective or a hoverer. I was more of an agonizer. I sweated my hundreds of big and small daily choices that, if fumbled, had the potential to squelch Matthew's creativity, thwart his self-confidence, hinder his development and send him into an underachieving adulthood full of therapy.

Until my daughter arrived (actually she didn't *arrive*; I had to go around the world to get her), I admittedly aspired to a ridiculously unattainable ideal of motherhood. I found myself swimming regularly in pools of guilt. Okay, not always swimming . . . occasionally sinking. And maybe not always pools, but more like tidal waves. Somewhere along the line I had become convinced that I had to do it all, and be it all and make life smooth for my son. I'm healed now, but nonetheless . . .

After trying a private school for his kindergarten year, I had decided to devote myself to homeschooling Matthew for his first-grade year. I looked forward to cozy days of stories and crafts and arithmetic by the fire. Harmony and bonding and focused, holistic learning would take place just under the surface of lots of fun. I was determined to create a thoroughly stimulating, creative and appropriately challenging program for Matthew. There were just a few slices missing in our well-rounded learning pie.

Social interaction was a concern, naturally, but I had a few homeschooling friends, and we planned regular outings with our kids. Problem solved. Athletics wasn't a big concern because I had a seven-year-old boy who was on the move from dawn until dusk most days. But often our outings were sporty: hiking, swimming, skating and such. We both looked forward to those outings the way kids crave candy.

We'd been hammering away at homeschooling for a few months, and somehow the cozy-harmony-and-bonding thing just wasn't clicking as I'd planned. Some days my carefully designed program became a launching pad for will-to-will combat. I wasn't achieving smoothness. After one particularly rough week of school, we were both panting in thirsty anticipation of a day of skiing at Lake Eldora with our group of friends. I was sure this day of sun and snow would ease the tension and put us back on track.

For me, the athletic part of the journey was getting the car packed by a reasonable time of the morning with lunches, gloves, hats, ChapStick, sunscreen, goggles, snacks, drinks, ski pants, ski poles, money, car keys, and—oh yes—skis and an energetic and impatient seven-year-old boy. My behavior that morning, specifically toward said impatient boy, was less than that of the serene, nurturing mother I sought to be. Somewhat.

But once in the car and on the road, I sighed and smiled for the first time that day and our excitement became mutual. Matthew had nagged, begged and pleaded all year to go skiing, and this was our first opportunity. Having grown up in the small mountain resort town of Breckenridge, I had been skiing since my earliest memory. If possible, I think I was even more eager than he was to hit the slopes.

We pulled into the parking lot after the hour-plus drive and began recklessly donning hats, gloves, scarves, boots and sunscreen. I helped Matthew get ready first and there he stood, smiling ear to ear with his little helmet on, waving his ski poles like swords. His glowing face boosted my confidence in my ability to provide happiness for my boy.

I began to accessorize myself and was well into the process when I ran out of clothing before I ran out of cold skin. In a panic I dove into the trunk, hoping for some hidden trapdoor or trick wall or something that could be hiding my missing essentials. I fought to maintain my smile, peeking over the side of the trunk. I realized in horror that on this very cold and windy day, I had forgotten my own coat and gloves.

Not only that, but by pure fluke I had actually cleaned out my car just the day before, ridding it of the many clothing items that regularly live and reproduce there. That's the only way my car ever gets cleaned out—by fluke. And this *fluke* had left no corner untouched. I found nothing, not even a wipe-rag to tie around my trembling fingers.

I sank into the driver's seat with my head in my hands, my eyes starting to sting. I grasped for any possible solution, came up empty and convicted myself as the champion day-ruiner of all time. What could I possibly say to my son, who was on his twelfth trip around the car, gleefully yelling, "Come on, Mom"? What kind of mother forgets her own jacket after yelling at her son twenty-seven times to put on his?

Suddenly this small crisis was about so much more than skiing. It was about my competency as a mother. It was about my increasing awareness that I just couldn't prevent those bumps in life's road. I didn't pray formally, but an anxious cry was pouring from my heart—and every other internal organ. I reminded myself to breathe, and in the process I somehow began to release my son and myself and to realize that God is the only Perfect Parent. He knows what Matthew needs. I can't pull it off, but He can. I needed to *stop striving*. I took a deep breath.

The agonizer in me was miraculously off the hook, but the other part of me still had to open the car door and face my son with the news. I had blown it and we were going to have to turn around and go home, without skiing. As I stepped toward him and met his big blue eager eyes, I forced the words out of my mouth.

"Matthew, I'm so sorry. I don't know what to do."

His face fell and crumbled into a hundred pieces.

I continued. "I've forgotten my . . ." but my confession was cut short by another voice from behind me.

"Betsey! Matthew! Hey, guys, how are you?"

It was a good friend of mine, Nancy. I vaguely remembered that weeks and weeks ago she had asked me to go snowshoeing and I had declined, knowing we had a ski trip planned.

"Hi, Nance! How cool to run into you. I remember now that you're snowshoeing today."

"I've already been. Oh, I had the most glorious time. It's beautiful up there. Have you skied?"

Ouch! Bad question.

"No. Actually, it looks like we won't be able to. I forgot my coat and gloves."

And of course, she said, "Take mine. I'm done. I'll get them from you in a few days."

Was this for real? Nancy had no idea that her presence, her words, her coat and her gloves had come straight from my Perfect Parent in heaven. What were the chances that we'd actually run into her—not a moment too late and not a moment too soon? I'm not a statistician, but I'm sure, given all the ski areas around Denver and possible timings of the situation, the chances are infinitesimally small. Impossibly small. *Divinely* small.

It's amazing to me that God was able to tame my perfectionism, show His detailed serendipitous provision to Matthew and to me and give us a fantastic day of skiing as the cherry on top—all in one smooth gesture. He makes it look so easy! School's still not perfect, just like life and just like me. But really, how boring would life be, anyway, without the moguls? The biggest thrills are in taking the bumps head on!

Who Knew?

Sami Austin

WHEN WE WERE KIDS, MY SISTER JANE AND I often went to visit our grandparents Tom and Nellie Newsome in Talladega, Alabama, a four-hour drive from our home in Columbus, Mississippi. We'd hang out in Grandpa Tom's country store playing I Spy; my sister would spot something in the store and I'd have to guess what it was. There was a lot to choose from: baskets of apples, jars of pickles or the cute little boy in a cowboy hat pictured in the huge advertisement hanging in the corner.

Then Mama New (she said the word *grandmother* sounded older than she felt) would lead us around the bend to their farmhouse and let us bake with her. By the end of the day, the kitchen floor would be blanketed with sugar and we'd be hoarse from telling stories. Mama New's favorites were miracle stories. She didn't just believe in miracles—she expected them.

"You just have to talk to God about what you need, and he'll take care of the rest," she told us.

As Jane and I grew up, our favorite topic of discussion with Mama New became romance. One by one our friends settled down, and Jane and I started to worry a bit about being single. After a particularly painful breakup, Jane announced she was giving up on marriage altogether.

"Be patient, Jane," Mama New said. "Your husband's just around the corner."

Jane rolled her eyes. "Really, Mama New," she said.

"I'm not just saying that. I've talked to God about it. Your husband's just around the corner."

Then one time Mama New came to visit us in Columbus. We set to baking, just like old times. Nothing had changed, including our marital status. But I had a steady boyfriend, and Jane had just met a nice-looking lawyer named Dennis. That night Jane introduced Dennis to us before they headed out on their first date. As soon as the door closed behind them, Mama New turned to me with a sparkle in her eye.

"That's him," she said, "the one who's been just around the corner."

Jane and Dennis have been married five years now. Sure enough, when they met, Dennis lived around the corner from our house.

And that's not all: When he was a child, Dennis modeled for advertisements. Remember the cute little boy wearing the cowboy hat in the poster that hung in Grandpa Tom's country store? He was none other than my sister's future husband!

Who knew? Mama New.

A Miracle Grows

Sue Ferguson

⁓⊰⊱⊰⊱⁓

Moving from Nebraska to northern California had sent me into shock. Our family's tiny, new, expensive house was impeccable structurally, but cosmetically I was forced to think only of potential. Finally it was time—time to pull out the ugly overgrown shrubs that hid the entrance to our home. After making essential aesthetic changes indoors, I was ready to see a portion of the yard transformed.

Neighbors told me the previous owner removed grass and a sprinkler system after one summer's drought. They were replaced with rocks, concrete, statues and bushes; my most positive description of the landscaping was sturdy. Our only hope in heaven was the long growing season and perfect climate. I longed for a yard that celebrated our location instead of denying the benefits that seemed visible in everyone else's yard. With a tight budget and a black thumb, I walked down the aisles of a nearby nursery. My husband and I knew the area where we'd pulled the shrubs would surely look better than before. With that comforting thought, I chose plants that would provide color and height variation, carefully reading the planting guidelines staked in each pot.

Later, standing on the sidewalk beside our garden plot, I was overwhelmed with disappointment. The new plants added to our walkway bed looked lonely and small. Maybe I shouldn't have asked my husband to remove those horrible bushes. Our garden looked hopeless, and I felt powerless. How do you create beauty in the midst of rocks and concrete? Gazing at my sparsely filled patch, I felt despair.

Suddenly an angel appeared. Joyce didn't fly in on wings, and she wasn't wearing a halo. No, she pulled into our driveway in her Mercedes and popped the trunk; soon she quietly stood beside me. I would have been embarrassed by our lack of progress, but her saintly spirit was gentle and her presence created peace. Without words, her quiet actions spoke the comforting command, "Fear not."

Joyce led me to her open trunk and I looked inside. I couldn't believe my eyes! Blooming plants filled the trunk so completely that not one young plant could have tipped over; each pot was held securely against the others. With calm assurance, Joyce began to empty the trunk, carrying the pots and positioning them in possible planting spots. Almost immediately, Joyce's gift restored my lost hope.

Joyce instructed and encouraged. She watched with gentle guidance and then left as quietly as she had appeared. My husband, shovel in hand, dug holes and I planted. We worked confidently as we repeated Joyce's words to one another, "You can always move it later if you decide it would look better somewhere else." Dirty and hot, we planted and planted and planted. Then I filled our watering can with water and added some Miracle-Gro. As I watered, I realized the miracle wouldn't come from our plant food; it had been delivered by the hand of a generous and capable friend. Our garden—the same garden that had seemed impossible several hours before—had the touch of an angel and now bloomed with beauty. From that day on, we have fondly referred to Joyce as our garden angel.

Over the months ahead, I continued to watch our miracle grow with amazement. The garden was strikingly beautiful, with vivid color and interesting variety. Joyce reappeared from time to time with angelic counsel and clippers for trimming, always encouraging and never scolding.

That lovely flower bed is no longer mine, and my thumb is still black, but the miracle that was planted by an angel in that garden is still growing. I often find myself looking for a desolate place in the life of another to plant my talents so I can watch, with wonder and delight again, a new miracle grow!

The Blizzard of '82

Zarette Beard

IT WAS CHRISTMAS EVE 1982. I WAS IN HIGH SCHOOL AND my only brother, Norm, was my best friend. He was quirky, funny, lovable and loyal. He had graduated three years prior and was already out on his own. I missed having him around, especially during the holidays. I was still living at home in a suburb north of Denver. Norm was living in a suburb south of Denver. I begged, I mean really begged him to come home for Christmas. He promised he'd be there. I knew without a doubt, barring a natural disaster, he would be home. *Did I say natural disaster?*

As is typical in Colorado, it started to snow. And snow. And snow some more. The entire city shut down. No cars were allowed on the roads unless they were four-wheel drives on their way to provide emergency services. The snow was simply too deep. I stared out the big picture window in the living room, helplessly watching the snow pile up. The drifts were already up to the window, and it was truly a beautiful sight. I wish I could have enjoyed it, but my heart was as lonely and quiet as the empty streets. I sighed and went to my room to read. I was grateful that, at least in our end of town, the power was still on.

I had just turned on another lamp for reading when I heard a knock at the front door. I rolled my eyes, tossed my book onto the desk and slowly headed for the front door, knowing full well it was yet another neighbor needing my energy and my shovel. I scolded myself for such a grinchy attitude at this time of year and decided to dig out whoever it was at my door.

I opened the door to the strangest thing I had ever seen. There stood a man wearing snowboots with wadded-up newspapers sticking out of the tops and frozen jeans. Puffy sleeves peeked out from beneath a big trash bag disguised as a poncho. His hat had a thick layer of frost on it, but it was his face that was intriguing. This man's face was red from the windburn, with white patches from being so cold. His eyebrows and mustache had tiny icicles dangling from them. We regarded each other for just a moment when he broke the silence.

"Meh-he-ree Ca–rist-mas, Zarette!" the frozen man yelled.

Taken aback, I looked closer to see which one of my crazy neighbors was at my door. And then I recognized something. Those eyes. Those soft, brown, caring eyes. I squealed in surprise and delight.

"Norm! You're here!" I jumped into his arms and almost knocked him off the porch. He just laughed at me, the way he always did. He was so cold he could barely speak. I dragged him into the house and helped him remove layer after layer of frozen clothes. I made some hot chocolate, and we sat down. I asked him how he made it all the way to my home in this raging blizzard.

He explained that a promise is a promise and no blizzard was going to stand in his way. He bundled up and started walking. A sympathetic trucker and a kind man in a four-wheel drive each gave him a lift. When they reached their destinations, he simply got out and walked. It took him nine hours to reach me, but he did it and gave me one of the best Christmas memories I will ever have. That was twenty-four years ago. My brother Norm spent this Christmas with me, and wouldn't you know, we had a blizzard. We looked at each other knowingly as we sipped hot chocolate together and watched the snow fall from the sky.

Paying It Forward

Holly Baxley

LYING IN A SUNNY PATCH OF LIGHT THAT FILTERED through the canopy of live oak branches overhead, he reposed in a furry white semicircle, with one pink padded paw in the air. His eyes were closed, and his upturned face seemed to wrinkle back in a smile, revealing two sharp little canine teeth. Besides the occasional puff of wind that wafted through the leaves and caused the little sunlight patch to dance, the only movement was one ear that twitched from the tickling breeze. He seemed to own the porch he was lying on, looking for all practical purposes as if he didn't have a care in the world. There was one problem, though. It wasn't his porch, nor his patch of sunlight, nor even his live oak tree. But I doubted I could tell him that.

As I quietly started up the sidewalk to my house, wondering how this peaceful puffball ended up at my home, my next-door neighbor hollered out, "He's a pretty one, ain't he?"

Startled by the voice breaking the silence, both the cat and I looked up in the direction of the voice. I smiled back at my neighbor and agreed.

"Yes, he is beautiful. Where did he come from?"

"Can't say. Just showed up this morning. I named him Snowball."

I looked back at the still reclining cat, who was staring at me with warm blue eyes. He was beautiful. He shook his head to get the remaining tickle out of his ears, stretched all four legs as far as they could go and then dropped back into a heap on the porch.

I sighed. My husband and I had no pets yet, and that was by choice. We were a young married couple in college, with hardly any finances to keep ourselves fed. We lived on Ramen noodles and a five-pound sack of mixed beans my sister had given us as a housewarming present when we moved to our off-campus housing. We had no way of affording any kind of pet food, we had told ourselves, so a pet was out of the question.

And yet I could see the cat's little ribs under his thin coat of fur. *He probably would not be picky*, I reasoned in my head. But I seriously doubted that this cat would enjoy a dinner of Ramen noodles, even the ones with chicken flavoring.

My neighbor spoke, as if reading my thoughts.

"He really enjoyed the leftover pieces I gave him from skinning my latest catfish. I caught a beauty this morning from my troll lines."

"Are you going to keep him?" I asked hopefully.

My neighbor looked at the cat fondly.

"He's not really the keeping kind, if you ask me. I think he likes his freedom. But I'm sure between us, we can keep him fed."

And that's how Snowball came to own us on our little street of Avenue D. He spent his mornings at our neighbor's house, enjoying whatever the catch-of-the-day happened to be. My neighbor was an avid fisherman who went out in the wee hours of the morning to fish. If he caught something, he'd bring it back and string it up in his backyard to filet. Snowball was at the ready before our neighbor got home, staring up at the hooks he knew a fat fish would soon be swinging on.

Then after his fishy breakfast, he'd slink silently off on whatever the day held for him, returning in the late afternoon. I'd get back from my classes to find him chasing that patch of soft sunlight on our porch, lying squarely in the center, soaking up all that sweet warmth—the only Snowball to absorb heat and not melt. My husband and I managed to finagle our finances just enough to add a small bag of cat food to our grocery bill and fed him that on days when our fishing friend's lures were empty.

The arrangement worked out quite well. Snowball seemed to enjoy it most of all. He wasn't pressured to be owned, we

weren't pressured to own him, and somehow through this process, we became closer to our neighbors as well.

But one morning Snowball needed an owner more than
he needed freedom. We woke up to find a very sick Snowball
on our porch. It was unusual enough to find him lying on our
porch in the morning, but things were far worse than that. He
had been in a fight. A very, very bad fight. His left ear was almost
torn off, and he was bleeding profusely. Our neighbors were
gone and time was of the essence. Brent quickly gathered into
his arms the almost limp kitty in his usual semicircle. Snowball
didn't move, but he did purr.

Brent transferred Snowball into my arms and deftly
cleaned his wounds and then wrapped his little head in a bandage. We thought he would struggle against it, but he had no
fight left in him. And that scared us. We took turns holding
him and talking to him from evening till late at night. We created a little bed for him beside our dryer on our enclosed back
porch and put out some food and water. Snowball lay exactly
where we put him and made no effort to move. We went to bed
that night wondering if we had done all we could.

The next morning we peeked out the kitchen door. Snowball
was standing over his water dish, trying to lap water in spite of the
restrictive bandage around his head. Then we heard him growl as
he pawed at the wound by his ear. That made us grin, for we knew
it was a good sign to see him a little put out by his circumstances.

As Brent and I prepared to leave for our respective classes,
we noticed our neighbor had his latest catfish conquest on a

line out back and was walking around his yard looking for his little white furry pal. Brent told him what had happened and pointed at our back porch. Mr. Stanley said Snowball was lucky to have someone watch over his nine lives and promised to save some fish for him.

In the afternoon, Snowball was lying once again in a sunny patch of light, this time on top of the dryer. But as soon as he saw us peeking at him through the back door's window, he started meowing loudly and fighting his bandage. We opened the door and he came streaking through the kitchen. His normally white, skinny tail was as thick as a bottlebrush held rigidly straight up in the air, not as a white flag of surrender but as a banner declaring war.

He howled, yowled and growled while running through every room of our small rented house. Every once in a while he'd stop to fight the ominous bandage that seemed bent on breaking his will. Like a prizefighter using light footwork while dancing around a ring, Snowball would stand on his hindquarters, weaving and bobbing and clawing at the dressing. He would not yield to the bandage's power over him, nor would he stop his crusade to rid himself of the evil thing. He would fight to the bitter end!

Until he heard the can opener. Upon hearing the mechanical whir, he stopped his one-cat campaign, sheathed his claws and padded back to the kitchen, dragging half of the bandage behind him. A victory dinner of tuna and milk awaited him. I figured he had worked too hard to settle for Ramen noodles with chicken flavoring. When Snowball had a full tummy, he became more docile. Brent picked him up once again, medicated his ear and applied a fresh bandage, much to Snowball's chagrin. But if he had been put out with us, he was just as quick to forgive, for the evening found him lying in that familiar semicircle repose on the couch between us as we studied. His eyes were closed and he was purring.

And that was the moment, the magical moment when something happened deep in my heart: I fell in love with him. He had weaved and bobbed his way into my heart with his bravery and courage, and I found myself wanting more than just a casual acquaintance with him. I truly wanted to be his owner. I put down my pen and scratched him under his chin—the only place the bandage didn't restrict him. His purr grew louder and deeper. Fish might get hooked on my neighbor's line, but Snowball had me hooked with that loud, precious purr.

All of a sudden, Snowball looked up at me, his eyes peering into mine. He winked, as if he knew some great secret. I think he personally could see how much I wanted him to become a permanent part of our family. For a mere moment, he leaned his head further into my hand to be scratched and then just as quickly leapt down and made his way through the kitchen to the back porch and his little bed. It seemed rather abrupt, but I was still learning his ways. Having owned dogs for most of my life, I didn't know how cats acted or responded, and to this day, I can't tell you why he did things the way he did. I have, however, thought about it a lot since then.

Perhaps he went to bed that night so soon because he was worn out from his battle with the bandage. Perhaps he was just ready to be alone for the night. But I honestly think that getting cozy with us was too much for his freedom-loving heart, and he didn't want to get too close to someone who wanted to own him.

The next few days, he'd repeat the above antics in a smaller version. Every day when we'd let him out for a while after class, he'd run like a crazed cat for a bit. Then he'd eat his food and let us undress and re-dress his wound. But when it came time for Brent and me to study, instead of hanging out with us, he'd head to the back porch and meow to be let out.

The first night he did that, we ignored his cries because he was too banged up to go out. But the next night, his cries were louder and a little angrier, so Brent took pity on him and let him outside. I was afraid we'd never see him again, but in the morning he was back in his bed, sleeping soundly. He must have been up all night. The next evening we let him out again, and when we woke up, he was happily eating fish next door. We caught him and took off his bandage for the last time as his ear was healing nicely.

After school, he was looking like the old Snowball, curled up on our front porch in his patch of sunlight. That evening he came inside, ate some cat food and hung out with us. He kept staring at me with a far-off look I couldn't read. It was as if he was trying to see through me or make up his mind about who I was as a person. I swear to you, I've never been so scrutinized as I was by this cat. I couldn't study, because I could feel him staring at me.

When he cried to be let outside, I watched him saunter out the door and wander off into the night. I didn't know we'd never see him again.

The next morning, we looked for him at our neighbor's, but he wasn't there. Brent went to the back porch to see if he was sleeping in his bed. And that's when I heard Brent call out, "Holly, come quick! You've got to see this!"

I ran back to the porch wondering if Snowball had been in a worse fight, but what I found amazed me as well. There in Snowball's bed was a tiny, long-furred orange kitten, whose eyes were barely open. This baby was too tiny to have been weaned from his mama. And there's no way he could have made his way all by himself even up our back-porch steps, let alone into Snowball's bed.

The kitten's baby-blue eyes peeked at us, and his tiny mouth opened as if to meow, but no sound came out. Not even a tiny squeak. Brent and I stared at each other in wonder as we tried to connect the dots of how this very thin and tiny precious kitten came to us. Later that evening, when there was no Snowball to be seen, we did our best to make our new baby welcome in our home.

And then Brent said, "I know what happened. Snowball didn't want to be owned, and he knew we wanted to own a pet. He also knew we took care of him when he was sick, so he found this kitten that needed both a home and someone to take care of it. I think he decided to help this kitten the way he had been helped."

We sat there stroking this new kitty and marveled at Snowball's thoughtfulness and sense of nurturing. Many years later I heard the term "pay it forward," which means that when a stranger provides a random act of kindness, you do a random act of kindness for someone else. Snowball was ahead of the curve. He knew how to pay it forward long before the term was ever coined. And I've been learning that lesson ever since.

Thinking with the Heart

Susan Ludwig

As a substitute teacher, I was recently assigned to a grade 5/6 class at a city elementary school. After checking in at the front office, I walked into the classroom. The students' chairs were stacked in a pile near the window. Lesson plans were on the teacher's desk. The chalkboard had a welcome message on it. It all smelled to me of a typical, mundane Wednesday in my substituting life.

I couldn't have been more wrong.

The first student in the room that day arrived in a wheelchair, and I quickly assessed that she had no use of her arms or legs and that she was deaf. Laura wore glasses and had a narrow, pretty face. A paraprofessional, assigned to work one-on-one with the girl, wheeled her to the back of the classroom and began tending to her. I left them alone and read the day's lesson plans.

In time, I wandered over and introduced myself. A sign language interpreter, who showed up a moment or two after Laura and her aide, filled the girl in on who I was and why I was there. Laura looked at me and smiled, and her aide told me Laura communicated only with her eyes—a blink for "yes," two slow blinks for "no"—and that her intelligence was not at all impaired. Students eventually streamed into the classroom, their loud, excited voices typical of preadolescents at 8:25 AM. By now Laura, her aide and the sign language interpreter were sitting at what looked to be their regular spots in front of the classroom. Laura was stretched out in a large reclining chair, her wheelchair folded in a corner. Most, perhaps all of the students took a moment to greet Laura and the two adults with a quick and friendly "Hello" or "Good morning" or "How are you today?" Many made sure to make eye contact with Laura, who could not voluntarily move her head to meet their gaze.

The morning progressed in what I'd consider a typical manner, and after the students came back from music class, I gave them ten minutes to read silently at their desks before lunch. Two girls immediately went over to Laura's chair and positioned themselves on either side of her. One girl read out loud from a book as the other girl used sign language to convey the story to Laura. The young signer's hand signals were fluid and seemingly perfect. Parts of the signing resembled a dance of her hands, and I was surprised at the beauty I found in the simple motions.

Occasionally the girl who was signing would ask a question of Laura: "Do you like this book?" "Is it too boring?" "Do you think Melanie will find her way home after this chapter?"

The girl waited patiently for Laura to respond, and after interpreting the communication, she'd tell the reader, "Laura doesn't like the way this story is turning out" or something of that nature.

The reader and the signer would switch places at what seemed to be prescribed times, each equally comfortable in either role.

At lunchtime, three girls and a boy stayed in the classroom to eat with Laura. I learned that she is fed through a tube in her stomach and, on the colder days, stays inside during recess. The students joked, told stories and discussed television shows and schoolwork. The entire time, one student was always seated by Laura's head to relate what was being said by those in the group.

Every so often, that signing student would report to the others, "Laura hasn't seen that show" or "Laura thought that was pretty funny." Occasionally someone would move a tendril of hair away from Laura's eyes or adjust her glasses so they weren't crooked.

As I watched the students and their interactions with Laura that day, I was touched by this unique situation and wondered if the students knew how wonderful they were. For all the talk we hear about troubled children, these students showed me an inspiring side of human nature.

And how fortunate, I thought, that in addition to learning about ancient Greece and how to turn fractions into decimals, these students are learning that disabled people are regular people. They're learning to think with their hearts as well as their brains. Indeed, their unconditional acceptance and affection for this particular student, and all of their fellow students, may turn out to be one of the greatest lessons these children will ever learn.

CHAPTER EIGHT

MIRACLES OF PRAYER

By day the Lord directs his love,
at night his song is with me—
a prayer to the God of my life.
—Psalm 42:8 (NIV)

Airport Angel

Christine E. Collier

I WAS A RUSTY DRIVER—THAT DAY, ANYWAY. BECAUSE OF a foot injury, I hadn't driven our car in over six months. My foot had been in either a walking cast or an air boot for months. Maneuvering the car pedals was difficult and unsafe. However, the cast was now off and my husband needed a ride from the airport.

In the past I often picked my husband up at the airport, and I decided this would be the day to break out my car keys again! I left our home early, with plenty of time to arrive at the airport before his plane landed. Instead, however, I had one of the most nerve-wracking trips I have ever had in a car. I couldn't have known that before the afternoon was over, I would meet an angel.

I am a person who never drives anywhere unless I know exactly how to get there. Daring I'm not! But for some reason, when I came to the traffic light where I should have turned to take the back route to the airport (I always took this route and knew it by heart), I kept driving straight ahead. As I said, I was a very rusty driver.

Soon I realized I had made a mistake and remembered where I should have turned. I became nervous and said a prayer that everything would be all right. I couldn't turn around at that point but knew where I would be able to do so. When I finally came to the place where I could turn around and retrace my path, I made an even more disastrous error. The highway exit allowed me to turn around; however, instead of going up the ramp and back where I had come from, I turned onto a major highway and immediately knew I was in trouble. I starting praying again but had to keep going once I was on the highway, even though I was already late.

After driving a few miles, I took an exit into a small shopping mall. My husband was probably landing at that time. I went into a restaurant and asked the manager if he would call a policeman for me. I explained I was lost and needed directions to the airport.

"You will be able to find it without the help of a policeman. Just go back through that exit, stay on the highway and you will come right to the airport."

"Okay," I said, my shoulders slumping and my confidence in my driving ability about as low as it could go. I got back on the highway, where tractor trailers were weaving steadily in and out of the lanes. This was the kind of highway driving I like to avoid at all costs. It was a nightmare, and I was growing more and more nervous by the minute. I couldn't believe one wrong turn was causing me so much misery.

In the back of my mind I knew time was rushing by and my husband had no idea where I was. I drove for what seemed like forever, but nothing looked familiar. I never used this highway, which was completely unlike the back route to the airport I always took. I worried that I might cause an accident as I wasn't driving fast enough. I decided this had to stop; I wasn't going to keep driving aimlessly.

I pulled off on an exit, prayed for help again and felt led to jump out of my car, my heart beating like a jackhammer. It was very dark by now, so this was a foolish thing to do, but I was desperate for help.

If someone stops, I'll ask if I can make a call on his or her cell phone to my husband or the police. At least I had a plan now.

I hadn't been out of my car more than two or three minutes when a truck with a cab pulled up by me. I believe a woman sat in the passenger seat but was never positive. The man driving asked if he could help me.

"Yes," I said. "Do you have a cell phone?"

"Yes, I do," he answered. "May I call someone for you?"

"Would you please call the police? I'm lost and can't find my way to the airport."

"There's no need for that, you are on the right path. I can tell you how to get there," he kindly replied.

"I think I'm too nervous to find it now. I know that sounds foolish, but I just don't think I can make it there," I answered.

"You can follow me; I won't lose you. Just go straight and the first road on the right is where you turn. You'll see the airport signs by then. You're on the right path; if you had kept going, you would have come to the road with arrows pointing to the airport. I'll wait on the road you turn onto and make sure you have made it. I will not leave you."

I thanked him over and over and said I would do that.

He drove back on the highway and I cautiously did as well. He was soon out of sight, but I knew to look for a truck with a cab and kept on driving.

Surely he's not still waiting for me. I'm driving too slowly. I did see a familiar airport sign, which gave me some hope, and I soon knew where he had told me to turn. There it was, the name of the road he had mentioned! A truck with a cab was waiting alongside the road.

He yelled out his window, "Will you be all right now? Do you want me to drive to the airport so you can follow me?"

"No, I'm fine now," I answered. "Thank you so much; I can't tell you how much I appreciate your kindness."

"No problem at all. Have a good evening."

The man drove away and I was able to find my way to the airport and pick up my husband. Needless to say, he had been very worried and had called our children, the hospitals and police trying to find out where I was. Our son went looking for me in the completely opposite direction from where I was, so he would never have found me.

I had a strong feeling that this man in the truck didn't just happen to drive by. I felt he had been sent to answer a desperate prayer and was my guardian angel that day. Did I make an error in judgment to trust a complete stranger? I was indeed vulnerable, and God protected me. I needed help and my prayers were answered so quickly it was as if an angel appeared from nowhere. This complete stranger took the time to ask me what was wrong and didn't judge my nervousness. He was encouraging and kind. Then he pulled onto the side of the road and waited until I made it there. Not everyone would do that. He truly was my angel unaware, perhaps an angel on earth.

Act of Faith

Richard H. Schneider

A S THE CAB THREADED ITS WAY THROUGH MANHATTAN'S East Side, I wondered about the man I was about to meet. Gian Carlo Menotti, the well-known composer, was a stranger to me, though I knew his works well, especially his opera *Amahl and the Night Visitors*.

Along with millions of others around the world, I had been captivated by its beautiful story of a crippled little boy and his careworn mother who are among the first to experience the love and healing power of the newborn Christ. Seen on television annually during the 1950s and 1960s, it is reported to be the most popular Christmas music offering next to Handel's *Messiah*.

But of its composer I knew little. Bits and pieces of his life gleaned from news clips and articles intrigued me. I was especially struck by one reference to something unusual, even mystical, behind the inspiration of this opera.

Fascinated, I wrote Menotti regarding a visit. It took fifteen months to come about. When he isn't composing, which is almost always, the maestro is traveling the world, overseeing musical events such as the Spoleto Festivals in Italy and Charleston, South Carolina. But now my cab drew up in front of the apartment building where he lives when in New York. A small elevator creaked to his floor, and I stepped out into the hall to be welcomed by the composer.

A lean man with penetrating eyes, Menotti ushered me into his living room, where eighteenth-century prints and marble statuary evoked a gracious Italian atmosphere. Now in his seventieth year, he spoke enthusiastically of his love of composing: "It is my life." When our talk turned to *Amahl*, his eyes twinkled, he leaned back and, in his soft Italian accent, told me the story behind the opera.

It all began, he said, in the New York Metropolitan Museum of Art. It was the fall of 1951 and Gian Carlo Menotti wandered gloomily through the museum, trying to take his troubled mind off the responsibility that was tormenting him.

Why did I ever sign that contract? he wondered. A few years earlier, the National Broadcasting Company had asked him to compose a one-act opera for television. Because he had already written several well-received productions and had fulfilled commissions for everything from ballets to operas, the assignment seemed perfectly feasible. He accepted a one-thousand-dollar advance payment and agreed to submit the opera in time for a Christmas production in 1951.

But he could not come up with a story. He tried and tried, discarding theme after theme. Finally giving up, he wrote to Samuel Chotzinoff, head of the NBC opera company, and asked if he could return the advance money and withdraw from the assignment. The NBC people called him in, concerned.

"We don't want the money," they pleaded. "We want your opera." They persuaded Gian Carlo to try once more.

He did, again and again, but still could not come up with an idea that inspired him. Not only did he feel he was disappointing other people, but he also wondered if his creative powers might be waning.

Now it was late fall, and seeking respite from his misery, he had entered the Metropolitan Museum. Wearily he climbed the stairs to its second floor and walked into a gallery with a collection of European masterpieces from the fourteenth to the eighteenth centuries. Something about one of them caught his eye, and he paused. The work was *The Adoration of the Magi* by Hieronymus Bosch, a fifteenth-century Dutch painter. Highlighted in the center of walled ruins was the Virgin Mary with the Baby Jesus in her lap. A shepherd knelt nearby. Three kings, robed in regal glory, offered the Child sumptuous gifts.

It was the kings that caught Menotti's eye. They reminded him of Christmas celebrations in his childhood home in Cadegliano-Viconago, Italy. Italian children at that time did not receive their holiday gifts from Santa Claus. Instead, the gifts were left by the wise men as they traveled toward Bethlehem on the eve of Epiphany, January 6.

Gian Carlo smiled, recalling how he and his little brother Tullio looked forward to that night, trying hard to stay awake to see the royal visitors. And though they never succeeded, it always seemed to Gian Carlo that just before he fell asleep he could hear them coming—the eerie cadence of their song in the distant blue hills, the camels' hooves crunching the snow of northern Italy, the jingling of the silver bridles.

In that quiet museum gallery, he again heard, coming from the distant hills of his childhood, the haunting music of the three kings. With the flame of an idea kindled, he went home to work. Composing, to the maestro, is an essential part of his daily life. He composes while shaving, eating, taking a walk ...

Undoubtedly, he mused as he worked, the kings had stopped at many houses during their long journey. Those ruins he had seen in the Bosch painting—perhaps someone was living there? Perhaps a poor widow and her child ... a little boy? The composer decided to call him Amahl after a name he dimly remembered from a childhood book.

He began to jot down ideas for the words, and the words immediately suggested some music, the sound of distant singing as the kings wound their way down from the hills. What were they like, these royal personages? Again his mind ranged back to childhood; his favorite then had been Melchior, because he was the oldest and had a long, white beard. His brother's favorite was Kaspar. Tullio insisted that this king was a little crazy and quite deaf—possibly because Kaspar never brought Tullio all the gifts he asked for!

As the characters took form, Gian Carlo let NBC know he was onto something. Immediately he was sorry. Though he had no idea how the opera would take shape, the television network confidently made plans to present it live on Christmas Eve. That was only a month away!

There was so much to do in developing the story. *Who was the little boy Amahl?* he wondered. *What was he like?* He gazed out his studio window and thought about himself. Here he was, a forty-year-old man whose childhood dreams, as the poet Wordsworth put it, had "faded into the light of common day." Lost with his dreams was a belief in such wonders as three kings who brought children gifts on Epiphany.

What had happened, he wondered, *to the faith of little Gian Carlo who had believed so completely?*

And then he remembered something special about his young beliefs. It had been so long ago he had almost forgotten. At age four, he was lame. The doctors could not cure what they called a "white tumor" in his leg, and he had difficulty walking.

In his household there in Cadegliano was a person of great faith: his governess Maria. She came from peasant stock and was adored by all the children in the family because of her incredible patience and sweetness. She was also blessed with great faith in God, which gave her surprising strength and understanding. Maria knew of a church high in the nearby

Lugano mountains, the Madonna del Monte, where it was said God worked miracles.

She asked him, "Gian Carlo, do you believe God can heal you?"

He nodded in earnest conviction. And so his dear Maria took him into the mountains to the place of God. And he was healed. The doctors had no explanation for why Gian Carlo was able to walk again. But Maria believed, and he believed, and the healing came.

Now, as the maestro gazed out his studio window, a picture began forming in his mind. It was the boy Amahl leaning on a crude wooden crutch. Of course! He was lame, as Gian Carlo had been. He needed a healing. And the story would be the miracle of the healing that comes when Amahl offers his crutch as a gift to the Christ Child. Days and nights blurred into an endless penciling of notes and orchestration, of crumpling music sheets and starting over.

Rehearsals in New York City were already underway. Feverishly writing a few pages at a time, Menotti gave them to his cook to rush to the railroad station, where NBC couriers picked them up. The excitement. The frustration. The exhaustion. Until finally one morning, with the green-shaded desk lamp still burning as his frosted studio windows glowed pink with the rising sun, Gian Carlo Menotti leaned back in his chair, totally spent. *Amahl and the Night Visitors* was a reality. The opera was finished.

"Inspiration," says Menotti reflectively. "How can one define it?"

I am still in the maestro's Manhattan living room. Menotti continues speaking: "It is as if God would send you a momentary flash of total recall—but a recall of what?" His eyes search beyond me. "Both St. Augustine and Plato have spoken of beauty as divine perfection," he resumes. "Only a few lucky artists can achieve that state of grace that allows them to have a fleeting glimpse of this beauty."

He is silent for a moment and then adds, "Was I one of the lucky ones? Perhaps I was."

The Healing of Maude Blanford

Catherine Marshall

THE WOMAN ACROSS THE DINING TABLE FROM ME HAD NO trace of gray in her reddish hair, though she was past middle age now, a grandmotherly type, comfortable to be with.

"How did your, ah, illness begin?" I asked, feeling foolish before this vision of radiant health. I had come to see Maude Blanford because a friend had told me about her. Twelve years earlier, she had been healed of terminal cancer.

"My leg had been hurting," Mrs. Blanford replied. "I thought it was because I was on my feet so much."

But when her family doctor examined her, his eyes were solemn as his hands gently probed several firm tumor masses on her left side. When he spoke words like specialist and biopsy, the patient read the unspoken thought: malignancy.

Mrs. Blanford was referred to Dr. O. J. Hayes, who examined her on June 29, 1959, and prescribed radiation treatments. The treatments began July 7, followed by surgery on September 29.

After the operation, when Mrs. Blanford pleaded with Dr. Hayes for the truth, he admitted, "It is cancer and it's gone too far. One kidney is almost nonfunctioning. The pelvic bone is affected—that's the pain in your leg. I am so sorry."

Maude Blanford was put on narcotics to control the excruciating pain and sent home to die. Over a six-month period she took stock of her spiritual resources and found them meager indeed. She had no church affiliation, no knowledge of the Bible and only the vaguest, most shadowy concept of Jesus.

The first week in January 1960, she suffered a cerebral hemorrhage and was rushed back to the hospital. For twelve days she lay unconscious; her husband was warned that if she survived the attack, it would probably be as a vegetable.

But Maude Blanford, oblivious to the world around her, was awake in a very different world. In her deep coma, a vivid image came to her. She saw a house with no top on it. The partitions between the rooms were there, the furniture in place, but there was no roof.

She remembered thinking, "Oh, we must put a roof on the house! If it rains, all the furniture will be spoiled."

When she came out of the coma, Mrs. Blanford's mind was very much intact but bewildered. What could the roofless house have meant? As she puzzled over it, a Presence seemed to answer her. Today she has no hesitation in calling Him the Holy Spirit.

"He seemed to show me that the house represented my body but that without Jesus as my covering, my body had no protection."

I leaned forward, excited by an insight. Wasn't this what I had always been taught about the Spirit—that his role was to show us Jesus and our need of him?

"At that time," Mrs. Blanford went on, "I didn't know how to get the roof on my house."

From then until July 1960, her condition worsened. Heart action and breathing became so difficult, she was reduced from normal speech to weak whispers. Even with the drugs, the suffering became unbearable. By July she knew she no longer had the strength to make the trips for radiation treatment.

"On July first, I told the nurse I wouldn't be coming back."

But that day, as her son-in-law helped her into the car outside the medical building, she broke down and wept.

"At that moment I didn't want anything except for God to take me quickly—as I was. I said, 'God, I don't know who you are. I don't know anything about you. I don't even know how to pray. Just, Lord, have your own way with me.'"

Though she did not realize it, Maude Blanford had just prayed one of the most powerful of all prayers: the prayer of relinquishment. By getting her own mind and will out of the way, she had opened the door to the Holy Spirit.

She did not have long to wait for evidence of His Presence. Monday, July 4, dawned beautiful but hot. That afternoon, Joe Blanford set up a cot for his wife outdoors under the trees. As the ill woman rested, into her mind poured some beautiful sentences:

"Is not this the fast that I have chosen? To loose the bands of wickedness, to undo the heavy burdens, and to let the oppressed go free, and that ye break every yoke? . . . Then shall thy light break forth as the morning, and thine health shall spring forth speedily. Here I am."

I stared at Maude Blanford over the rim of my coffee cup. "But I thought you didn't know the Bible?"

"I didn't! I'd never read a word of it. Only I knew this didn't sound like ordinary English. I thought, *Is that in the Bible?* And right away the words came: *Isaiah 58.* Well, my husband bought a Bible for me. I had to hunt and hunt to find the part called Isaiah. But then when I found those verses just exactly as I had heard them—except for the last three words, 'Here I am'—well, I knew God Himself had really spoken to me!"

Over the next weeks, Maude Blanford read the Bible constantly, often until two or three o'clock in the morning, seeing the person of Jesus take shape before her eyes.

Along with the hunger to meet Jesus in the Word, the Holy Spirit gave her an intense desire to be out-of-doors, close to His world.

"Joe," she told her astonished husband one day, "I want to go fishing."

This made no sense to him. The terrain to the lake was rough. She would have to be carried down and then back up a steep hill.

But some kindly neighbors offered to take her, and her husband acquiesced. She could not fish, of course, but she could look—at a breeze rippling the water, at the wheeling birds and the distant hills. And as she looked, a response grew in her, a response that is another of the Holy Spirit's workings in the human heart: praise. All that first day she praised Jesus for the world he had made. That night, she slept like a baby.

After that, the lake trip became routine. A month or so later Maude Blanford was walking up the hill to the road by herself. At home she had begun very slowly climbing the stairs, praising Jesus for each step attained. Or she would sit in a chair and dust a mahogany tabletop, saying, "Thank you, Jesus. Isn't this wood beautiful!"

Next she tried putting a small amount of water in a pail. Sitting in a kitchen chair, she would mop the floor in the area immediately around her, scoot the chair a few inches, mop again. "Thank you, Jesus, for helping me do this!"

Her daughter-in-law, who was coming over almost daily to clean house for her, one day asked in great puzzlement, "Mom, how is it that your kitchen floor never gets dirty?"

The older woman twinkled. "Well, I guess I'll have to confess: The Lord and I are doing some housework."

But their chief work, she knew, was not on this building of brick and wood but on the house of her spirit, the house that had been roofless for so long. Gradually, as her knowledge of Jesus grew, she sensed his protective love surrounding and sheltering her. Not that all her pain and difficulties were over. She was still on pain-numbing narcotics, still experiencing much nausea.

"The will to live is terribly important," she commented to me. "It takes a lot of self-effort just to get out of bed, to eat again after your food has just come up. This is when too many people give up."

One Saturday night, when the pain would not let her sleep, she lay on her bed praising God and reading the Bible. About 2:00 AM she drifted off to sleep with the Bible lying on her stomach. She felt she was being carried to heaven, traveling a long way through space.

Then came a voice out of the universe: "My child, your work is not finished. You are to go back." This was repeated three times, slowly, and then she was aware of her bedroom around her again. The rest of the night she remained awake, flooded with joy, thanking God.

When her husband woke up in the morning, she told him, "Honey, Jesus healed me last night."

She could see he did not believe it; there was no change in her outward appearance. "But I knew I was healed and that I had to tell people." That very morning she walked to the Baptist church across the highway from their home and asked the minister if she could give a testimony. He was startled at the unusual request from someone who was not even a member of the congregation, but he gave permission, and she told the roomful of people that God had spoken to her in the night and healed her.

A few weeks later she insisted on taking a long bus trip to visit her son in West Virginia. Still on narcotics, still suffering pain, she nonetheless knew that the Holy Spirit was telling her to rely on Jesus instead of drugs from now on. At five o'clock on the afternoon of April 27, 1961, on the return journey, as she popped a pain-killing pill into her mouth at a rest stop, she knew it would be the last.

And so it turned out. In retrospect, physicians now consider this sudden withdrawal as great a miracle as the remission of cancer cells.

It took nine months for her bad leg to be near normal, two years for all symptoms of cancer to vanish. When she called Dr. Hayes in 1962 over some small matter, he almost shouted in astonishment.

"Mrs. Blanford! What has happened to you! I thought you were—"

"You thought I was long since gone," she laughed back.

"Please come to my office at once and let me examine you! I've got to know what's happened."

"But why should I spend a lot of money for an examination when I'm a perfectly well woman?" she asked.

"Mrs. Blanford, this one is on us!"

What the doctor found can best be stated in his own words:

I had lost contact with Mrs. Blanford and had assumed that this patient had expired. In May of 1962 she appeared in my office . . . her last X-ray had been in July 1960.

The swelling of her leg was gone. She had full use of her leg; she had no symptoms whatsoever, and on examination, I was unable to ascertain whether or not any cancer was left. . . .

She was seen again on November 5, 1962, at which time her examination was completely negative. . . .

She has been seen periodically since that time for routine examinations. . . . She is absolutely asymptomatic. . . . This case is most unusual in that this woman had a proven, far-advanced, metastatic cancer of the cervix and there should have been no hope whatsoever for her survival.

The miracle of Maude Blanford reminds me of that scene on the night before His Crucifixion when Jesus said quietly to His despairing disciples, "Ye have not chosen Me, but I have chosen you. . . ." He is still saying that to us today, while His Spirit—always working through human beings—sometimes confounds us, often amazes us and is always the guide to the future who can bring us joy and exciting fulfillment.

The Therapy of Prayer

William Wilson, MD

B ILL? GOT A MINUTE?"

I looked up from my desk to see an old school colleague standing in the doorway of my office at Duke University's Medical Center. He was an internist; I was a psychiatrist.

"Sure," I said, pushing aside the patient reports I'd been working on. "Come in."

It was late, nearly seven, and the cold fluorescent lighting cast thin blue shadows across my friend's usually warm and animated features. He looked tired as he sat down in the chair facing me.

"What's up?" I asked.

"Well," he said, with a tight little smile, "my life is a drag." He hesitated. "I don't understand it. I mean, you'd think I had everything. Like you, I've just been appointed as a full professor here at the University. I have unlimited access to a huge laboratory, research facilities and library. Journals publish my papers, the government awards me grants. I've got a great wife and nice kids.

"So why," he asked, leaning back with a wry grin, "do I feel so empty inside?"

I wished I could have given him an answer that would offer real help. But all I could say was, "The way you're feeling isn't unusual. If it's any consolation, I often feel the same way."

My friend grinned ruefully.

"Don't let it get you down," I said.

"Yes," he agreed, rising from the chair to go. "Guess you're right."

The interlude had left me feeling vaguely depressed. *Why, I wondered, did I feel like my friend more often than I cared to admit?*

"Fatigue," I told myself. "You've been working too hard."

It had been an unusually long day. I was anxious to get home to my wife Elizabeth and the kids. In two weeks I'd be joining my oldest son and his friends on an eight-day Scouting trip deep in the wilds of northern Minnesota's Quetico Superior Wilderness Area. The trip, a canoe expedition, would take us close to the Canadian border via a 169-mile circular route, culminating with a twenty-four-hour nonstop survival paddle. Tonight, therefore, I was beginning a self-prescribed emergency program of jogging and sit-ups to get in shape.

"You know, Dad," commented my son a week later during one of these workouts, "I think you're looking forward to this trip as much as I am."

He was right.

As a boy I'd spent most of my childhood hunting, fishing and exploring the wonders of North Carolina's woods. I'd never been a religious person, not even as a kid, but something about those quiet times in the forest was, well, special.

Yes, I was looking forward to the trip. The change, I knew, would do me good.

The moment I shook hands with our expedition leader Ray Mattson, I liked him. A tall, lean-muscled college student with copper-colored hair and beard, he took a liking to us too. With unflagging enthusiasm, Ray led us on an unforgettable journey that challenged the strength and skills of the hardiest troop member.

The seventh day fell on a Sunday. That morning, according to Scout rules, Ray gathered us together for a brief outdoor worship service. Standing atop a craggy boulder, he gave a little talk based on the twenty-third chapter of Matthew.

"Blind Pharisee!" he recalled the words of Jesus. "First clean the inside of the cup and of the plate, that the outside also may be clean" (Matthew 23:26, rsv). He went on to compare the wilderness, in all its splendor and untouched beauty, to the way the inside of our lives should be. Then he led us in a sing-along of simple religious songs that rang out pure and clear in the cool morning air. Listening to that sound, I felt something—some untapped emotion—stir deep inside me.

It had been a long time, I realized, since I had thought about God.

That evening, as the sun was setting, I walked to the edge of Basswood Lake, immense and sparkling beneath a pastel-painted sky.

I kicked off my moccasins and let my bare feet play along the pebbly shore. My thoughts wandered back to the morning worship service and the strange effect it had had on me. As a man of science in a field where religion was often viewed with skepticism, the idea of a living God had always seemed remote and archaic. But there was nothing outdated about the morning's message: God wanted us clean and healthy, inside as well as out, so we could be the kind of human beings He had designed us to be. Inherent in that concept, pure and simple, was the essence of modern psychiatry.

It suddenly became apparent that the only way to clean up your life and be completely fulfilled wasn't through science, wasn't through medicine and wasn't even through psychiatry—it was through God. And looking out over those placid waters, I knew that was what I needed and wanted more than anything in the world: for God to come into my life and make me whole.

Before I knew it, tears were streaming down my face. As the sunset melted into a golden blur, I was overwhelmed, flooded with God's love. He was truly with me. His Presence filled me with a peace and reassurance I'd never known. I savored the experience as long as I could, but soon it was time to go.

That night, as we paddled in the moonlit darkness, I remained silent—lost in thought about what had happened. I knew I had changed.

Back home, it seemed I loved my wife more deeply and was more tolerant and kind with the kids. And I found myself going back to church. I actually wanted to go. This, in turn, led to new friends and fellowship that further nurtured my newfound faith.

But work was a different story. The prevailing attitude of the hospital staff was generally negative where religion was concerned, and I chose not to "rock the boat." After all, all of us doctors were familiar with the deranged old character who thought he was the prophet Jeremiah. And all of us had treated patients—pathetic cases—who suffered under self-imposed burdens of hate or guilt they insisted on justifying by Scripture. In fact, we had a rule that incoming psychiatric patients were not allowed to have Bibles.

Once these long-held professional attitudes had seemed logical enough to me. But now I had increasing difficulty resolving a growing inner conflict: I knew without a doubt that God was helping my personal life. *Why*, I wondered, *couldn't He do the same for our patients?* Still, I didn't have the nerve to speak out.

"Lord," I prayed, "give me the courage to do something about this."

He did.

The changes in my work were subtle at first, but soon I found myself ignoring the no-Bible policy. And if a patient wanted to talk about religion, I encouraged him. The Lord led me slowly, no faster than I could handle, to the appropriate people and situations.

I remember one case in particular. At Duke's Medical Center in the late 1960s, I had been treating a young man named John with traditional psychiatric therapy and techniques. John was a drug-addicted physician. When he was first admitted, he was taking up to forty tranquilizers a day—that's a paper cupfull of pills.

After two months of treatment with no discernible progress, there was really nothing more I could do. I told him so.

"Please," he begged. "Please don't say that. I'm standing here craving drugs just as badly as the day I checked in here. Please," he said, to himself as much as to me, "there's got to be something else."

"John," I said, "there's nothing else I can do . . . but maybe there's something God can do."

"God?" whispered John, a glimmer of hope in his voice.

"Yes," I said. "God." And I recalled that day in my office when my good friend had needed help—and I had nothing to offer. Never, I vowed, would that happen again.

Since returning from the Scouting trip, I had never spoken much about my experience to anyone. But now I told John everything. He listened intently. My advice, when I left him, was simple.

"Pray," I said. "Just get down on your knees and pray. And don't get up until you've felt God in your life. He's waiting for you. And He wants to help."

The next morning when I looked in on John, he returned my gaze with eyes as clear and untroubled as the waters of Basswood Lake.

"You can send me home now," he said. "Everything's going to be all right."

So remarkable was John's recovery, I felt it best for him to remain in the hospital for a short period of observation. For three days he stayed. Then he went home.

Prayer, to this day, remains my most effective tool in psychiatric treatment and counseling. Now I pray regularly for every person in my care before and after sessions. I often pray silently during our conversations together. The power of prayer never ceases to amaze me. And its power has not gone unnoticed by others.

News of my success with heretofore hopeless cases such as John's spread rapidly. Soon associates were dropping by my office to chat about this "new" technique. Professional organizations began asking me to speak on the subject of Christian psychiatry at their meetings. Perhaps the most exciting development was the growing interest my students expressed in the subject. As a result, I began offering a course called "Christianity in Medicine and Psychiatry" that proved to be extremely popular and is now being taken by students from all over the country.

But this is just the first step toward our ultimate goal. We are working now to establish at Duke University a formal Program of Christianity in Medicine, which will eventually offer complete curriculum, research and regular counseling on this new and exciting frontier.

I do not consider myself an innovator in this field; other dedicated and farseeing people were pioneers long before I entered it. But it's exciting to share with them a wonderful discovery and a wonderful conviction: that religion and psychiatry really can work together to mend broken lives.

When Papa Asked God
for More Mules

Gustavia Raymond-Smith

A S THE WIFE OF A FOREIGN SERVICE OFFICER, I'VE TRAVELED all around the world, living mostly in developing countries. When I looked at lush fields in Zaire or green rice paddies in Laos, I thought of the farm I grew up on in Natchitoches, Louisiana, with its neat rows of crops, the tall brown sugarcane shimmying in the breeze, the cotton blooming white like popcorn. I found that no matter how far I traveled, I took a bit of my childhood with me, especially the bedrock faith of my father.

Jerusha was what my father always called me, using my middle name. "Jerusha," he'd say, "what did you learn at school today?" or "Jerusha, please get me a glass of water." Jerusha was the mother of a Judaean king in the Bible. Papa wanted us to have strong names so we would stand firm against the adversities of life.

Papa couldn't read very well. He'd dropped out of school in third grade to toil beside his father, cutting trees and hauling logs to the sawmill. When he and my mother met, he was working in a lumber mill. Then he bought the small forty-acre farm where they reared their children. With fourteen of us, Papa and Mama's work was never done. He labored in the fields from dawn till dusk, and she was on her feet all day in the kitchen or vegetable garden.

What Papa couldn't read about his faith, however, he more than made up for by living it. He was a deacon in his church and was often called upon to be the song leader. He chanted each line in his mellifluous baritone and the congregation repeated it. At home he led us in a weekly prayer and singing time. We got down on bended knee in front of our chairs, sinking our elbows into the caned seats, our heads bowed, hands clasped.

Then Papa spoke to God as though the Lord was right there in our front room with us: "Listen to Your children here on bended knee, calling on Your grace and mercy . . ."

Papa's first exhortation to us in the morning was a prayer. He and my brothers were up before dawn, feeding the animals in the barn. Then he came inside and called to us, "Rise, shine, give God the glory." We splashed water on our faces and feasted on breakfasts of eggs, bacon, grits and Mama's hot biscuits.

As hard as things were in the 1930s, we knew we were fortunate. Ours was one of the few Black-owned farms in the parish. Folks came to us to buy fresh vegetables or drink a glass of water cooled by ice chipped from a hundred-pound block. Papa sold the main crops: corn, soybeans and sugar.

With the money he made, he went to Mr. Nelkins' general store and bought shoes and fabric to be sewn into clothes for us. There were so many of us, the neighbors used to tease my parents.

When one lady spotted us gathered around the kitchen table, she exclaimed, "Look at all those chilluns. They can eat the heads off the angels and drink the Jordan dry!" But we never went hungry. We had horses that got us back and forth from town and mules that helped with the heavy plowing and hauling.

Some people were envious of Papa's success. One night our barn burned down in a suspicious fire. There were rumors about who did it and why, but the chances of a Black farmer successfully pressing charges were slight. And anyway, that wasn't Papa's way.

Early one morning I listened, half asleep, to the whistle of a passing train and the commotion my father and brothers were making as they tromped out to feed the animals.

Papa's shout made me jump out of bed, wide awake: "The mules are gone!"

Our mules were part of the family. We had given them names— Mink, Squirrel, Pet and Tilldi. They worked hard, and I think they looked forward to the trips into town as much as we did, pulling the wagons with the harvest to be traded for provisions. I ran into the kitchen, where Mama was stirring grits and cutting biscuits. But there was no joy in the sizzling bacon or the steaming coffee. None of us could eat a thing till we heard about the mules.

"Lord, have mercy," Mama kept muttering under her breath.

And when Papa finally came inside, he didn't even utter his usual, "Rise, shine, give God the glory."

He sank onto his chair, tears rolling down his weathered cheeks. We children were shocked. None of us had ever seen Papa cry. Even when the barn burned down, he hadn't shown any sign of discouragement. "The Lord don't give us any more than we can handle," he'd reminded us at the time. But now he looked like a beaten man.

"Rollie Raymond," Mama finally whispered. "What happened?"

"They're dead," he said. "The mules are dead. Run over by the train." Someone had opened the barnyard gate and let the mules out. They'd gone their usual route, following the train tracks to town. But without Papa or my brothers to guide them, they were killed by the locomotive.

Even though I wasn't much bigger than a bean plant, I knew how serious our loss was. It was planting time. We needed mules to plow the fields. If we didn't get the crop in soon, there wouldn't be any harvest and we wouldn't be able to pay the annual installment on the farm, not to mention barter for provisions at Mr. Nelkins' store.

That night we gathered on the front porch for an emergency prayer meeting. We sang as we had never sung before: "Amazing Grace," "Walk in Jerusalem Just Like John" and especially "He Knows Just How Much We Can Bear." We got down on our knees, our elbows on our chairs.

"Dear God," Papa prayed, "You know how much we needed those mules. So, Lord, please give us a way to plant the crops and plow the fields . . ."

Papa borrowed a team of mules from another farmer for a couple of weeks until the man needed the animals back for his own plowing. After that, Papa tried hitching up our horses, but they couldn't do the job. Every evening we gathered for singing and prayer.

"God, it says in the Bible that faith can move mountains," Papa prayed. "I won't ask You for that much, but if You can see it in Your wisdom to give a poor farmer a few more mules . . ."

With all the courage he could muster, he went to the bank. Perhaps he could borrow enough money for some new mules, using the farm as collateral. The owner of the bank turned down Papa's request with a flat no. Two days later Papa went to the mule farmer. Maybe they could work out a deal.

When we looked up the lane and saw the speck that was Papa coming toward us, we were filled with hope. Had God answered our prayers? As Papa grew closer, we could see his downcast head and slumped shoulders.

The news was bad. That evening we returned to our singing and praying with renewed vigor.

"Jesus," Papa said, "in the parable of the persistent widow you showed us how God hears us when we are constant in our prayers. So tonight, heavenly Father, we come to You once more with the same request . . ."

"Amen!" we answered.

The next morning Papa went to the general store. He knew Mr. Nelkins did not lend money—there was a policy against that. But maybe this one time Mr. Nelkins would make an exception. After all, Papa always paid his bills on time. Mr. Nelkins was a good, decent man. He would be sympathetic to Papa's request. Papa put on his best shirt and hat and headed into town.

I could hear Mama murmuring prayers as she ground meat for sausages. The rest of us prayed, too, while we were doing our chores—gathering eggs, drawing water from the cistern, hanging clothes on the line.

I hummed, "He knows just how much we can bear . . ." *Well, Lord, I sure hope so,* I thought, *because we can't take much more than this.*

Finally I saw Papa's figure far down the lane. I squinted into the dust for some hint of what had transpired. Was he walking with his head held high and his hand swinging jauntily at his side?

Oh, Lord, let it be true! When he was close enough so we could see the expression on his face, he broke into a radiant smile. It was the most beautiful thing I'd ever seen.

"You got more mules!" Mama exclaimed.

"No," he said. "It's better than that. We've got a tractor!"

True to his policy, Mr. Nelkins would not lend Papa money to buy more mules. But he agreed to lend him a tractor that we could pay for over time. You can't imagine how thrilled we were, especially my brothers. A tractor! It could do the work of a whole team of mules! There was plenty of celebration and prayers of thanksgiving that night. As I bowed my head with my elbows on my chair, I listened to Papa and heard his faith at work.

"Thank You, God. For a moment there I doubted You, but while I was praying for mules, You had something even bigger and better in mind. A tractor! Thank You, God, in Your mercy!"

"Amen!" we all shouted.

The harvest was good that fall. Papa was able to make the annual installment on the farm, repay Mr. Nelkins and have enough left over to buy us some good things to eat and fabric for new clothes.

"Jerusha," Papa said, "don't forget what you learned here. God does not promise us a bed of roses, or even ice cream and cake, but He does say our bread and water shall be sure. He answers prayers."

He does indeed, and I've never forgotten.

The Girl Who Was Frozen Solid

Jean Hilliard Vig

I GRABBED MY PURSE AND THE CAR KEYS, THREW ON MY
new green waist-length parka and started toward the door.

Mom called, "Jean, aren't you going to take your boots and
snowmobile pants? It's supposed to get colder tonight."

I'd lived on a farm in northern Minnesota all my life and
was used to cold weather.

"I'll be fine, Mom. Just driving into town to meet some
friends. It's not that cold."

I was nineteen years old and thought cowboy boots and blue
jeans were more appropriate than warm clothing for a night out
with friends. Besides, I had no idea that in just a few hours the

temperature would plummet to twenty-five degrees below zero with gusts of fifty-mile-an-hour blizzard winds.

Around midnight, after a fun evening in Fosston with my friends, I was driving home in Dad's big white Ford LTD. I usually took the four-wheel-drive pickup, but tonight it was low on gas and Dad had said I could take the car.

The snow sparkled festively in the beams of my headlights. I decided to take the old country gravel road because it was a few miles shorter than the blacktop. Besides, I had always loved that road, which meandered through a forest of tall pines. Every couple of miles a house or a farm dotted the landscape, but the rest was pure picture-postcard scenery: icy-blue Minnesota lakes, tall trees and the narrow, winding, hilly gravel road.

Because of the new snow, I didn't see the small patch of ice in the middle of the road. Before I knew what was happening, the car skidded off to the side and the front wheel slid precariously close to the ditch. I tried to back up slowly, but the tires were spinning. When I put the car in forward gear, the front tire slipped off the shoulder and the car became helplessly marooned.

I wasn't frightened, but I sure was disgusted! I could just hear Dad's booming voice when he found out what I'd done with his good car.

I knew there was a house a half mile or so ahead, so I got out of the car, slammed the door and stomped off down the road, forgetting my hat on the front seat.

I was steaming over the mess I had gotten myself into, and my anger kept me warm for a few hundred feet. Then the wind forced me to zip up my jacket collar over my nose and mouth. I shoved my hands deep into my pockets and dug into the snow in my pointy-toed leather cowboy boots.

I walked on a little farther and then remembered Wally's place in the opposite direction. It should be just a half mile or so, I thought. Wally was an acquaintance of my folks and I knew he had a four-wheel-drive truck and could pull my car out of the ditch easily.

As I passed the car, I felt like kicking the tire, but I trudged on. After a half mile or so, I passed a house. It was dark and there were no tracks in the driveway.

Probably out of town, I thought.

I walked on another half mile or more. The next house was also dark and the driveway filled with snow without a tire track to be seen. (I found out later that both of these families were home that night and the wind had blown snow over all the tracks an hour or so before I became stranded.)

I pressed on. The wind whipped and whistled through the pines. My feet were starting to bother me. My dressy high-heeled cowboy boots were not meant for hiking. Why hadn't I listened to Mom and taken my warmer boots?

Where was Wally's house, anyway? I thought it was just over the next hill. I kept walking, but the fronts of my legs, protected only by my thin blue jeans, ached from the cold. Down another hill. Why had I taken the shortcut? At least on the blacktop there'd be cars on the road this time of night.

I struggled up another hill. Finally, I thought I saw Wally's farm in the distance. *Yes!* There was the long lane leading to his house. I was breathing harder. And then . . . I blanked out.

Although I don't remember it, apparently I half-walked, half-stumbled, falling at times, down that long lane. I crawled the last hundred feet or so on my hands and knees, but I don't remember doing that, either.

By now the wind chill factor was seventy to eighty degrees below zero. Right at Wally's front door, I collapsed and fell face forward into the snow. And that's where I lay all night.

The next morning Wally came out his front door just before seven o'clock. Normally he didn't go to work until eight, but thank God, he decided to go in early that morning. Wally saw my body in the snow, leaned down and tried to find a pulse. There was none. My swollen face was a gray, ashen color. My eyes were frozen open. I wasn't breathing.

Wally still doesn't know how he managed to pick me up and get me into his car. He said it was like struggling with a one-hundred-twenty-pound cordwood stick or a big piece of meat out of the freezer.

At the hospital in Fosston, Wally yelled through the emergency room doorway for help. He picked me up under my arms and a couple of nurses lifted my ankles. My body didn't bend anywhere.

As they were putting me on a stretcher, one nurse exclaimed, "She's frozen solid!"

Another nurse, the mother of one of my best friends, said, "I think it's Jean Hilliard! I recognize her blonde hair and the green jacket!"

Mrs. Rosie Erickson, who works in bookkeeping, ran out in the hall when she heard the commotion. She leaned over my body.

"Wait! Listen!" A hush fell around my stretcher. "It's a moaning sound . . . coming from her throat! Listen!"

I was wheeled into the emergency room, where Dr. George Sather, our family doctor, was on duty that morning. He was unable to hear any breathing or a heartbeat with his stethoscope. Then he attached a heart monitor, which picked up a very slow, faint heartbeat. A cardiologist said it seemed to be "a dying heart."

"We have to get these boots off! Bring some blankets! She's still alive!" The emergency room sprang to life. My boots and jacket were the only clothing items they could get off immediately. The rest of my clothes were frozen on me.

When they cut my jeans off, they saw that my feet were black and there were black areas on my legs and lower back. My feet and legs were swollen. The tissue damage seemed so severe that when my parents arrived, Dr. Sather told them that if I did live, my legs might have to be amputated. He wanted my parents to be prepared.

Dr. Sather ordered oxygen, and a nurse suggested trying Aqua-K-pads. Just the day before, a new kind of water-filled heating pad had arrived at the hospital. Quickly the nurses unpacked one heating pad box after another. Fortunately, the only nurse on the staff who knew how to connect them to the special water-filled machines was on duty and she directed the operation.

My body was frozen so hard they couldn't pierce my skin with a hypodermic needle. At first there was no way to give me any medication to speed the thawing process or to prevent infection. But the medical team didn't know what Rosie Erickson was about to do.

Rosie found my parents in the hall. "Mr. and Mrs. Hilliard, do you mind if I put Jean on the Prayer Chain at our church?"

Mom, completely bewildered at the scene before her, answered quickly, "Yes . . . please do!"

Mrs. Erickson hurried to her office and made a phone call to the Prayer Chain chair at the Baptist church where her husband is pastor. The Prayer Chain was set in motion: The first person on the list called the second, that person called the third and so on.

My heart started beating slightly faster. Even though still far slower than the normal rate of about seventy-two times a minute, the doctors were overjoyed. Slowly I started breathing on my own.

The Prayer Chain was lengthening. Mrs. Erickson called the pastors of the Lutheran, Catholic, Methodist and Bethel Assembly churches in Fosston. They, in turn, called the chairs of their Prayer Chain groups, who passed the word along.

During the first hours that the Prayer Chain was under-way, my legs and feet, instead of getting darker as Dr. Sather expected, started to lighten and regain their natural color. One after another, the doctors and nurses filed in to marvel at the pinkish tinge appearing at the line of demarcation where the darkness started. (That was the line on my upper thighs where Dr. Sather said he thought they might have to amputate.)

The Prayer Chain spread to the nearby towns of Crookston and Bemidji and to Grand Forks, North Dakota. Soon hundreds and then thousands of people were aware that a young woman had been brought in to the Fosston hospital frozen solid and was in desperate need of God's miraculous healing.

One of the nurses, on her way to get more blankets, poked her head into Mrs. Erickson's doorway and said, "She might make it! Her legs are starting to regain color at the top! And her heart is beating stronger!"

Mrs. Erickson looked up at the clock and thought, *The Prayer Chain is in full swing now. God is answering those prayers already. Of course she's going to make it!*

At that moment the whole attitude in my hospital room changed. Now, instead of "She probably won't survive," the feeling was "Perhaps she'll live, but she will surely lose her legs from the knees down."

Before noon that day I stirred and moaned a word that sounded like "Mom." My mother and oldest sister Sandra stayed near my bed, holding, squeezing and patting my hands.

"Jean, Jean, wake up! Jeannie, can you hear me? It's Mom. Sandra's here too. Jeannie, we love you. Jeannie, can you hear?"

Around noon I mumbled a few words to them.

All over the area, the Prayer Chain was continuing.

By mid-afternoon I woke up and started thrashing in bed. The doctors told me later that I moaned and yelled so much they were convinced I had severe brain damage.

All day the nurses and doctors watched in amazement as the blackness in my legs and feet disappeared inch by inch.

By late afternoon Dr. Sather thought perhaps my legs would be saved and that only my feet might have to be amputated. A few hours later he was astounded to realize that perhaps it would be just my toes. In the end I did not lose any part of my body! Normal color and circulation came back to even the blackest parts of my legs, feet and toes.

Dr. Sather had also thought he would have to do numerous skin grafts where huge blisters covered my toes. But these places healed, too, without skin grafting.

Indeed, after watching my body become whole again, I am convinced a miracle did occur.

Even Dr. Sather said, "I just took care of her. God healed her."

The doctors kept me in the hospital seven weeks to make sure of my recovery from frostbite and to lessen the possibility of any infection in my toes. And that entire time I never once experienced any fear. I'm convinced it was the Prayer Chain that kept me calm and filled me with a positive faith that I would be healed.

The night I nearly froze to death was over three years ago: December 20, 1980. Since then I met a wonderful man, got married, had a beautiful baby girl and am expecting our second child in February. My husband, daughter and I live on a farm outside Fosston, and my life is a tranquil, happy one. But not a day goes by that I don't think about the night I nearly froze to death.

I've become a different person because of that experience. Last winter I joined forces with a civil defense expert, an army sergeant, a highway patrolman and a doctor from Crookston who is an expert in hypothermia (subnormal body temperature). We give talks to people in many towns and counties around here about winter survival. I tell them my story and point out what can happen when you go out in the winter unprepared for the weather.

I'm surprised I can do this, because in high school I was absolutely terrified of speech class. The thought of standing in front of people with all eyes on me almost made me sick to my stomach. But now I feel none of that. I'm proud to share my story with the hope that I can help even one person avoid the mistakes I made. I believe this is the reason God spared me—so I can help other people learn how to survive the changeable and very cold winters.

I've changed in other ways too. My family and I are much closer now. I appreciate every day I'm alive, and I have an enormous respect for the power of prayer.

I believe the Prayer Chains saved my life. Thousands of people I didn't even know bombarded Heaven with powerful prayer requests in my behalf, and against all medical odds I survived. I not only lived, I survived as a completely normal, whole human being without so much as a skin graft. In fact, unlike most people who have suffered from frostbite, I now experience no ill effects from the cold. As one minister reminded me in the hospital when we spoke of the Prayer Chain, we as God's children have been commanded to pray without ceasing. (1 Thessalonians 5:17). And I'm sure that's what caused my miracle: all those people praying unceasingly for me.

Wednesday Night Special

Jackie Scott

EVERY WEEK A BUNCH OF US HAVE DINNER. NOT AT THE food court or the local steak house, but at church. For a few nights, at least, everyone eats healthy. That can be a struggle, as my daughter Diane and I know a little better than most. But we found a solution.

Flash back five years. I weighed 250 pounds. Diane was over 350. She couldn't even use a normal scale. When I met my husband Brett in college, I was a svelte 127, but I thought nothing of eating fast food every day. I never exercised, and eventually my metabolism couldn't keep up with my appetite. Diane copied my eating and exercise habits, graduating from college heavier than I had ever been. How was she going to have a normal life?

That summer the three of us moved from Michigan to Kentucky for Brett's new job. Lexington was wonderful. We joined the church choir, made new friends. But my weight caused some embarrassing situations. Like when I visited the DMV to get a Kentucky license.

"Age?" The woman asked.

"Forty-seven," I replied.

"Height?"

"Five-two."

"Weight?" I stared at the ground.

"One-seventy-five," I mumbled. The woman gave me a look but didn't say anything.

I knew what she was thinking: *Yeah, right.*

I told Brett what had happened. "Maybe now is the perfect time for all of us to go on a diet," Brett said. We'd tried all the diets before: the Zone, Sugar Busters. We didn't need a diet; we needed a miracle.

In church that week I prayed, *God, please help Diane and me lose weight. Please let it be different this time.* As soon as I finished, a thought jumped into my head. *What will you do different this time?* Why had all our diets failed? Why had we?

I hit the books. It all seemed to come down to two things: calories and exercise. We burn about 1800 calories a day; if you eat fewer calories than you burn, you lose weight. Simple. Most diets cut too many calories. We're starving! That's not healthy. The key was making smart food choices.

Diane and I started cooking our own calorie-conscious meals. We studied nutrition labels on every package. We walked. Whenever one of us was tempted to wolf down a bag of chips, we had the other to keep us in line. We were losing weight slowly and steadily. Eventually I'd lost almost a hundred pounds, and Diane had lost nearly two hundred!

"You guys look great!" our choir buddy David told Brett one morning after church. Then he turned serious. "I wish I could lose weight. The doctor says I'm at risk for another stroke. I've been praying for a miracle." The same miracle I prayed for.

I called him up. "We're making dinner tonight," I said. "Why don't you and your wife Jackie join us?"

We started cooking and eating meals with David and Jackie. They lost weight.

Soon other people in the choir were asking, "Hey, can we join you guys too?"

That's how our dinners started. We'd cook healthy meals and serve them at church five days a week. Chicken simmered in a honey-mustard glaze. Creamy orzo pilaf and roasted asparagus. Soon everyone was involved. Later we took over the regular dinners before Wednesday night services for the whole congregation. Not only were we eating better, but we were also encouraging one another in good habits. Just what a church should do. The minister himself came up to thank me.

"My wife lost sixty-five pounds! She's so happy, confident, full of energy. We're all eating healthier."

We put together a cookbook so everyone can make healthy meals at home. Maybe some eating education will help people change their lives, the way it did ours. Diane just got married to a wonderful guy. I don't need to fib about my weight anymore. God gave us good food to eat; we just have to make the right choices.

Why I Did Not Pray to Be Rescued

Samuel A. Mann

⁂

I ONCE FOUND MYSELF IN DANGER OF DYING, YET DID NOT pray to be saved.

I was a lad of nineteen then, and I had no more religion in me than an alley cat. One day, down in North Carolina, I was trying to take a shortcut through a bit of swampland. I had on hip boots and didn't mind plodding through the saturated, muddy ground to save myself miles of detour around the swamp. But at one point I stepped onto what seemed to be a cleared plateau of sand when I suddenly sank down almost to my knees. As I tried to back out, a powerful suction gripped my legs like a vise, dragging me down deeper. *Quicksand!*

The first thing that flashed through my mind was something the natives had been telling us: "Nobody ever gets out of those quicksands alive!"

Here, I thought, *is certain death*. If ever there was a time to pray, this was it. Yet I hesitated. I did not believe in such things. What could I have expected to come from praying—that God would reach down and lift me out bodily? Or that God would cause some supernatural miracle to take place that would free me? It is the nature of quicksand to engulf people, and I could not believe God would disrupt the nature of things simply because I asked for it.

There's no way out of this, I thought; *I've just got to die*. But I realized with some terror that I wasn't brave enough for that. Then it came to me that perhaps here was something I could ask of God. My prayer was simple: "Sustain me for this ordeal!"

At that moment all fear and panic left me, and in its place came a strange, no-fear of death. I did not have that sweet calmness before; it had just been given to me.

I had not asked God to save me. Yet it was that very calmness and freedom from panic and fright, with its resulting presence of mind, that enabled me to save myself.

Being able to think clearly now, I was able to see something I had not noticed before. Close by, but just beyond reach, some tall marsh grass was growing in blades about one inch wide and over four feet high. If only I could get to that. A single blade of grass is fragile, I knew, but "in union there is strength"—ten or fifteen of those blades joined together would have the strength of a sturdy rope. But I could not move toward them, for powerful suction gripped my legs, and any movement I attempted made me sink more rapidly. When I stretched out my arm, the nearest blade of grass was about twenty-five inches beyond the tips of my fingers.

A daring plan suggested itself to me, and now I had the courage for it. I would let myself fall forward (to give my hand the needed distance), try to grasp a handful of the grass and at the same time pull myself over onto the firmer soil in which I knew the grass must be rooted. If I failed, I would plunge head-first into the quicksand. However, even that alternative seemed preferable; if I must die, why not get it over with quickly, rather than wait to be swallowed up in slow, tortuous suffocation?

In the new calmness of my mind, another thought followed. By now I had sunk till the quicksand was almost over the top of my high hip boots. The quicksand, I suddenly realized, was not actually holding *me*; it was holding my boots, which in turn were holding me. I unfastened the boot straps so if I succeeded in catching a sufficient amount of grass I might pull myself right out of my boots.

Taking a deep breath, I lunged forward full length across the treacherous sand, my fingers stretching desperately for a grip on the slender grasses. With my face almost buried in the sand, I wound the handfuls of thin blades around my wrists and slowly, carefully inched my way to safety.

In the years since, I have never forgotten the prayer lesson I learned that day. "Please, God, help me to help myself." I believe this prayer for increased personal powers—spiritual strength, greater inspiration and greater confidence—is one that God always answers.

CHAPTER NINE

MIRACLES OF JOY

*Splendor and majesty are before him; strength
and joy are in his dwelling place.*
—*1 Chronicles 16:27* (NIV)

Roadside Rescue

Bernadette Fuller

I HAD BEEN INJURED AT WORK AND HAD TROUBLE WALKING. Even sitting could be painful. Efforts to be compensated and get needed help had proved futile. The frustration of knowing that an employer had used me but did not take responsibility for my welfare needled me. The ordeal not only affected my physical well-being but also our family's pocketbook and my inner spirit. Was I to face life injured and poor? Time passed and things did not change for the better.

During the same period, my eight-year-old son with severe diabetes was being put at risk in the school system. Because I was unable to homeschool him, he attended an elementary school where no provision was made for children who are ill. Even though the school district had been allotted funds for each school to have an infirmary with a full-time nurse, that allocation mysteriously ended up funding the high school football team. Monthly I showed up at the school board meeting asking, pleading, even begging for a nurse at my son's school. The board did everything to silence me short of kicking me out. At times like this I was tempted to think I had no value. But worse still, I felt alone against an uncaring world.

I was driving up Route 18 in the San Bernardino, California, mountains in the middle of a cold day in July. Our winding four-lane highway covers nineteen miles from the bottom of the mountain to my hometown. Because it had not rained in a while, the wet deluge coming down left the road especially slippery from layers of car oils covering the incline. Thick fog enclosed me on all sides on this most unusual of days.

About halfway up the grade, my back tires skidded out of control on a curve, sending me spinning across two lanes and turning me a hundred-eighty degrees in the opposite direction.

As I lost control of the car, I cried out, "Help!" When the car came to a halt, I found myself in the far lane pointing directly into oncoming traffic and pinned against the rocks on the side of the road.

I tried to move the car. Not only was it wedged in place, but also a tire had blown out. With my Plymouth Voyager minivan locked securely in place, a white car sped past me, missing me by inches. Other cars, traveling at fifty-five miles per hour, would be rounding the curve momentarily. Without notice and with my van obscured by dense mist, a collision seemed unavoidable. Until now, I hadn't tried to move. With my injuries from work I was afraid I would throw something else out of kilter. *Hadn't the work accident been enough? Now this!* I wondered if I had further injuries as a result of this jarring accident. But worse than that, I couldn't maneuver my body to get out of the car without jarring pain. I couldn't reach safety. I was panicky!

Then a pickup truck, traveling down the mountain, pulled into the turnout across the road. I could barely make it out through the fog. A young man jumped from the car with a handful of flares. I saw him hurry to place them strategically to divert traffic away from me to the middle lane. Almost simultaneously another car pulled into the turnout. This time a woman leapt out and traversed the dangerous road, calling out to ask if I was all right. Reaching me and sizing up the situation, she crossed the street again to obtain a blanket from her vehicle. Four small children waited for her as she returned to comfort me. All this happened in less than three minutes.

In another couple of minutes the nice man who had set up the flares approached me with a cup of hot coffee and the announcement that he had called for police assistance on his ham radio. He took my husband's ham radio number and tried to reach him as well. Until the police arrived, I sat quietly in my car, watching cars whiz past me in the dim light. When the tow truck arrived, police held back traffic as they towed me to the other side of the road and changed my tire.

Then, as I realized I had not been hurt further by the accident, they sent me on my way. Not, however, before I promised to return the blanket to the wonderful lady and took the number of the kind young man—both strangers who seemed miraculously prepared for this unexpected emergency. Indeed, the man told me he had decided to leave work early and go out into the hills to chat with friends on his ham radio. Hence the warm java. Before he left, the police gave him eight new flares and thanked him.

I tried to thank him later as well, but to this day I have never been able to reach him. This incident of kindness assured me I am not alone. And it helped me get through the months ahead as my situation slowly worked itself out.

A Hatful of Miracles

John Gleason

I HAD JUST GRADUATED FROM NORTHWESTERN UNIVERSITY and wanted to see something of the world before settling into a career. With three hundred fifty dollars saved from a summer job—quite a lot in those days—I was heading for Puerto Rico and the Virgin Islands, places that seemed romantic to me. It was October 1938. In New York I boarded a rusty old coal-burning freighter. At first there seemed to be just three passengers besides myself: a bright young civil engineer from Michigan; a worried-looking old man in a white linen suit; and a stately, charming woman who turned out to be Mrs. Charles Colmore, wife of the Episcopal bishop of Puerto Rico, who was returning there after a visit to relatives in the United States.

We made friends quickly, the way you do on a sea voyage. Then, two days out of New York, a young woman with dull blonde hair appeared on deck for the first time. She was in her early twenties, much too thin. She looked so pale and wan that we instantly pitied her. She seemed a bit wary of us male passengers, but she accepted Mrs. Colmore's invitation for tea in her cabin.

"It's a strange story," the bishop's wife told us later. "She comes from a little town in Pennsylvania and she's on her way to the West Indies to look for her husband. He evidently left home several months ago after a violent quarrel with her mother over his drinking and his inability to find a job and support his wife properly. She finally heard a rumor that her husband had gone to the West Indies. She still loves him, so she left her old dragon of a mother, and now she's on her way to find Billy—that's her husband's name: Billy Simpson."

"You mean," I said incredulously, "she's going to leave the ship when we get to San Juan and start looking? Why, that's crazy! There are hundreds of islands in the Caribbean."

"I told her that," the bishop's wife said, "but it didn't seem to make any impression. She just says she'll find him. How, I don't know. But she seems absolutely sure of it."

"It would take a miracle," the old man said, thin and intense in his white tropic suit and brown wool cap.

"It would take a whole hatful of miracles," I muttered.

"Does she have any friends where she's going?" asked the young engineer. "Does she have any money?"

"No friends," said the bishop's wife. "And almost no money. Ten dollars, I think she said. Not even enough to get her back to New York."

When we heard this, the rest of us dug into our pockets and raised twenty-five dollars to give to this strange waif of a woman.

"This will help you find a place to stay when we get to San Juan," the bishop's wife said when she presented the money in front of all of us. "And I'm sure our church there will help find enough for your return passage home."

The girl murmured her thanks. Then she said, "But I'm not going home. I'm going to find my husband."

"Where? How?" asked the old man. He had been fired from his bookkeeping job after thirty years with the same company. Now he was moving to Puerto Rico, where he hoped his experience would outweigh his age when it came to finding a job. I couldn't help thinking he was seeking an answer to his own *where and how* as much as to the girl's.

The girl shrugged and smiled a little. She had the oddest smile, sad, fateful, dreamlike. "Prayers," she said. "My prayers. A few years ago I asked God to send me someone to love, and He did, and I married him. Now I'm asking God to help me find my husband again. That's all. Just asking. And I'm sure He will."

Time passed, trancelike, the way it does on shipboard, the girl leaning against the rail watching the flying fish skitter across the cobalt sea, the engineer and I on the fantail, the old man asking the bishop's wife for ideas about getting a job in Puerto Rico.

We docked in San Juan early one morning. I was scheduled to catch another boat that afternoon for St. Thomas in the Virgin Islands and so had a few hours to kill. The others were going to look for an inexpensive hotel where the young woman could stay while she figured out her next move, whatever that might be. The engineer and the old man needed places to stay too. The bishop's wife had delayed her own trip to Ponce, where the bishop was, to give some reassurance to the young woman.

"I've got to see her settled somewhere," she said to me privately. "And then I'll ask some people at the church to keep an eye on her."

In the smothering heat of midday we walked all over the old city of San Juan, finding the cheap hotels—all run-down establishments infested with fleas and bedbugs. Finally the bishop's wife suggested getting on a bus for the little neighboring town of San Terce. She thought accommodations might be more attractive and more available there.

So we clambered onto a bus for San Terce, but all the hotels we found in this pleasanter suburb were too expensive. Finally, exhausted under the hot sun, the bishop's wife, the old man and the young woman sat down on a sidewalk bench. The engineer and I continued the search and, amazingly, we found a pleasant, clean and inexpensive hotel within a block.

We tried to register for the group, but the clerk insisted that each person should register individually. So the others lined up before the registration book. When it was the woman's turn to sign, she picked up the pen, glanced at the page, dropped the pen—and fainted.

The clerk dashed for some water. The engineer and I put her on a couch, and the bishop's wife bathed her forehead while the old man patted her hand. She came to slowly.

"Heat too much for you?" I asked. She shook her head.

"No . . . Billy."

"Billy?"

"He's in the book," she whispered.

We jumped up to take a look. There, scrawled after a date two days before, we read "Billy Simpson."

"What room is he in?" I asked the clerk. I couldn't believe it.

"Simpson?" the clerk said, "Oh, he got a job. He come back after work. Not here now."

"This can't be," the old man said almost angrily. "She must have had some idea that he was here!"

The bishop's wife looked at us. "No, I'm sure she didn't," she said. "Otherwise she would have come directly to this hotel on her own, wouldn't she?"

Nobody could answer that.

Now, I know that in a good story the narrator does not remove himself from the scene just when the climactic episode is coming up. But this is the way it all happened. Real life doesn't always write the script the way a good playwright would. Anyway, I had to be on the boat that sailed to the Virgin Islands. The engineer shook my hand and wished me well. The bishop's wife gave me a letter of introduction to the Episcopal minister on

St. Thomas, a Reverend Edwards. The old man said he would come and see me off. The boat was belching smoke, more of a ferry than a ship. As we neared the gangway, the old man spoke.

"The real reason I wanted to come along was to ask you something. Do you think prayer really led that girl to her husband?"

"I don't know," I replied uneasily. "There's always coincidence. But this is certainly a big coincidence."

"I wonder if prayer could help me?" he said. "I don't know much about it."

"Neither do I," I said. "Why don't you ask the bishop's wife?"

"Do you think I should? I've been a bit afraid to."

"Sure," I said. "Ask her. And if I hear of any jobs in the Virgin Islands, I'll write you at the hotel."

"Thanks," he said. "Have a good trip."

When I arrived, Reverend Edwards invited me to stay with him, charging only ten dollars a week for room and board. Settled in, I spent my time sightseeing, chatting with natives at the docks, writing, relaxing, learning all I could about the islands. I often visited with Reverend Edwards after dinner. One night I told him about the girl on the boat and the missing husband and the prayers. I'm sure my tone indicated my doubts.

The old clergyman said, "Don't ever be afraid to believe, John. You're too young to have a closed mind."

With time, the girl and Billy Simpson almost slipped from my memory. But one day I mentioned the incident to two new friends of mine, deaconesses who lived next door to the church.

"Why," said one of them, "that sounds like a Mr. Simpson we had here at the clinic. He came from Antigua with a bad case of the DTs. We practically had to chain him to a bed."

"And then," said the other, "one day he suddenly became alert and insisted on getting up. Our Danish doctor said he'd better stay with us for a time, but Mr. Simpson was adamant. He said he had to get to San Juan to see someone. When we asked who, he said he didn't know; he just had to get to San Juan. That night he caught a small powerboat going to Puerto Rico. We gave him twenty dollars to get him there and maybe enough for a room. That's the last we heard of him."

We compared dates, and this "Mr. Simpson" would have landed in Puerto Rico three days before my group arrived. He could have reached that hotel before we had, as the register showed.

I had to find out. I wrote to the bishop's wife, gave her my news and asked for hers. In two weeks, her answer came.

"Yes, it was the right Billy Simpson. His reunion with his wife was one of the most touching things I've ever seen. Now there are several events to consider, miracles possibly. One, Mr. Simpson's sudden cure from alcoholism in St. Thomas, which he confirms; two, his strange compulsion to get to San Juan, which he couldn't understand at the time; three, the guidance that led him to that hotel; four, his finding a good job within twenty-four hours after not being able to get a job for months; five, the guidance that took our group to that hotel. For me, these events add up to a hatful of miracles that can be explained in only one word: prayer. The Simpsons are living happily in San Juan now. Not long ago they gave me fifty dollars to use for charity, so I am enclosing twenty dollars for your friends who helped Mr. Simpson while he was ill."

A week later, I received a letter from the old man. He had gone to Ponce with the bishop's wife, found a good job, joined the church and become very happy in it.

He wrote: "When we were at the hotel that day, Mrs. Colmore said maybe there was a lesson in the experience we had shared. I believe there was. For me, the lesson was that some people instinctively know the power of prayer, but others have to learn it."

I couldn't argue with that. These days my mind is no longer young, it is no longer closed and I am no longer afraid to believe.

The Miracle of Friendship

Betty R. Graham

PAPA DIED TWO MONTHS AGO AFTER NINETY-EIGHT YEARS
of a full, happy, productive life. He wasn't my real father.
Both my real parents had died more than thirty years ago while
I was living abroad where my husband's foreign service job had
taken us.

We had been posted to Honduras when my mother died,
and I returned to the States for her funeral. I remember feeling
very much alone when I returned to Honduras after the funeral.
But then one day in church I met an elderly couple who had just
come to Honduras. The woman, Dorothy Keithley, looked so
much like my mother that we were immediately drawn to each
other. That was the beginning of a long and wonderful friendship. Her husband Preston did not look much like my father,

but his sincere welcome drew me close to him as well. Thus began a friendship that grew into love and lasted to the present time. In fact, we became so close that I began calling Dorothy "Mom" and Preston "Papa."

That first day in church, I noticed they had a little Latin girl with them. She was not much bigger than my own son Brian, who was then only three years old. I thought at first she was their granddaughter, but I soon learned they had adopted Elena in their previous post. It seems the Keithleys had room in their hearts for both of us. As the years went on, Mom and I spent much time together, working on local projects, helping to build a new church and attending women's meetings together. That closeness helped me through the grief I'd felt at losing my real mother and laid the foundation for a beautiful relationship.

We remained like a family for the years we lived in Honduras and kept in touch by mail when my family was posted to Venezuela. Four years later, when my family and I returned to the States, I was happy to learn that the Keithleys had already returned to their home in St. Michaels, Maryland, only a two-hour drive from my Virginia home and just a telephone call away. Each time I visited, I learned how active Papa was.

He had already completed two careers, retiring from both, and he still actively taught celestial navigation to students working to qualify for their licenses. The word *retirement* had no meaning for Papa. He read avidly and took an interest in many things. We talked on the phone every week, and I drove down to see them several times a year.

At the close of each telephone call, Mom would always say, "Remember, I love you. You're precious to me." Do you know how wonderful those words made me feel? I try to say them now to my own sons.

Whenever I had a problem, I could talk it over with Mom. She was always there to comfort me through troubles and to celebrate with me in the good times. She even drove up to attend my college graduation, after I'd spent six years studying at night to get my degree. She had encouraged me through all those years when at times I felt inadequate to grasp some of those courses. And I drove to St. Michaels to help her and Papa celebrate their fiftieth wedding anniversary and to attend the wedding of their adopted daughter. I don't think we could have been closer if we had been blood kin.

Each time I visited them, Papa would greet me at the door with open arms and a broad smile, and while I was there, a steady stream of family and friends always came to the door, each greeted by Papa as warmly as I had been. I can still hear his jolly chuckle as he welcomed each person into his home. He had a boundless supply of energy and enthusiasm. It made one feel good just to be in the same room with him. Papa loved to tell stories of the past. Whenever he started to reminisce, I would be all ears, listening to his humorous adventures and hearing of his antics in his youth. Mom would scold him at times, but she enjoyed reliving his tales as much as I. She said he was a rascal, which always brought a twinkle to his eye.

In 2006, Mom suffered a bad fall and was taken to the hospital in St. Michaels. I knew something was wrong when the phone rang and it was Papa's voice I heard. He had never called me before. I talked to him each time I called, but if I ever received a call, it was from Mom. Papa was very worried about Mom, especially when she was transferred to a hospital in Baltimore for several operations. It was then I was thankful Elena and her family had moved in with Mom and Papa. Elena was there to take Papa to the hospital each day, and when Mom was able to leave the hospital, she was transferred to a rehabilitation hospital in Easton, Maryland, which is much closer to their home.

Another miracle happened to me at that time. I had put Mom on the prayer list at church, and her name was in the bulletin. I can't drive as much now as I used to, and I longed to visit again with Mom and Papa. A kind lady in my church approached me and volunteered to drive me down to see Mom. I was so happy to be able to visit Mom in the rehab hospital. When I called and told Papa I would be coming, he was delighted and said he would join me in the hospital. But when we got there, Papa didn't show up. Mom was happy to see me and to meet my friend, but she said Papa had been ill and was not able to come that day.

In the next few weeks, Papa was taken to the hospital. This time he did not return. I was able to call him on the phone in the hospital, and he sounded as cheerful as he always did. While Mom and I openly said "I love you," Papa was more reserved. I had never said that to him before, but I know he knew how I felt. Yet somehow that day, I was moved to tell him on the phone that I loved him. He replied with, "I love you too." I never spoke to him again. The next phone call I received told me of Papa's death. I was so glad I had said those words to him.

I was very sad, but even more, I worried about Mom. After she had lived more than sixty years with the man she loved, I was afraid she might have a relapse. She was ninety-six years old.

Another friend in my church drove me to the funeral. He and his wife knew Mom and Papa because they had driven me down to see them in recent years. Thank God for kind friends. Mom didn't look well when I saw her in a wheelchair, but it was to be expected. The church was packed with family and friends. A few days after the funeral, Mom had to return to the hospital. I was afraid she was giving up, but Elena told me that Mom said "Don't worry. I'm not a quitter." And I knew she would survive.

Many times I thank God for my good fortune in meeting these two wonderful people who accepted me into their lives as if I had been born to them, and for the long and happy relationship I've had with them these many years. I know Papa is now in heaven, waiting with open arms to welcome all of us as he always did in his own home. I thank God also for all the kind friends who went out of their way to drive me to see my loved ones. To me, the miracle of friendship is something to cherish.

Canned Soup and Wedding Cake

Mary Hollingsworth

<hr/>

THE LATE SPRING RAINS HAD BEGUN, AND IN MONROE, Louisiana, that meant several things. First, the azaleas exploded into hot-pink and white blossoms everywhere you looked, and lavender wisteria cascaded in massive waves from the tops of trees to the ground and along fences. Combine that with the ever-present swampy bayous full of cypress trees and draping Spanish moss, the largest pecan-tree orchards in the world and thick foliage in a multitude of green hues, and I was often overwhelmed by the glory and mysterious charm of it all. Second, spring rains brought warm, muggy days and sticky nights. Black Bayou, near where I lived, was almost full, the native alligators floating like brownish-green logs near the shore and the giant man-eating mosquitoes hatching and buzzing. The mosquitoes were so large, in fact, that I often joked I heard two of them on the end of my bed, discussing whether they should eat me there or take me home.

On a particular rainy Thursday morning I dressed, stopped at Marianna's Café for breakfast, as usual, and headed over to the University Church of Christ where I worked. Our church occupied several buildings across the street from Northeast Louisiana University (NLU), one of which was our large student center that reached out to serve the NLU students. My office was in the student center, where I served as receptionist, Bible teacher, assistant to the two ministers and anything else that came up.

The center was a busy place, with dozens of students coming and going every day. They came to the center for lots of reasons: to study, to meet their friends, to watch TV or play games, to use our library, to receive advice and counseling or just because they liked it there. Many of them were far from their families, and the center's warm, welcoming atmosphere felt like their home away from home. It was in that setting that many students found Christ and became Christians.

Because it was raining, we didn't have as many students in the center that day. So by mid-afternoon, I found myself alone except for one of the ministers, whose office was at the other end of the hall. I was busy typing some letters, and because our front door opened and closed a hundred times a day, I didn't notice when a stranger came in and stood quietly in my office door waiting for me to see him.

Finally, he said softly, "Excuse me."

I turned to see a scruffy-looking, middle-aged man smiling shyly at me with his cap in his hands. His clothes were soaking wet, and his shoes and pant legs were muddy. His hair hadn't been washed in weeks, it appeared, and his beard was shaggy. He had on a black cloth jacket with holes in the arms, and on his back was a large backpack that seemed to include a bedroll, among other things.

"Well, hello," I said warily. "I'm sorry, I didn't realize you'd come in. Won't you sit down?"

"Oh no, ma'am, my clothes are much too wet and dirty to sit on your pretty furniture."

"Then how can I help you?"

"My name's Bob Jordan, ma'am, and I just need a place to rest for a little while, dry off and clean up, if that's possible. I saw your church, and some of the students directed me here. But I'll understand if you don't want a stranger in here."

"Nonsense, Bob. Of course you're welcome here. Perhaps you'd like to use our men's locker room and showers to clean up."

"Oh yes, ma'am!" he smiled. "That would be wonderful. And I really do appreciate it."

Looking at his water-soaked backpack, I asked, "Say, I hope you won't think I'm trying to pry, but do you have clean, dry clothes to put on?"

"Not really, ma'am. I've been on the road for about three weeks now, and it's been raining for so long that everything I have is soaked completely through."

"May I ask why you're on the road?"

"It's sort of a long story."

"Well, that's all right. How about giving me the short version?"

"Yes, ma'am. Well, it's this way: I live in Oregon, but my son lives in Florida. He called me about three weeks ago to say he's been diagnosed with cancer and asked me to come stay with him during his chemo treatments."

"I'm sorry to hear that."

"The problem is, my company downsized a few months ago, and I lost my job. So far, I haven't been able to find another one, and my cash reserves have run out. In fact, I had even sold my car to make ends meet, just before my son called. Naturally, I didn't have the money to fly to Florida; so I decided I'd hitchhike."

"That's a long way to walk and hitchhike."

"Don't I know it. I had no idea how hard it would be or how long it would take when I started. But I'm making good progress and hope to be at my son's house now in just three or four more days."

It was obvious this man was the real thing. He wasn't a panhandler or a troublemaker. He hadn't asked for anything except some hot water and a place to rest.

"Listen, Bob, you wait right here for just a couple of minutes, and I'll be right back with a nice dry towel you can use."

"Thank you, ma'am. I sure will."

My house was next door to the center, so as I headed out the back door toward home, I asked the minister down the hall to please go visit with Bob. I got two big towels, some soap and shampoo and a man's robe that was hanging in the guest bath and went back to the center.

"Bob, I have an idea. Why don't you take off your wet clothes and hand them out to me. You can wear this robe after your shower, and I'll take your clothes next door to my house and run them through the washer and dryer. While they're washing, you can rest. How's that sound?"

"Oh, I don't want to put you out, ma'am. You've been too kind already."

"Well, never mind about that. Just give me your clothes and anything else in your backpack that needs washing. I'd really like to do this for you, if you'll let me."

About an hour later, I came back with Bob's clothes that were now clean and dry. He'd had a long, hot shower, washed his hair and trimmed his beard. He'd also cleaned off his shoes and laid his bedroll out to dry in front of the fireplace in the center's big lounge.

I handed him his clothes and asked, "Have you had anything to eat lately?"

"No, ma'am. I ran out of money and food about three days ago."

"Well, I think we've got some leftovers back in the kitchen. I'll go fix something for you while you get dressed."

"Thank you, ma'am. I don't know how I'll ever repay you for your kindness."

I found several cans of soup in the cabinets in the large kitchen, as well as some cake left over from a wedding. I also found some cheese, crackers and iced tea. So I heated the soup and set a place for him to eat in the lounge. When he came in, I was amazed at the difference a little soap and water had made for both him and his clothes. He looked like a new man. A hungry man! He wolfed down the soup quickly, along with the cheese and crackers, and ate a giant piece of the wedding cake. Then he laid down on one of the lounge sofas and slept for a few hours.

Before he left that afternoon, I tucked the other cans of soup into his backpack, along with some crackers and several more pieces of cake wrapped in tinfoil. The minister gave him a twenty-dollar bill from our church emergency fund and prayed that God would watch out for Bob as he traveled on to his son's.

He thanked us over and over and promised to send the twenty dollars back just as soon as he could. We told him it wasn't necessary to send the money back because it was a gift from God, but he insisted he would send it back in case someone else needed help as he had. I was happy to notice, as he walked out the door toward the freeway, that the rain had finally stopped and the sun had come out.

I stood in the door for several moments, watching him go. I thought back over Bob's visit, wondering if he was "one of the least of these" that Jesus talked about. I was glad we could give him a cup of cold water in His name, but I figured that was the last we'd ever see or hear from Bob.

About three months later, as I was opening the mail for the church, I came across a small square blue envelope. I opened the envelope and pulled out a piece of blue stationery. As I unfolded the note, two twenty-dollar bills fell out on the desk.

The note was from Bob. And it said, *You may not remember me, but about three months ago I came to your student center. You let me take a shower, you washed my clothes, you gave me something to eat and you let me rest. I'm now at my son's house in Florida, and we're both doing very well. He has completed his chemo and is now cancer-free. And I've found an excellent job so that I can stay here with him. Enclosed is forty dollars—God's original gift to me through you and my gift back to Him. Please use it to extend kindness to others as you did to me. You literally saved my life . . . and my soul, because my son and I have now both become Christians. Gratefully, Bob Jordan.*

Grocery Cart Angel

Susan Sundwall

B OY, WAS I FEELING SORRY FOR MYSELF. A GOOD FRIEND
and her husband had just told us of their encounter with a
waitress who wanted to know what Good Friday was all about.
We were all ears as we sat in our Thursday morning Bible study,
and a few others related similar experiences where God had
used them to help or inform others. As I listened, something in
the back of my mind began to nag at me.

*Why do these chance opportunities to bear witness to God's
love never happen to me? Perhaps I'm such a poor example of what
a believer should be that I'm not worthy of such moments.*

That nagging thought occurred again a few days later as I
sat at the traffic light next to the grocery store where I almost
always stopped each week after services. My focus diverted for

a few seconds, and I did a quick note-to-self to run in for the Sunday paper, cold cuts and milk on my way home that day. Later, as I zipped through the store aisles, I thought about another phenomenon we talked about in the Bible study. The pastor spoke of looking at the world with our spiritual eyes so we can see others as God wants us to see them. I paid for my paper, cold cuts and milk and hurried for the exit. It was a beautiful summer morning, and I couldn't wait to get home and get on with the day.

As I passed through the automated glass doors, I noticed a woman standing on the sidewalk near a line of grocery carts. As she gripped one tightly by the handle, her face was a picture of agony. Her eyes were squeezed shut, her mouth hung open and tears oozed from her eyes. I slowed down for a moment, although I usually take little notice of other shoppers when I'm intent on getting home to a hungry family. I'm ashamed to say my first thought was to rush past and head for my car. I almost turned away, but somehow I couldn't take my eyes off her face. This woman drew me to her for reasons I would only fully understand later.

"Are you okay?" I asked, approaching cautiously.

"No," she wailed, tears spilling down her cheeks. "I just talked on the phone to my father."

"Oh dear," was all I could think of to say. She wasn't a young woman, perhaps forty, and I wondered what about their conversation could have caused this outburst.

"He hates me!" She gagged the words out. I looked around quickly to see if anyone else had noticed her distress, but the other shoppers were oblivious, scurrying by as though nothing was amiss. I moved a little closer.

"I'm sure he doesn't," I said, trying to be sympathetic. Her breath escaped in big gasps, and it was then I noticed the strong smell of alcohol. *Oh, great,* I thought, *what am I getting into?* My mind went into overdrive. I could offer some kind word such as "things will work out" and leave her there, or maybe I'd ask if I could call someone for her. She didn't seem like a street person. Her clothes were clean, her hair was combed and she didn't have her hand out for money. She was a middle-aged woman in deep distress, and I was the one who had noticed. I felt rooted to the spot.

I stood with her for about twenty minutes as she told me of her stormy history with her father. Today she had only wanted to call and tell him happy birthday and got nothing but hostility from his end, or at least that was her side of it. I had no idea if what she was saying was true. I didn't give in to the temptation to mention her substance abuse as a possible reason for his hostility.

In her next breath she also told me she'd just been released from the hospital. "They let me out too early," she said, "and I need my medication. I wish I was still there."

This gave me pause, and I wondered if I should call the rescue squad. During similar nerve-jangling situations in the past, I had always looked for a way out, but this time, amazingly, I felt graced with a peculiar calm. Maybe it was because I was in a public place and could literally walk away without consequence. Maybe it was because this woman wasn't a friend or relative, so I had no real responsibility toward her. *Or did I?* The discussion at Bible study popped into my head. Was it possible I was drawn to her because on some level I was actually using the spiritual eyes we had spoken of? I looked at her again and suddenly wanted to tell her how much God loved her. I made up my mind to do whatever it was that this poor woman needed.

"How did you get here?" I asked, ready to provide transportation if she asked for it.

"I have a car out there," she said, waving vaguely in the direction of the parking lot.

"Would it help if I took you home?" I asked.

"No, I don't live very far from here." She sniffed back a few more tears and looked around. "I think I'm feeling better now," she said. Then she smiled at me. "You're a very nice person," she said.

"Well, I hate to think of your being all alone," I said. "What can I do?"

"Thank you for just standing here and talking to me," she said, sighing. "I really love my father so much. I hope he has a happy birthday."

I leaned forward a little. "Do you know how much God loves you? He loves your father too," I said.

"Sometimes I pray," she said. Her voice sounded less tear-choked and she smoothed her hands over her dress.

It was as if she had come out of a fog and was now aware of her surroundings. "Is there a place in here where I can get a cup of coffee, do you know?" she asked, nodding at the grocery store doors. I told her to look for the small lunch counter near the produce section at the back of the store.

"Do you need some money?" I asked.

"No, I have money," she said, patting her pocket. "Maybe I can get a muffin or something too," she said. "I'm hungry."

I realized that probably all she had needed was someone to listen to her. At that moment I did something I never, ever do with complete strangers, especially ones with alcohol on their breath. Just before she turned to walk away, I reached over and gave her a hug.

"God really does love you," I said.

She hugged me back and wiped her hand over her eyes. She smiled again, straightened her shoulders and walked through the automatic doors of the grocery store. I never saw her before or since, and in a small town like ours, that's saying something.

It's only been a few years since I had that encounter with the grocery cart angel, and you may ask why I call her that. You see, I know the methods by which God works don't always fit into our strict notion of what those methods should be. It's not hard for me to believe that I encountered a being in the guise of a disturbed woman with alcohol on her breath. The Bible says the first emotion one experiences when an angel shows up is fear. My grocery cart angel had indeed produced a fear in me, the fear (and annoyance) of stepping out of my own time constraints, for one. Remember, I had a hungry family waiting for me. I was also afraid I wouldn't know what to say to her, and that fear was exaggerated when the scent of alcohol rose around me. But every fear took a backseat to the need the woman presented on that sunny sidewalk in front of the grocery store. When it was time for me to witness to His love, God gave me the words I needed to speak, and just like my friends with the Good Friday waitress, I was able to voice and—more important—to show the love He has for all of us.

It turns out in that particular encounter I was the needy one. Sure, this woman needed to have a listening ear for her current woe. But as I stood with her, I realized she was answering a need in me too. God had counted me worthy of sharing His grace with her. The angel at the grocery cart allowed me to step out of my own tidy world and into hers, befriending her for ten minutes on a busy Sunday morning. She helped me understand the necessary use of our spiritual eyes as the instrument God gives us for seeing His way in the world.

My Own Life Is Proof

Dan Wakefield

I KNOW THE TRUTH OF EINSTEIN'S WORDS, "I HAVE LIVED both ways." Growing up in Indiana in the 1940s I saw the world with wonder, in the frost on windowpanes, in the winter constellations, in the flowers called four-o'clocks that opened around that hour on summer afternoons. Attending Baptist Bible school, I watched in awe as a young preacher and his wife made miracles come to life by using a brown paper bag over a drinking fountain to reenact Moses' drawing water from a rock.

As a young writer living in New York City's Greenwich Village in the 1950s, numbing myself with bourbon and Freud (the former a daily habit and the latter a six-year five-times-a-week psychoanalysis), I saw the world through a darker lens. With sincere, if self-conscious cynicism, I adopted an Ernest

Hemingway character's prayer of nothingness: *Our nada who art in nada.* My newfound view of Bible stories was expressed by a pseudo-jaded friend, who had gone to a more enlightened sort of Sunday school where she was taught scientific explanations of the miracles in the Bible. Just how had Moses led the Israelites across the Red Sea? She explained while exhaling two tusks of cigarette smoke: "Low tide."

Clearly, I was at low tide myself by 1980. Several years earlier I had left my home in Boston and the woman I had hoped to spend the rest of my life with and had moved to Hollywood to write an NBC series called *James at 15.* Before that, I had worked as a journalist and author for publications such as *The Atlantic Monthly, Esquire, Harper's Magazine* and *The Nation.* I had had four novels published, and one of them, *Starting Over,* was made into a movie starring Candice Bergen and Burt Reynolds.

But in Southern California, surrounded by palm trees and people whose satisfaction in life was dependent on Nielsen ratings and box office revenues, I felt things falling apart. When *James at 15* was canceled, I stayed on in California to struggle at the entertainment business, constantly drinking to soothe the stress. That created even greater stress and a resting pulse of a hundred twenty, a condition called tachycardia. I tried to write, but it became impossible. My attention span was getting shorter and my money was getting lower. My life consisted of the nothingness Hemingway's fictional character discovered. Yet mine was real.

I was a few dreary weeks away from my forty-eighth birthday when I woke up screaming one morning. It was more than a nightmare. Wide awake I got out of bed and screamed some more. In misery and despair I groped among a pile of old books and pulled out a Bible I hadn't opened since high school except for research. I turned to the Psalms, that source of comfort and sustenance to people for more than two thousand years, and read out loud the Twenty-third Psalm.

Throughout the weeks ahead, I repeated that psalm again and again. *He leadeth me beside the still waters.* . . . In the spring of 1980 I got on a plane and returned to Boston, where I went like a homing pigeon to sit on a bench beside the still waters of the pond in the Public Garden.

A new journey for me had begun. I joined a church called King's Chapel and began attending an adult Bible study. I started a steady program of exercise and a healthy diet. By 1984 I was able to give up the constant drinking that had been my addiction, indeed my very identity. But even more amazing, I became free of the desire to drink. The need that had once consumed me was gone, lifted. One of the definitions of the word miracle is an extraordinary event "considered as a work of God," and that's how I felt—and still do—about my release from alcohol. I had no doubt I had experienced a miracle.

Step by step I continued on my way. My minister, the Reverend Carl Scovel, pointed out that the translation of conversion in both Hebrew and Greek is "turning." When you turn even slightly, you are going a different way, and the farther you go, the more distant your old way becomes. Instead of a driven, frantic existence, I was gradually changing my perspective, looking inward and focusing on a healthier and more spiritual way.

At the King's Chapel parish house I sat with nine others around a table as Carl Scovel led us in a class about writing a spiritual autobiography. Difficult as it was in the beginning, I slowly began to share my most intimate fears and struggles— and learned that others had also gone through a dark night of the soul. Eventually I started leading workshops myself.

I now saw that a spiritual path really is a path, a genuine ongoing journey, and not just a metaphor. My new path was taking me to churches and adult-education centers around the country to guide others in writing their own spiritual autobiographies. I helped people of all ages and backgrounds as they poured out their deepest feelings on paper.

My personal satisfaction was enormous. But by 1993 I was running out of writing ideas—and cash. All spring I had worked on a novel, and when people I trusted told me it wasn't good, I threw it away.

"I'm in trouble," I said to a friend. "I need a miracle."

One day not long after, my phone rang. It was a call from an editor in San Francisco.

"We've got a great book idea and we want you to write it," he said. What was the subject? Miracles.

"I've got a head start on this one," I told the editor excitedly. I contacted the people I knew from my workshops and asked them to send me stories of what they considered miracles in their own lives.

Next I set out to interview on my own. A woman in Atlanta told me her daughter had suffered a traumatic brain injury when hit by a car and was given little hope for recovery. Yet with prayer from family and friends and Bible study groups around the city, the girl came out of her coma and returned to school and a full life.

A friend in Los Angeles who had suffered third-degree burns and was scheduled for skin-graft operations met with psychologists and medical assistants who were experimenting with alternative healing. The morning after the group had moved their hands above her body in "energy techniques," the burns were gone. (The surgeon who was to do the skin grafts insisted there was no way such a healing could have happened. It happened.)

Rabbi Nancy Flam, one of the founders of the Jewish Healing Center in San Francisco, believes healing can occur through "the ministry of presence," by clearing one's mind to be fully present to another human being. When we give others our full and loving attention, we become "a conduit for Divinity to express itself." Or, as Thérèse of Lisieux put it in the nineteenth century, "Whose hands are God's hands but our hands?"

In Athlone, Ireland, I met a glowing, rosy-cheeked woman named Marion Carroll. Others attested to the fact that she had multiple sclerosis, was blind in one eye, had lost control of her bodily functions and had been paralyzed in her legs for three years. In 1989 she was taken on a stretcher to a shrine in

Ireland. She heard a whispery voice tell her to get up, and when she did, "My legs weren't even stiff!" She hasn't needed a wheelchair or catheter since.

"My healin' does not belong to me," she reported. "It's a special gift to people . . . to let them know . . . God's work is happenin' now—like when He walked among us."

But what about people who are not cured? I discovered an even deeper kind of miracle in their stories. Lloyd Kantor, a Vietnam vet who lost both arms and legs and one eye in the war, married and went to Paris on his honeymoon and then took a trip to Tahiti. He and his wife Loretta returned to Mount Vernon, New York, to do volunteer work, arranging to have ramps put in the city hall and an elevator in the town library and to have a memorial erected bearing the names of local men who died in Vietnam.

"All in all, things have worked out well," Lloyd told me in a firm, strong voice. "I have to believe it has to do with God."

I discovered that many artists consider their creativity miraculous. While on a visit to Germany, writer Marcie Hershman was dramatically struck by "a silence full of voices still calling out" that reminded her of relatives who had died in the Holocaust, and it led her to write two searing novels about that time, *Tales of the Master Race* and *Safe in America*.

"In the Bible, miracles aren't confined just to blessings of joy," Marcie told me. "Some are about evil and how to confront it rather than turn away." Marcie's ability to deal with such a challenge was, to her, a miracle.

Other artists described to me the state of grace they felt on occasions when they transmitted something higher—or what William Blake described as the feeling that his poems were dictated by the angels.

At the same time, we are surrounded by miracles every day. "We see people looking for weeping statues," Frankie Murray, a curate in County Longford, Ireland, pointed out to me. "They miss the every morning miracles—like the sunrise and friendship."

Or the frost on the windowpane in my long-ago Hoosier boyhood. In a sense my path has taken me full circle, back to the simple wonderment at God's mighty hand in the winter constellations. As Willa Cather has written, "Miracles . . . rest not so much upon faces or voices or healing power coming suddenly near to us from afar off, but upon our perceptions being made finer, so that for a moment our eyes can see and our ears can hear what is there about us always."

As for me, I proceed day by day on my journey as a writer and teacher. I have no doubt that miracles abound. The path my own life has taken is proof.

Pennies from Heaven

Judy Gordon Morrow

A COASTAL WIND RIFFLED MY HAIR AS I SAT OUTSIDE our small stucco tract house in Lompoc, California, and I wondered for the millionth time if we should move. The house seemed to squeeze tighter around us as our three active sons, ages thirteen, ten and six, kept growing. I longed for more room. My husband Patrick and I often looked at larger homes, yearning yet hesitant. The question hounded me again: *Should we try to move?*

I prayed for guidance. While reading my Bible one day my heart quickened when I came across Psalm 18:19 (NIV), which read, "He brought me out into a spacious place; he rescued me because he delighted in me." Did I dare believe what I sensed God was telling me? My heart said yes, and I wrote in the margin, "December 2, 1987—God's promise to me for a spacious home."

More than three years later I was wondering if I had misunderstood. The year before, we had tried to buy a larger home contingent on selling ours, but our house wouldn't budge. After discovering a new home for sale, we decided to try again.

In spite of our efforts, the For Sale sign stubbornly remained. No one could understand it, least of all me. After all, God had given me a promise—hadn't He?

Evening strolls with my friend Arlene provided welcome diversion. During one brisk walk Arlene abruptly stopped and squealed with delight.

"Look," she exclaimed, "a penny!"

I laughed. "Arlene, I've never seen anyone get so excited over finding a penny."

"Oh, but it's not just a penny," she explained. "My grandma taught me that every time I find a penny to think about the inscription on it, 'In God We Trust.' It's my special reminder from God to trust Him."

I smiled as she pocketed the coin and we continued our walk.

Surprisingly, not long afterward I began to find pennies myself—on the sidewalk and in parking lots. *Lord, are these from You?* I thought.

Yet the tedious routine of cleaning for open houses and impromptu showings dragged on for months with no offers.

Our real-estate agent was as baffled as we were. We agreed to drop the asking price well below market value. Still nothing happened.

Weary in spirit, Patrick and I went for an evening walk. I had told him about Arlene and her pennies, and how since then I had been finding the coppery coins myself. When Patrick spied a penny a split second before I did, he scooped it up. He teased me when I whined that the penny he had picked up was mine. "Nope, this one's mine," he said with a grin.

Inwardly I complained, *I know it's silly, Lord, but I really needed that penny tonight. I don't understand why this is taking so long.*

I still felt disgruntled later when I started to transfer a load of laundry into the dryer. The clothes were strictly underwear and socks, so I was amazed when a shiny penny appeared amid the pocketless clothing. It was as if God had wrapped His arms around me and whispered, "I haven't forgotten you. Just keep trusting Me."

As our housing problem continued, I reluctantly listened to Patrick's suggestion that we consider moving to a rural area in northern California. His job with the California Highway Patrol allowed for statewide transfers. We had already planned to make such a move when Patrick approached retirement, because his seniority would guarantee our choice then. Now I balked at the thought of leaving our friends and church and my school library job. Yet I sensed an unmistakable peace as we chose towns to visit during our June vacation.

Before our trip, Patrick and I took a walk around a nearby field and found a dirt-encrusted nickel. I scraped off the grime with my fingernail and uncovered the familiar "In God We Trust." I wondered, *Is this supposed to give me five times the hope, Lord?*

After a day's drive we traveled through high desert and into the rugged Sierra Nevada Mountains. Deeper in Plumas County we admired the majestic evergreens, cascading streams and pristine lakes. The quaint downtown of Quincy with its historic buildings charmed me.

This is the setting I've dreamed of all my life, I thought.

I turned to Patrick and said, "I feel like I'm coming home." Is this why nothing would work out before? While we wandered around the town, a penny shined up at me, and I sensed God's smile and answer.

Do I dare hope for this to happen? I wondered again.

Back home, Patrick submitted his transfer request. Although our hearts had been captured by Plumas County, we knew it might be years before the transfer could occur. Yet I couldn't help but hope and pray for a miracle as I kept finding pennies reminding me of God's trustworthy care.

October brought the announcement of that very miracle: Patrick had made the transfer list! Our hearts burst with joy and gratitude. On Thanksgiving Day he left to find us a home. With Quincy's population of only five thousand, coupled with the onset of winter, few houses were available. Patrick bought the last one he saw, a refurbished Victorian-style home. Its warmth embraced me when I arrived in January 1992, and I knew it was the house God had in mind all along. It had large rooms and ten-foot ceilings; the word spacious described it perfectly.

And there was more to God's promise-keeping. Our old home sold at its market value. Patrick reported to his new job four years to the day of God's promise to me—December 2, 1991. And a library position at the nearby elementary school opened up for me the following August, replacing the same dream job I had left. God's promise held more blessings than I ever imagined.

I rarely find pennies these days. But when I do, I add them to all the others in the clear glass container that sits on my desk. I call them my pennies from heaven. They serve as small reminders of a big God who loves me and who can be trusted every time.

Big Trouble in Paradise

Wanda Davis

I'LL GO FIRST," MY FRIEND KATHY SAID. I'D ASKED KATHY to accompany me on a cruise to the Bahamas. Our cruise ship had stopped for an afternoon in Freeport, and Kathy and I had just gotten up the nerve to try parasailing over Pelican Bay. Now we were waiting at the dock for our turns.

"It's like being flown on a kite," a woman who'd gone before us said. "It's a blast!" Harnessed to a sail, we'd fly high in the sky tethered securely to a speedboat by a six-hundred-foot towrope. The crew on the dock assured us it was absolutely safe, scores of tourists like us had done it every day for sixteen years. And this day of all days looked perfect—clear blue sky, soft tropical breeze, only the slightest chop in the water.

I'm a careful person, never one to take risks. I like to feel in control. But now that I'd worked up my courage, I was determined to try parasailing. Still, I watched nervously as Kathy pulled on her life vest and was strapped into the parachute's harness. The speedboat roared to life and Kathy was lifted into the air, borne by the breeze.

I could see the look of exhilaration on Kathy's face. *The view must be incredible*, I marveled. The boat pulled her around the bay for five minutes, finally swinging around to the dock in front of the Grand Bahama Beach Hotel. Two guys grabbed the towrope and guided it under a hook. Still pulling, the boat motored away from the dock, lowering Kathy toward the outstretched hands of the crew. She landed with a hop and a whoop, grinning from ear to ear. It looked so fun.

Relax and enjoy this, I told myself. *You're here to have a good time.*

My heart raced as I was strapped into a life jacket and then clipped into the fabric harness attached to the parachute.

Okay, Lord, I asked silently, *You wouldn't let me do anything foolish, right?*

The boat eased forward until the towline was taut, the guys on the dock held the parachute up and, whoosh, I was off.

I shut my eyes as the towrope was let out farther, taking me higher and higher into the sky. As the warm tropical air rushed against my face, I got enough courage to open my eyes and look down. I gazed at the shimmering water below. I could see clear to the bottom.

Thank You, Lord, for letting me see the island in such a beautiful way. At last I relaxed. I was completely at the mercy of the wind—and it felt wonderful, so wonderful to let go of my fear.

Then, well out over the bay, a strong gust abruptly pulled the parachute. My harness jerked. Another gust and a jolt.

Was this supposed to happen? I glanced toward the horizon. Dark, angry clouds boiled up out of nowhere, rolling in my direction—fast. The sun disappeared and the breeze became chill. Below me the water had turned frothy with whitecaps.

God, get me down, I thought, *and I'll never try this again!*

The boat turned sharply and started back to the dock. The wind knocked me from side to side. My stomach churned. *Hurry,* I urged. At last we approached the dock and the crew members stood ready to grab my towrope.

The crew had just hooked the rope to the pole on the dock when—*whaap!* A powerful updraft hit the parasail. The speedboat spun around, almost capsizing. The crew unhooked the rope from the pole and, as I swung terrified in the darkening sky, shouted frantically for help. They couldn't reach my towrope and the boat didn't have the power to fight the wind and waves.

Another speedboat roared toward us. The two boats were lashed together. The drivers revved their motors and used their combined power to pull on the towrope, trying to get me close enough to the dock so the crew could hook the rope. Then the wind hit gale force, hurtling the two boats toward shore, sweeping them out of the water and onto the beach.

"Help!" I shouted. Palm trees bent toward the ground under the force of the wind. On the beach, people stopped to stare and point at me; others came running from the hotel below. A woman screamed. As I clung to the straps above me, I felt a sickening snap. The towrope broke! My parasail shot straight up. Up, up, up, over two hundred feet in a matter of seconds.

People scrambled to catch the end of the rope, but it was far over their heads and I was going too fast. I sailed over the five-story Grand Bahama Beach Hotel, the rope dragging behind me like the leash of an errant dog.

A man working on the hotel roof gaped at me as I shot by, a look of astonishment frozen on his face. The parasail dropped and the rope dragged across a construction area hundreds of feet below. Still the parasail zoomed on, with me dangling help-lessly beneath it.

The rope end was bouncing along a four-lane highway. Ahead of me was the Port Lucaya Marketplace, a row of flat buildings we'd visited earlier that day. Suddenly I was dropping. *I'm going to hit them!* I squeezed my eyes shut and kept saying, "God, please save me" over and over. Just as suddenly, the wind lifted the para-chute, barely missing the last building in the complex.

Even though I'd been in the sky for only minutes, it seemed like hours. My legs were numb from hanging in the harness. My left arm had been jerked so hard I couldn't move it. Emergency sirens wailed below. I could see ambulances darting around traffic as they sped after me. Crowds of people were running along, too, tiny frantic figures.

I was being blown closer and closer to the ocean. What would happen if I was blown out to sea? They'd never find me.

God, You created the wind and the waves. Please control this parasail. Then I grasped what I was saying. You created the wind. God was in the wind. It was in His power to turn this gale into a gentle breeze that would drop me safely to the ground. Just as I felt completely at the mercy of the wind, it was necessary to give myself over completely to the mercy of God. I had to relax and let Him take control, to let go and let God.

Lord, I'm in Your hands. I trust You to carry me where You want me to go.

I looked down and saw a sliver of water ahead of me.

"There!" I shouted out loud. "God, please drop me there." At that moment the wind gave a final bellow and then calmed. I was coming down fast, headed right for what seemed to be a canal. In the next instant the wind died completely and the parasail floated downward like a petal. Giving a final flutter, it gently collapsed into the water about ten feet from the seawall.

I floundered to free myself from the sinking sail. Had I gotten this far only to drown? *Relax*, I reminded myself. *Remember who's in control.*

A man came running.

"Unhook your life jacket from the parasail!" he shouted. I managed to hold my left arm across the vest, pushing it down, and with my other hand squeezed the clasps. As the water rose around me, the clasps clicked open and I was free.

Moments later, rescue workers pulled me out of the canal. As they carried me toward an ambulance, someone asked me where I was, to see if I still had my senses.

"What time is it?" he then asked, tapping his watch.

"Honey," I said, "I'm over forty. I can't see that dial without my glasses."

He grinned. "She's got a broken arm but she's okay!" The crowd who'd been following me cheered.

A man showed me his red and blistered palms. "Rope burns," he explained. "I tried to catch your rope when you passed over." Everyone seemed amazed I wasn't dead.

"I want you to know that you just witnessed a miracle," I said.

A lady touched my arm. "You are mightily blessed," she said with an island lilt that made me laugh with relief and joy.

At the hotel the next day, people saw my arm in a sling and kept asking if I was "the parasailing lady." Others filled me in on what had happened on the ground while I was in the air. The broken towrope had been dragged across a moving taxi, startling the driver off the road; fortunately, no one was hurt. A construction worker said the debris I'd flown over had been set with dynamite, and he was surprised they hadn't been blasting. Later, I talked to the parasailing crew, who said that in all their years on the island, they'd never seen the weather change so abruptly.

I gave a shudder of fear. If an accident like this could happen out of the blue, what other uncontrollable event might next befall me? Then I reminded myself who it was that made the wind and the waves. And that night on the ship as I drifted to sleep, lulled by the faraway sound of a gentle breeze, I relaxed knowing that no matter what happened, I was in God's hands.

A NOTE FROM THE EDITORS

We hope you enjoy *When Miracles Happen*, created by the Books and Inspirational Media Division of Guideposts. In all of our books, magazines and outreach efforts, we aim to deliver inspiration and encouragement, help you grow in your faith, and celebrate God's love in every aspect of your daily life.

Thank you for making a difference with your purchase of this book, which helps fund our many outreach programs to the military, prisons, hospitals, nursing homes and schools. To learn more, visit GuidepostsFoundation.org.

We also maintain many useful and uplifting online resources. Visit Guideposts.org to read true stories of hope and inspiration, access OurPrayer network, sign up for free newsletters, join our Facebook community, and follow our stimulating blogs.

To order your favorite Guideposts publications, go to ShopGuideposts.org, call (800) 932-2145 or write to Guideposts, PO Box 5815, Harlan, Iowa 51593.